DANCE IN THE CITY

Also by Helen Thomas

DANCE, GENDER AND CULTURE (*editor*)
DANCE, MODERNITY AND CULTURE

First published 1997 by
MACMILLAN PRESS LTD
Houndmills, Basingstoke, Hampshire RG21 6XS
and London
Companies and representatives
throughout the world

ISBN 0–333–64960–5 hardcover
ISBN 0–333–64961–3 paperback

A catalogue record for this book is available
from the British Library.

This book is printed on paper suitable for recycling and
made from fully managed and sustained forest sources.

10   9   8   7   6   5   4   3   2
06   05   04   03   02   01   00

Printed and bound in Great Britain by
Antony Rowe Ltd, Chippenham, Wiltshire

Published in the United States of America by
ST. MARTIN'S PRESS, INC.,
Scholarly and Reference Division
175 Fifth Avenue, New York, N.Y. 10010

ISBN 0–312–17453–5 cloth
ISBN 0–312–17454–3 paperback

Dance in the City

Edited by

Helen Thomas
Senior Lecturer
Department of Sociology
Goldsmiths' College
London

For Stephen and Jim McDonald

Contents

List of Plates

Preface

This book was conceived as companion volume to *Dance, Gender and Culture* (Thomas, 1993) which was also published by Macmillan. Just as that collection demonstrated that dance is an important site for understanding the relations between gender and culture, so this edition locates dance within the spectrum of urban life in late modernity. The focus here is specifically concerned with Western concepts and practices of dance. Like the first collection, the papers were written specifically for this volume and express a variety of theoretical approaches. Although by no means comprehensive, the book highlights a wide range of dance forms and styles that have been forged through or may be witnessed on a routine basis in and around our contemporary urban landscapes: from dance halls to raves and the club striptease; from set dancing to ballroom dancing and ice-dance shows; the waltz, the lancers, swing, hip hop and ceroc; the ballet class in the local hall, step aerobics in the fitness centre, and 'art' dance, for which the contemporary fragmented city is a centrifugal force for the mapping of bodies in space and time. By taking dance as its focus, the book attempts to illuminate the divergent possibilities inscribed in the spatio-temporal features of urban life from a different angle to other recent books. At the same time, the collection weaves across the interface of performance and social dance, dance and fitness regimes, dance and sport, raising questions about the tensions surrounding the boundaries and margins of dance.

The intention is to locate theoretical issues surrounding: individual bodies and social space (Prickett, Pini); gender (Briginshaw, Pini, O'Connor, Dodds, Prickett, Sayers)/race (Gilroy, Back, Roy)/age (Thomas and Miller, Ward, Prickett) representations; local/global (Roy, Back, Gore) interrelations; rural/urban (O'Connor, Roy) trajectories, high/popular (Jordan and Thomas, Sayers,) culture divide, and modernity/postmodernity (Gore, Briginshaw), within *case-study* material on dance. There is also a concern to begin to address *why* and *how* people dance and point to differences and similarities in dance practices (Ward, O'Connor, Pini). The book brings into focus other cultural systems connected with dance such as music and dress (Gilroy, Back, Sayers, Ward, Thomas and Miller), but unlike cultural studies analyses of youth cultures, the activity of *dancing* is central to the discussions.

I have divided the collection into three parts, and although the chapters in each section should not be seen as either inclusive or mutually exclusive, there is, nevertheless, a certain rationale to the structuring of the book. The first section mostly deals with some aspect of performance (except

for Gore), and the chapters also raise many of the theoretical issues indicated above that are addressed at a more substantive level in the other two
sections. Part II is more directly focused on *case-study* material of people
who dance, as opposed to representations of dancing, using ethnographic
methods and/or ethnographic history. Here the issues are directed largely
towards 'social dance' contexts, although notions of performativity are also
raised. The third section is called *Border Country* because the chapters
point up and challenge the traditional boundaries and margins between
dance, music and culture, dance and the fitness regime, performance dance
and stripping, and dancing and ice-skating.

One of the most interesting and encouraging aspects for me in bringing
this collection together was that it was relatively easy this time round to
persuade people who do not usually write on dance to join in this venture.
Perhaps this says something about the emergent profile of dance in academe
in this country, on the heels of the interest in the body in society. Moreover, and without being overly parochial about this, the fact that all the contributors either work or were trained on this side of the Atlantic is a further
testament to a developing dance studies in the UK and Ireland. I would
like to thank all the contributors for producing such stimulating and thought-
provoking chapters, which I feel certain will add to this field and further
demonstrate the import of dance as a focus of research for a variety of
theoretical perspectives and intellectual traditions.

Helen Thomas, August 1996

Notes on the Contributors

Les Back is a lecturer in Sociology at Goldsmiths' College, University of London. He has written extensively on racism and popular culture and his book *Urban Culture and New Ethnicities* will be published by UCL Press. He has also written two books with John Solomos on *Racism and Society* (Macmillan) and *Race, Politics and Social Change* (Routledge).

Valerie A. Briginshaw is a Principal Lecturer and Head of Dance at Chichester Institute of Higher Education. Her recent publications include a chapter on postmodern dance and politics in the book *Analysing Performance* and a plenary paper in the Surrey University *Border Tensions* Conference Proceedings. Her research interests are in feminism, postmodernism and the body in performance.

Sherril Dodds gained an MA (Dist.) in Dance Studies at the University of Surrey in 1993. She then took up a position as Lecturer in Dance at the City of Liverpool Community College. In 1994, she returned to Surrey to commence a Ph.D. Her area of research is 'dance for the camera'.

Paul Gilroy works in the Sociology Department at Goldsmiths' College, University of London.

Georgiana Gore is based in France as a full-time lecturer and writer in Dance and Anthropology. She has recently been appointed Maître de Conférences at Blaise-Pascal University, Clermont-Ferrand. Previously, she was Lecturer in Dance Anthropology at the University of Surrey and spent the 1980s in Nigeria establishing a dance section in the Department of Theatre Arts, University of Benin.

Stephanie Jordan is Professor of Dance Studies at Roehampton Institute. She has taught both practical and theoretical aspects of dance in Europe, North America and Australia. Her books include *Striding Out: Aspects of Contemporary and New Dance in Britain* and *Parallel Lines: Media Representations of Dance* (co-edited with Dave Allen). She has contributed many scholarly articles and conference papers on dance and has been awarded a research grant from the Radcliffe Trust to write a book on music and dance.

Nicola Miller is visiting tutor in Sociology at Goldsmiths' College, University of London. She is currently writing up her Ph.D. research which considers the relationship between late capitalism and state-funded dance.

Barbara O'Connor is a sociologist and teaches in the School of Communications,. Dublin City University. She has published articles on the representation of women in Irish television drama and film and has written on audience responses to television soap opera. She is co-editor of *Gender in Irish Society* and *Tourism in Ireland: A Critical Analysis*. She is currently researching the role of dance in the construction of cultural identities in Ireland.

Maria Pini is currently registered as a Ph.D. student at Goldsmiths' College, University of London, where she is doing research into articulations and embodiments of femininity within contemporary social dance cultures. Other forthcoming publications include 'Women and the British Rave Scene' in Angela McRobbie's collection *Back to Reality* (Manchester) and 'Dance Classes: Dancing between Classifications' in the journal *Feminism and Psychology*.

Stacey Prickett wrote her MA and Ph.D. dissertations on the American revolutionary dance movement at the Laban Centre for Movement and Dance. She recently lectured at the University of California, Berkeley, and she currently lectures on dance at Sonana State University, California. She has published in journals such as *Studies in Dance History, Dance Research, Dance Theatre Journal*, and *Dance View*.

Sanjoy Roy read biology at the University of York, later studying contemporary dance at the Laban Centre for Movement and Dance, and Bharata Natyam at the Academy of Indian Dance. In 1993 he graduated with an MA in Communication, Culture and Society from Goldsmiths' College. He currently works as an editor, designer and writer for Dance Books, and is co-editor of *Dance Now* magazine.

Lesley-Anne Sayers is a freelance writer and dance critic. After graduating in Drama and Classics she undertook postgraduate study at the Laban Centre for Movement and Dance during the 1980s. Since then she has been a regular contributor to *Dance Theatre Journal* and *Dance Now* magazines and has contributed to a range of publications including programmes, encyclopedias and books on dance. Her research interests include British dance history, Western theatre dance during the 1920s, and the history of dance criticism.

Helen Thomas is Senior Lecturer in Sociology at Goldsmiths' College, University of London. She has published a number of articles on dance in journals and edited collections. She is editor of *Dance, Gender and Culture* (Macmillan) and recently published *Dance, Modernity and Culture* (Routledge). She is author of two large-scale surveys, *Equal Opportunities in the Mechanical Media* (Equity), and *Unequal Pay for Equal Parts* (with Martina Klett-Davies), which was funded by the Leverhulme Trust.

Andrew Ward has taught Sociology at Goldsmiths' College, Oxford Polytechnic and Thames Valley University. He has lectured throughout the UK and well as in Cyprus, Thailand and the USA. He is currently involved in an extensive project on morality, part of which was published as *A Good Old Morality Tale: Back to Basics and its Aftermath* (IPPR, 1996). Now employed as head of Corporate Relations at TVU, Andrew has long given up the struggle to reconcile his professional, intellectual and sybaritic interests.

Part I

Dance in the City/
The City in Dance

1 Dancing around Meaning (and the Meaning around Dance)

Andrew Ward

INTRODUCTION

I want to begin this chapter with a statement from a recently published text on the 'philosophy of dance'. This statement is included here because it alerts us to a significant feature of dance and urban life that informs much of this chapter. We are told that when walking

> through the City, indoors or outdoors, one is everywhere confronted with the worn-down forms of distinctively artistic activity. There is architecture all over the place, of course. But also there is music everywhere, a background privately or publicly generated; there are sculptural and graphic forms, and literary language. One is surrounded, not indeed by artistic masterpieces, but by signs and symbols used in ways that could not be what they are without the direct influence of self-consciously artistic practice. But there is no sign of dance anywhere, other than in actual dances which have to be located and sought out. (Sparshott, 1995, p. 6)

It is clear, I believe, that the writer's concern here is not merely with the literal visibility of dance or just with the status of dance as a fine art. The physical relationship of dance to the urban built environment, and its particular spatial requirements (in contrast to those of other forms of expression), are not the principal issues here. Moreover, even though this writer tells us that dance has to be 'located and sought out', he is not saying that dance is an unusual or infrequent activity in Western culture. On the contrary, he tells us that 'it seems that people everywhere dance' (Sparshott, 1995, p. 3; see also Hanna, 1987, p. 3). His point, rather, is that dance is not strongly codified within the cultural fabric of our institutions or interpolated within public discourse, so that in going about our daily business we do not commonly see (or use) signs of dance.

This passage is important, then, because it brings our attention to a curious and paradoxical feature of dance. This is that despite being 'pervasive and intrinsic' (Sparshott, 1995, p. 6) to modern industrial societies dance largely remains, or is made, invisible. Hence the paradox: dance is 'every-where and nowhere', 'ubiquitous' yet 'elusive' (*ibid.*). This means that in coming to terms with dance in the city or anywhere else today we should not be surprised to encounter a deep-rooted reluctance (or inability) to bring dance into focus, even if at the same time 'dance mania' may be 'sweeping the country' (Bishop, 1995).

RAVE – A HIGHLY SIGNIFICANT PHENOMENON

Nowhere is this reluctance (or paradox) more strikingly demonstrated than in the ways rave culture has been discussed and conceived. Rave is a highly significant phenomenon: indeed it is perhaps the most extraordinary of all contemporary social movements. Extraordinary, first of all, simply because of the scale of its appeal. It is extremely difficult to give an accurate figure for how many people are involved in rave events. This is because of issues of definition (what counts as a rave?); of accessibility (raves occur as both commercial and private activities, which can be either legal or illegal); of the character of raves (however they are specifically defined, their general nature precludes accurate headcounts). However, research reported in 1993 in *The Times* suggested that more than one million young people attended raves each week and that this was probably an underestimate, given that the figure only includes legal events.[1] But even if this figure was, on the contrary, an extreme overestimate (say by 50 per cent), rave culture is still a most remarkable phenomenon. For, on the basis of this calculation, nearly one in nine of those aged between 16 and 24 attended a rave event on a regular (i.e. weekly) basis in 1993[2] and, if anything, the indications (given, for example, in the press) are that rave is even more popular three years later.

This is an astounding figure in itself but it becomes even more astonishing when set against other factors that have accompanied rave, such as its systematic demonisation within the media (Redhead, 1993, pp. 7–27), the framing of new prohibiting legislation (the Criminal Justice and Public Order Act, 1994) and the involvement of organised crime in rave events.[3] Add to all this the logistical difficulties that characterise rave – the need to travel to out-of-the-way venues by a section of the population who have limited access to the means to make such journeys – and its popularity is truly remarkable.

Yet the response to rave by serious commentators has been at best muted but generally non-existent (an exception here is McRobbie, 1993 (reprinted in McRobbie, 1994); see also Gore and Pini in Chapters 4 and

7 of this volume); whilst those who have a sense of its importance adopt a strange, semi-myopic approach to the topic. Consider, for example, two recent books on the subject: Steve Redhead's *Rave off: Politics and Deviance in Contemporary Youth Culture* (1993) and Nicholas Saunders's *Ecstasy and Dance Culture* (1995).

These are very different in style and content (the first being a collection of academic papers; the second an information handbook), but each is characterised by a curious failure to discuss what is the defining feature of their subject-matter – namely dance. This is not to say that, for example, in the Redhead volume dance is never mentioned – it is (approximately 50 times in fact); but the point is that dance is only mentioned: there is no sustained address of dance *per se*. Moreover, when the term dance does appear it does so most frequently as a descriptor or qualifier as in 'dance drug', 'dance craze', 'Indie Dance crossover', 'groovy dance single', 'psychedelic dance hall', etc. This usage tends continuously to move attention away from dance. And on those few occasions when dance does get a mention as a phenomenon in its own right, no clear or emphatic view of dance or the centrality of dance to raves emerges. Indeed, on the contrary, in at least one paper in the book it is implied that dance is a secondary and accidental feature of raves (albeit as they appear in a different context). The argument here is that because particular music forms 'derived from unlicensed and under-age clubs in ghettos, where alcohol was not sold', an 'open market' was 'created' for 'punters faced with *no other option* than to dance' (Redhead, 1993, p. 123; emphasis added). This view of dance, as a phenomenon that arbitrarily results from other primary conditions, sits comfortably within the general approach expounded within the book where, if it is mentioned at all, dance is glossed and its importance and centrality to raves is effectively ignored. Indeed, it would be quite possible to read most of the Redhead book and have no clear idea of what happens at raves.

Despite the appearance of 'dance' in Nicholas Saunders's title, *Ecstasy and the Dance Culture*, those seriously interested in dance will have to look hard to find any material on dance *per se*. Indeed, if anything, dance is even more elusive in this text than it is in Redhead's. True, Saunders makes it quite clear that his concern lies squarely with Ecstasy, and that his intention is 'to satisfy Ecstasy users' thirst for knowledge, to help them avoid its dangers and to stimulate further research' (1995, p. 3), but it is still reasonable to expect dance to receive some specific attention in a book concerned, even secondarily, with dance culture. As it is, Saunders implies that the one aspect of dance culture that need not be considered is dance itself. Paradoxically, Saunders seems to be aware that this emphasis on drugs is misleading. This is shown by his (apparently) supportive reference to

Steve Hillage's contention that 'the dance music scene is belittled by the "concentration on drugs"' (1995, p. 198). It is also shown by his mention of a study which reports that only 6 per cent of those interviewed identified drugs as being the motivation for getting involved in rave culture (1995, p. 41). Drugs, and Ecstasy in particular, are undoubtedly a core defining feature of rave events and for many commentators, particularly within the press, rave equals drugs. The terms can virtually be used interchangeably. But if in talking about what are dance events, dance gets lost from view or glossed over, then we surely need to ask why this happens? When those who are clearly well-informed and are in no way hostile to rave culture pay so little attention to what is the irreducible feature of the culture they are discussing, there must be a fundamental reason for their perspective which goes beyond oversight or lack of concentration. It appears, rather, that dance is literally unaccountable.

Both Redhead and Saunders, then, exemplify that dance is, indeed, 'everywhere and nowhere'. Given this, and given a commitment to dance (as a 'pervasive and intrinsic' human activity), how should we respond? How do we capture in words that which is so often silently passed over in public discourse? What do we need to say and write to bring dance into focus? What should we do to make dance visible?

DANCING AND WRITING

Unfortunately, such questions are not easily settled. This is so not least because writing about dance is itself a paradoxical pursuit; one that involves traversing the ontological faultline that inevitably divides dancing from writing. Indeed, there can be few people who have seriously tried to write about dance who have not been daunted by the self-evident truth that dancing is not writing. Skilful authors may be able to create sensations that summon up memories of dance events; they may be able to illuminate the nature of dance and (re)orient our views of what dance is; but when all is said and done, writing is simply not dancing.

Of course, this is not just an issue for dance commentary. The gulf between writing and 'doing' applies equally to sex, swimming, playing the flute and indeed innumerable other more or less commonplace activities. We can never escape this dilemma. But it is of the utmost importance that we find ways of talking about dance that do dance justice. Although several writers have recognised the need, for example, to develop an 'enlarged and enriched critical literature' on dance (Redfern, 1988, p. 20), the issue here is not just one of plugging an academic gap (or 'ensuring that the standing of dance as fine art rises' (*ibid.*). It is much more crucial than this. Indeed, we need to be clear that at stake here are ethical issues that are every bit as serious as those raised by genetic engineering and biomedical technologies. For we are concerned with tendencies and assumptions that distort our humanity and which therefore have to be counter-balanced (see Seidler 1989, 1991 on this theme; e.g. 1989, p. 156). We must vigorously repudiate the constraining of our nature that occurs when the non-rational is deprecated and treated as an alien or primitive characteristic which we would be better off without. Yet, paradoxically, to do this we have no option but to deploy rationalist means; that is, we must use rational devices to emphasise and if necessary to reinstate activities judged to be non-rational as vital, positive and defining features of being human. It is our responsibility (as scholars, dancers and citizens) to argue for the inherent meaningfulness of dance and for the place of dance as an essential human practice.

DANCE AS A NON-RATIONAL ACTIVITY

In pursuing this responsibility, let us look at the identification of dance as a non-rational activity. We do so because this characterisation seems to be a generative issue within a great deal of dance scholarship. Indeed, the view that dance is marginalised in our culture and that this is a result of its non-rational character appears to be a common starting-point for dance commentators, regardless of their roots and intentions. There would also seem to be general agreement that this attitude to dance is part of a broader cultural syndrome in which characteristically the body is disregarded (or even, according to one commentator, 'despised' (Seidler, 1989, p. 45)). This disregard arises because 'verbal forms' are 'prioritised' in 'logocentric western societies' which leads to the 'marginalisation of the body' (Burt, 1995, p. 44).

But this observation, crucially important as it is, contains a self-negating implication. For in recognising and exposing the marginalisation of dance the danger is that we imply that dance is categorically marginal in (or to) our society (or, to use Durkheim's term, that dance is now a *pathological* phenomenon). If this implication sticks it becomes difficult to argue that dance is integral to our culture and, therefore, to do what it is held here as vital that we should do (i.e. reinstate the non-rational as an irreducible human quality).

So, for example, when Errol – one of the respondents in Helen Thomas's research of a community dance project – told her that dancing 'is the exact opposite of what society is in a sense' (Thomas, 1993, p. 83), he might simply be seen as reflecting the opposition between the non-rational (as represented by dance) and the rational (which dominates society); reflecting, that is, the opposition that is so widely acknowledged by dance scholars. But equally, Errol's comment could be taken to indicate something more than this; it could be seen as confirming that dance *lies outside society*: that it is beyond the pale and does not belong!

The same issue arises when Ted Polhemus tells us that 'we are rapidly coming to realise that by our excessive dependence upon verbal-arbitrary language, oral and written, we have allowed ... our resources of bodily communication (to atrophy)' (Polhemus, 1975, p. 30). If this is so, and he persuasively argues that it is, he may be seen as giving legitimacy to views that he not only does not support but which he was directly trying to repudiate. Indeed, it becomes difficult to see how 'we may regain our full complement of communicative powers', as he urges we should, if our 'resources of bodily communication' 'have atrophied' – that is, 'wasted away' (*Collins Paperback English Dictionary*, 1990).

The problem here is that through the very means of alerting us to a danger Polhemus helps to actualise this danger, so his warnings concretise precisely that which he is warning against. It is not that our 'resources of bodily communication' have literally atrophied; it is that in the dominant ways in which the body is addressed (if it is acknowledged at all in rational discourse) imply that this atrophication has taken place. We must always beware of reinforcing or reflecting such hegemonic viewpoints. The issue here is not simply that these dominant views are partial, representing only particular perspectives and sectional interests; it is that they frequently deny the actual practice of those they are presumed to represent or protect. There arises, then, a tension between what people say and what they do (as well as that between what *some* people say and what *others* do). But because certain forms of discourse tend to set our agendas does not mean that the vocabulary and syntax of bodily communication disappears.

DANCING MAKES THE NEWS

This tendency for non-verbal communication and dance not to register in general consciousness is what is meant here by the invisibility of dance. The point is not that dance *is* invisible; it is that in the context of dance's patent visibility – a context in which with a 'resurgence of dancing' (Wolffe,

1995) 'about five million people go dancing each week' (Gledhill, 1995), and in which there have been explosions of interest in tea dances (Roffey, 1994), ceroc (Woolf, 1995), flamenco (McLeod, 1995), folk dancing (Bishop, 1995), tango (Norman, 1995), ballroom dancing (Gledhill, 1995) and the doop (Halpin, 1994) – there is a pervasive tendency to make dance invisible. So, as we have seen, texts concerned with dance culture mention dance only in passing and discourse is generated which typically glosses the non-rational as an essential and positive element within everyday life, despite the 'seemingly endless popularity' of dance music and dance (Bellos, 1995). And paradoxically this tendency can be identified even at those moments when dance is made highly visible. Take, for example, those rare instances when dance makes the news and becomes the subject of a pro-minent press photograph. Such images, perhaps because they are so few and far between, tend to stick fast in the memory. Images such as Margaret Thatcher dancing with Ian Gilmour at a Tory Conference ball only a few weeks after she had sacked him from the Government; or Wayne Sleep dancing with the Princess of Wales on a dance-floor emptied for their benefit; or much more recently (and the one of concern here) Salman Rushdie dancing at the launch party for a new Martin Amis novel.

Undoubtedly, as far as the media are concerned, the government and the royal family are inherently newsworthy (this is especially the case if the figures centre-stage are icons such as Thatcher and the Princess), but the focus on Rushdie was surprising and the way in which what would seem to be a trivial instance was treated was extraordinary.

Of course, Rushdie does have his own newsworthiness, not so much because he is an author but because he is living under the threat of a *fatwah*. This was well illustrated in the reporting that accompanied the photograph when – for example – Rushdie was introduced as 'he of the long-forgotten book but never-forgotten Fatwah' (Mouland, 1995). Fair enough perhaps, but why this newsworthiness should extend to his dan-cing is less apparent. And it was his dancing that was important here: it was not just that he was out enjoying himself whilst there is 'a £1.3 million bounty on his head' (*ibid.*) (although as we shall see this was a key issue too). We can conclude that this is so because, although he is appar-ently 'a regular on the Capital's cocktail circuit' (PHS/*Times* Diary, 1995), there have not been photographs published in the daily press of Rushdie just because he was having a drink at this or that fashionable venue. No, the crucial factor that caught the journalists' attention here was that he went to a party and *danced*!

This tells us that at least as far as journalists are concerned Rushdie and dancing (both separately and together) have a significance that goes way beyond that normally attributed to an author or a leisure activity (or an author in pursuit of a leisure activity). And if there is one message that emerges from this strange episode it is that Rushdie should not have danced at all. A variety of reasons was given why he should not have done so. Firstly, it was pointed out that Rushdie 'can't dance' (D'Souza, 1995). He was, we were told, too old. Indeed being 'born in 1947 (apparently) he belongs to a generation . . . that has unquestionably produced some of the worst and most cumbersome dancers of all time' (Walker, 1995).

Secondly, some of the media – it was contended – are against Rushdie 'having any life at all'. Indeed, 'it sometimes feels as if sections of the media tacitly support the fatwah against . . . Rushdie' (Moore, 1995). To be seen dancing at a party was a 'crime' (*ibid.*) which he should not have committed. In other words, to be the subject of a *fatwah* means, apparently, that it is unseemly to dance. Thirdly, whilst Rushdie was dancing, we were told, Special Branch 'officers of a team of six permanently assigned to the author at a cost of £1 million pounds a year continued to do what they always do on these occasions. They watched. Unobtrusively, guns on safety' (Mouland, 1995). The 'snide' (Lawson, 1995) implication here is only semi-veiled: it is that we the taxpayers, who have already forked out '£6 million' whilst he manages 'to enjoy a globetrotting lifestyle' (Mouland, 1995), are now having to pay to protect Rushdie whilst he dances. This style of reporting led one journalist (who was one of Rushdie's partners at the Amis party) to ask: 'What do people want? For him to stay locked up out of sight?' (Lawson, 1995). Fourthly, he should not have danced because he could not keep up with the 'tall' 'Amazonian' 'younger' and 'more agile' (Walker, 1995) women who were his partners.

Fifthly, Rushdie was wrong to dance because he was inappropriately dressed: 'his clothes were so big and baggy they made him look like a small farm animal desperately struggling to escape from a potato sack' (*ibid.*); furthermore, he was 'dressed all in brown' whereas the other party goers were clothed in a 'fashionable black' (Mouland, 1995).

In telling us that Rushdie should not have danced, the writers of these accounts are effectively asserting that this instance of dancing should – in an absolute sense – have been invisible. At the very moment that the spotlight is turned on this dance event those who made it so visible suggest that it should not have occurred at all. Moreover, this simple event – someone dancing at a party – served to trigger a sinister litany of implication. Rushdie would have been better off back in hiding (D'Souza, 1995); he should have been out of sight (Lawson, 1995); he should not have stood out amid the crowd (Mouland, 1995). He should, in other words, have been invisible. And why? Because he danced!

THE RATIONAL/NON-RATIONAL DICHOTOMY

The treatment of this incident would seem to confirm that, as one writer tells us, our culture 'carries a deep unease about bodily experience' (Seidler, 1989, p. 97). Indeed, such experience 'needs to be controlled' (*ibid.*). So that in dancing, Rushdie, the writer (and moreover the writer who 'we-the-taxpayers' support), failed to show this control: he departed from the rationality that defines our (and particularly men's) identities. This implicit and pervasive perception of non-rational behaviour as inappropriate and dislocated within public contexts effectively makes us strangers to ourselves. Yet because this repudiation of the non-rational is routinised (and indeed ritualised) we accept this estrangement as an everyday fact of life. In this sense, this repudiation is unproblematic – which is precisely why trying to speak for the non-rational is so difficult but also so urgent.

But what is stopping us here? Surely, in recognising the pervasiveness of this perception of the non-rational we have taken the first crucial step necessary in order to do what we have to do – that is, to focus on the non-rational, to become more familiar with the non-rational, to identify and establish a positive place in our lives for the non-rational? However, the issues here are not just a matter of commentators taking the decision to adopt a different attitude. They are far more fundamental than this. Indeed, we have to take on board something that is highly inconvenient and this is that there is no one way of establishing the parameters and content of what is non-rational. We could never produce a workable delineation that directed how much of our behaviour should be rational and how much should be non-rational; neither can we establish definitively when we should and when we should not be non-rationally oriented. But then it is important to realise that treating the rational and non-rational as discrete realms is in any case an analytic procedure, a way of talking, which undoubtedly simplifies a much more complex, interrelated relationship. As it is, the rationalism/non-rationalism dichotomy is too limited for our purposes here. We need also to draw a distinction between non-rationalism and irrationalism. This is necessary because the term 'irrationalism' carries such negative baggage now that it could never be used other than derogatively. Consequently, we definitely would not want to assert that dancing is irrational (even though this is frequently the implication of – for example – press reporting of dance events). Yet dance commentators appear to be quite at ease (and on occasion enthusiastic about) talking of dance as a non-rational activity.

But the term 'non-rational' is itself not trouble-free. For it is clearly a contingent term: it exists and derives its meaning from being counterposed with rationality. This makes the non-rational secondary to the primacy of the rational, with the implication that the non-rational deviates from the rational. The rational/non-rational dichotomy is not, then, a contest of equals. And, as such, it is hardly a fruitful device for our purposes here.

We might (I think rightly) conclude from these discussions that debating where dance stands in relation to rationality does not do much for dance. How then should we proceed? Clearly, in principle there is any number of options available. But we need to find a focus that relates to our experience as dancers and to the need to argue for dance as an integral and enduring part of being human. The proposal here is that perhaps we can meet these aims through turning our attention to *meaning*.

DANCE AND MEANING

However, we should be warned: meaning is an 'elusive and slippery' (Sparshott, 1995, p. 54) topic. (One that we would be well advised to 'steer clear of' – or so I was told in a private conversation with one of the contributors to this volume.) And just a casual glance over the (sociological) literature reveals how tricky meaning is; for it quickly becomes apparent that the relevant discussions seem to be predominantly concerned not with meaning after all but rather with the *problem* of meaning. Indeed, meaning is hardly ever discussed without reference to its status as a problem – which means that for many writers meaning is inherently problematic.

If this is so, how should we pin down meaning? How do we begin to find out what any dance – or indeed any expression, gesture or word – means? This may seem a foolish question: surely we should just ask the dancer what his or her dancing means (in the same way as we might ask whoever it is who is doing any expressing, gesturing or speaking what they mean)? Not according to some commentators. Indeed, there are those who argue that the meaning of dance is not available verbally at all but can only be grasped *through dance*. For example, Sparshott tells us that there are meanings in dance 'that cannot be articulated in words at all'. Indeed, 'we have no way of identifying them otherwise than by dancing them for each other' (Sparshott, 1995, p. 80). Similarly, Peter Brinson tells us that we find it hard to penetrate the inner feelings expressed through dance; so that 'often when discussing such problems a dancer will say, "I cannot *tell* you. I can only *show* you. I must dance it"' (Brinson, 1985, pp. 208–9). And several of the dancers in Thomas's Lewisham study made the same point: Mark 'can't put into words' what dancing 'brought out in him';

whilst 'for . . . Dawn, Nessa and Trisha [dance] enables them to express themselves in a way they cannot with words' (Thomas, 1993, pp. 82, 79). Why is it that dancers cannot articulate verbally what their dancing means to them? It might be that because they are dancers they are simply not adept enough with words to express their meanings adequately. But commentators such as Sparshott, Brinson and Thomas indicate that this is not the issue. Rather, it is that dance meanings *cannot* be produced in words: they are of a different – although equally valid – order. So the ordinary linguistic competence or otherwise of dancers (or indeed of anyone else) is irrelevant.

THE DIFFERENT SITES OF DANCE'S MEANINGS

Yet we all know that dance is not just meaningful to those who are dancing. For example, those who are observing dance (whether in a social or performance context) will attribute meaning to what they see. They will do this in both a general and a more specific sense. For dancing is meaningful as a general activity whilst particular dances (or dance events) may express or convey a specific meaning. But an observer does not attribute meaning either to dancing or to a dance as a purely individual achievement. Rather, observers draw on a common stock of knowledge which enables them to recognise a set of movements (and accompanying factors) as dance. This stock of knowledge cannot be reduced to the meaning-making of any individual dancer or observer. It is a collective possession.

Let us take a simple scenario: let us say that we look into a room and see people moving about. Because we are familiar with what counts as dance in our society (in other words, because we have access to this common stock of knowledge) we can rapidly decide from the clues we pick up about what is happening here. We could quickly conclude, for example, that these movements are not pain-induced gyrations, sexual couplings or a competitive sport but rather that they are dancing. And more or less simultaneously we would be able to classify what variety of dance event we were witnessing – whether it was a dance performance, a formal social celebration, a party, etc. So that in the process of recognising what is going on as the activity we know as dancing we also attribute to this particular instance of dancing a specific meaning. (Although exactly how specific (or detailed) this meaning was would depend upon how much information was available at the time and how familiar (or routine) the activities were that were being observed.) However, we arrive at these judgements through drawing on a range of evidence and not just on the basis of the movements alone.

If there was no music, for example, or if the room had not been prepared for dancing (through, say, rearranging the furniture), then we would need some further information to know what was 'really' going on. In other words, there is other evidence extrinsic to the movement *per se* that needs to be detected before we as observers could make an event meaningful as dancing, and before we could establish the specific meaning of *this* (instance of) dancing.

Activities become meaningful as dance, then, when we recognise a range of factors as occurring in a certain combination. There is no one phenomenon whose incidence will ensure that what takes place will be identified as dance. But then it is not the occurrence of these factors in itself that determines whether this or that event will be a dance-event. The key defining element is our decision (or recognition), whether as dancer or spectator, that this activity *is* dance. It is our capacity to make such decisions (and to do this recognising) which is all-important. There is no absolutely fixed or pre-figured repertoire of what counts as dance. Rather, we operationalise this general capacity to 'ring-fence' phenomena and realise them as dance.

The little bare-boned scenario outlined here takes the viewpoint of the spectator but might just as easily have looked at things from the dancer's perspective. And equally we might have focused on this event from both the dancer's *and* the spectator's positions together. This would be interesting because we cannot presume that a dance will have the same meaning for a dancer as it does for the spectator (or, indeed, for this rather than that spectator). But even this approach might not give us the whole picture. For, as we have seen, the meaning of dance is not always simply a matter of the attribution of meaning by an individual dancer or observer/audience. And it is certainly not always appropriate to explain the meaning of a dance in terms of a dancer's inner feelings. Indeed, these feelings are not necessarily reflected in the dance at all and a dance's meaning might be quite different to the feelings a dancer is experiencing. As – for example – Sparshott tells us: 'a dance that is an act of public penitence will have that meaning, even though it is danced by dancers none of who are the least bit sorry for anything' (Sparshott, 1995, p. 54). And Suzanne Langer makes the same point when she tells us that 'no one . . . has ever maintained that Pavlova's rendering of slowly ebbing life in the "Dying Swan" was most successful when she actually felt faint and sick' (Langer, 1953; Spencer, 1985, p. 7). In other words, the meaning of a dance can be independent of (and starkly different from) the feelings the dancer is experiencing. But then equally within their cultural contexts the meaning of a penitential dance or 'The Dying Swan' are not dependent on, nor derived from, any particular audience at any given time. The meaning of such dances is a diffused cultural (and therefore collective) product. Consequently, these dances have a meaning which stands apart from these or those audiences or, indeed, this or that performance. In this sense, dance is autonomous.

THE ANALYST'S PERSPECTIVE

In this discussion we have considered three sites (i.e. the dancer, spectator and culture) where the meaning of dance can be seen to reside. But there is one more perspective (or site) we need to be concerned with here: that of the analyst (or critic or commentator). For dance is not only meaningful for dancers, spectators and members of a particular culture or sub-culture. It can also be meaningful for analysts, etc., who may be from outside the culture and who are not involved in any given dance-event.

The analyst's task is to construct or capture meanings of the strange and interesting phenomena under consideration. But the analyst is never categorically only an analyst. Analysts can also be dancers and (non-analytic) dance observers, whilst they will always have emerged from, and be working within, a cultural context. Consequently, the meaning of dance for the analyst may be different than the meaning of dance for the same individual as dancer, spectator or citizen. Of course, these different roles may inform one another (see, for example, Grau, 1993, p. 96) but it would be highly unusual if the analyst did not make some kind of distinction between the sense of dance he or she has as a member of a particular cultural grouping and his or her work as an analyst.

Consider, for example, Paul Willis's treatment of breakdancing in Walsall. Although only a few paragraphs long, Willis's account is significant. This is so, firstly, because his breakdancers exhibited features more usually associated with performance dance or with anthropologically interesting dance than social dance; and, secondly, because what he says illustrates some of the key issues relevant to the analyst's perspective. Willis describes how the young men he studied produced 'routines' with 'clearly apparent narratives to them'. These boys had no formally defined status as performers yet this is certainly what they were. As 'serious' dancers, they 'invest considerable work and training in their dancing' and indeed 'formalise a bodily grounded aesthetic of their own' (Willis, 1990, p. 66). And their dancing incorporates obvious features of performance dance: 'they go on stage'; they are 'acting'; there is a 'story behind their dance; they have an 'audience' who they 'leave to fill in' the meaning of their dance (Willis, 1990, p. 67).

However, Willis indicates that the meaning of dance for these dancers is not just contained within the stories they dance. Rather, they had a wider perspective on their activities. They were – apparently – 'perfectly sure that what they were doing was worth something, culturally and aesthetically'. Indeed, 'to them it was an achievement to have reached a certain level of competence and skill in their dancing, a lasting achievement that would be remembered and even passed down to subsequent generations, rather than just a passing fad of youth' (Willis, 1990, p. 68).

What is interesting about Willis's account is its portrayal of different meaning perspectives. He directly reports the words of the dancers; he distils what he thinks they are thinking; but he also gives an analytic meaning to this dancing. Of course, the direct reporting of what individuals say in a particular context is always a selective process: not only does Willis select out of all that these individuals say what he wants to record but the dancers themselves only say what they want to say. He is, however, at least implying a difference between what the dancers say they are doing and his account, as an analyst, of what is happening. At the same time he appears to presume that his distillation of what they are thinking does accurately reflect the dancers' understanding of their practices. And in providing a distinct analytic account Willis is implying, presumably, that the dancers' understanding of their own activities – the meaning their activities have for them – should not be treated as complete: there is another dimension of meaning which needs to be added if these activities are to be sufficiently explained and understood. This analytic account is that for these dancers 'dancing . . . affords a sense of personal power, energy and control through bodily movement and the flaunting of a unique style which can provide some kind of displaced resolution to the powerlessness of the dole' (*ibid.*). To Willis the analyst, then, the meaning of this dancing rests with its compensatory effects to the experience of unemployment. Willis thereby provides a structural context for a set of cultural practices. And taking it as a given that he views his analysis as worth making, we can conclude from the approach he adopts that the entire meaning of any dance event is never wholly available to the dancers involved.

ATTRIBUTED AND INHERENT MEANING

Where do these discussions take us? Certainly from what has been said here we can claim that dance is meaningful from a variety of perspectives. Indeed, through looking at different sites of dance's meaning we have mapped at least some of the territory that it would seem appropriate to cover when seriously considering meaning and dance. But, necessary as this mapping has been, the identification of dance as meaningful is not after all the key issue here. For to say that a phenomenon is meaningful can be either a significant or an empty claim. Empty because we can make everything meaningful: nothing can be absolutely meaningless (even the state of meaninglessness itself has some meaning for us). Indeed, as Merleau-Ponty put it, as humans 'we are condemned to meaning' (1962, p. xix): we cannot stop ourselves making the world and our experience meaningful. So that to say that dance is meaningful, in the sense that we can make dance meaningful, is to say no more than that dance is a perceivable phenomenon: an activity like any other activity to which we can attribute meaning.

However, the claim that dance is meaningful becomes significant once we assert that dance itself constitutes meaning. And we can make this assertion, that is, dance events can be said to be inherently meaningful, when they have a meaning that exists independently of those meanings that the events have for critics and observers. So the issue here is not the methodological capacity of non-dancers to attribute meaning to dance but rather it is the discovery of, and the connections that can be made to, the meaning produced through dance by and for dancers. In other words, our focus must turn away from how non-dancers can make sense of dance to the meaning dance does make for dancers. Indeed, when the spectator, critic and ordinary community member make sense of dance (i.e. render it meaningful), their involvement will be exclusive of precisely that which is crucial about dance, and this is that it is embodied experience. The body is the vehicle for sensing the inherent meaning of dance. The body (apart from in the most trivial sense) is not involved in being a critic or the member of an audience.

But this brings us directly back to the key dilemma that is the leitmotif of this chapter: how do we capture the inherent meaning of dance when this is only available through dancing and cannot apparently be presented in a verbal or written form without distortion or loss? How can we talk about embodied experience and not end up ignoring or explaining away precisely that which is being considered?

CONCLUSION

The proposal here is that a focus on inherent meaning *does* allow us to speak *for* embodied experience. It does so on the grounds that if any range of activities is inherently meaningful this can be taken as the guarantee that these activities do belong to their particular social context (and that they are categorically human), and as such they are worthy of analytic attention. And once dancers' meanings are identified as the key concern it is social dance in particular that should be topicalised. This is so because generally speaking social dance is accessible to us as a practice in a way that performance dance and anthropological dance are not. (The former being available to the majority of us only as spectators; the latter only via the reports of specialists.) In other words, there is a categorical divide between dancers and the audience in performance dance and between the dancers and spectators in anthropologically interesting dance that does not exist between dancers and spectators in social dance, where these roles are interchangeable.

A corollary of this attention to social dance is that *all* social dance activities are potentially worth considering. This is important. For although it might well be that the dancing of Paul Willis's breakdancers is richer both choreographically and in terms of its inherent meaning than that of inebriated uncles at nieces' weddings, this in itself is no reason to ignore such dancing or to presume it has no significance. To do so would be like a botanist refusing to acknowledge the existence of a monocellular organism because it is not as complex and therefore as 'important' as, say, a flesh-eating plant. Of course, in Britain today not every uncle at every wedding dances and those that do may not always be entirely comfortable acknowledging that they did so. But a phenomenon does not have to be universal or even widely representative to demand our attention, whilst this sense of embarrassment, if anything, makes the dancing and what this dancing meant even more interesting.

It follows from these discussions that a focus on inherent meaning requires thinking about meaning in different terms than those the analyst (-qua-analyst) or the observer (-qua-observer) might routinely use when they make sense of dance. This means, for example, that it is no longer appropriate to approach this or that dance as if it had a message to reveal, or as if it was a discrete narrative moment, or if it was the mirror of, or cipher for, some more real or fundamental (social, economic or psychological) phenomena. We have to begin to think about dance not just as an activity but as a form of life or as a way of being. To do this we must recognise that dance enables us to access a different plane of experience that is in itself meaningful, where this meaning is continuous, diffuse and pervasive. In other words, quite different from the sense of meaning implied in the question: 'what does this dance (or dancing) mean?' For generally when we ask such a question we presume the working of a process in which dance is isolated from its context and freeze-framed, so that its single, specific and definite meaning can be recognised.

To develop a sense of the inherent meaning of dance, then, we have to move away from reading dance as if it was an assembly of hidden messages. We should also realise that in social dance meaning resides not so much in this or that dance as in dancing *per se*. More fundamentally we need to realise that embodied experience is not an optional extra, or a quaint or unwanted anachronism; rather it is an essential component of being human which needs to be fully recognised. The issue is not that such experience no longer exists, it is that we gear our engagement with one another both institutionally and personally in ways that deny the centrality and integrity of such experience. No one could seriously argue that dance, for example, is not empirically significant as a recurrent phenomenon in Britain today; yet at the same time dance seems to have only a very marginal place within public discourse.

The challenge that this situation poses had been the focus of this chapter. The contention here is that there is work to be done in coming to terms with social dance and its inherent meaning. In undertaking this work, we cannot avoid directing analytic attention to the individual. We have to try to grasp what dance means from those who are the sites of this meaning. But it is this subjective plane that sociology and cultural analysis cannot cope with at all. Indeed, it is no coincidence that at the same time as dance is so often made invisible within our culture, subjective experience is nearly always glossed, discarded or simply just does not appear in social and cultural analyses.

NOTES

1. The research was carried out by the Henley Centre for Forecasting. See Pierce, 1993.
2. These figures are extrapolated from the CSO's *Monthly Digest of Statistics* (October 1994), Table 2.2, where it is estimated that there were 7 015 590 young people aged between 16 and 20 in the UK in 1993.
3. The involvement of organised crime is a regular feature of press reports of raves. See, for example, Redhead, 1993, pp. 14–21; Goodwin, 1990; Lavelle, 1994, etc.

REFERENCES

A. Bellos, *Guardian*, 24.10.95.
C. Bishop, *Sunday Times*, 30.9.95.
P. Brinson, 'Epilogue: Anthropology and the Study of Dance' in P. Spencer (ed.), *Society and the Dance* (Cambridge: Cambridge University Press, 1985).

R. Burt, *The Male Dancer: Bodies, Spectacle, Sexualities* (London: Routledge, 1995).

Collins Paperback English Dictionary (Glasgow: William Collins, 1990).

CSO, *Monthly Digest of Statistics* (London: HMSO, October 1994).

C. D'Souza, *Sunday Times*, 2.4.95.

R. Gledhill, *The Times*, 19.8.95.

S. Goodwin, *The Times*, 10.3.90.

A. Grau, 'Gender Interchangeability among the Tiwi' in H. Thomas (ed.), *Dance, Gender and Culture* (London: Macmillan, 1993).

T. Halpin, *Daily Mail*, 8.3.94.

J. L. Hanna, *To Dance is Human* (Chicago: University of Chicago Press, 1987).

S. Langer, *Feeling and Form* (London: Routledge, 1953).

P. Lavelle, *Northern Echo*, 2.7.94.

N. Lawson, *The Times*, 4.3.95.

J. McLeod, *Daily Telegraph*, 15.7.95.

A. McRobbie, 'Shut Up and Dance: Youth Culture and Changing Modes of Femininity', *Cultural Studies*, 7, 3 (1993), pp. 406–26.

A. McRobbie, *Postmodernism and Popular Culture* (London: Routledge, 1994).

M. Merleau-Ponty, *The Primacy of Perception* (London: Routledge, 1962).

S. Moore, *Guardian*, 30.3.95.

B. Mouland, *Daily Mail*, 29.3.95.

N. Norman, *Evening Standard*, 26.6.95.

PHS/Times Diary, *The Times*, 29.3.95.

A. Pierce, *The Times*, 27.10.93.

T. Polhemus, 'Social Bodies' in J. Benthall and T. Polhemus (eds), *The Body as a Medium of Expression* (London: Allen Lane, 1975).

B. Redfern, *Dance, Art and Aesthetics* (London: Dance Books, 1988).

S. Redhead (ed.), *Rave Off: Politics and Deviance in Contemporary Youth Culture* (Aldershot: Avebury, 1993).

M. Roffey, *Independent*, 2.6.94.

N. Saunders, *Ecstasy and the Dance Culture* (London: Nicholas Saunders, 1995).

V. Seidler, *Rediscovering Masculinity: Reason, Language and Sexuality* (London: Routledge, 1989).

V. Seidler, *Recreating Sexual Politics* (London: Routledge, 1991).

F. Sparshott, *A Measured Pace* (Toronto: University of Toronto Press, 1995).

P. Spencer (ed.), *Society and the Dance* (Cambridge: Cambridge University Press, 1985).

H. Thomas, 'An-other Voice: Young Women Dancing and Talking' in H. Thomas (ed.), *Dance, Gender and Culture* (London: Macmillan, 1993).

T. Walker, *Daily Mail*, 30.3.95.

P. Willis, *Common Culture* (Milton Keynes: Open University Press, 1990).

R. Wolffe, *Financial Times*, 1.7.95.

M. Woolf, *Independent on Sunday*, 9.7.95.

2 Exer(or)cising Power: Black Bodies in the Black Public Sphere
Paul Gilroy

> The circle of the dance is a permissive circle: it protects and permits. At certain times on certain days, men and women come together at a given place and then, under the solemn eyes of the tribe, fling themselves into a seemingly unorganized pantomime which is in reality extremely systematic in which by various means – shakes of the head, bending of the spinal column, throwing the whole body backwards – may be deciphered as in an open book the huge effort of a community to exorcise itself, to liberate itself, to explain itself. There are no limits – inside the circle.
>
> Frantz Fanon

I have been asking myself, whatever happened to breakdancing? Where did the acrobatic dance form that legend tells us evolved in the South Bronx as a competitive alternative to gang violence go? I can still recall the awe with which underground London beheld Ritchie 'Crazy Legs' Morales perform a head-spin so devastating that it transformed the way that we heard the Rock Steady Crew's celebrated signature tune. Thirteen years later, no breakers have become stars. The most visible dancer operating in the hip-hop spotlight is Heavy D, and for all his skill, breaking is not part of his repertoire, which has a far more orthodox show-biz lineage. Where dance sequences appear in black music videos they stay close to the rules established by Hollywood musicals and endorsed by prominent crossover performers like Michael and Janet Jackson and Mariah Carey, whose latest video-led assault on the charts – *Fantasy*, a bizarre collaboration with the Wu Tang Clan's Ol' Dirty Bastard – includes a particularly leaden-footed set-piece.

Concern over the African origins and components of black diaspora cultures has recently re-emerged as a vital political issue. Because dance is regularly identified as one of the most reliably and authentically African elements in the black vernacular, this seems an appropriate point to ask why the innovative dance practice in early hip-hop culture faded away so quickly,

21

why the delicate initial balance which that wild, revolutionary style struck between music and dance shifted so emphatically away from the latter and why dance did not remain a more significant part of the mood, attitude and power of the movement as it conquered our planet's popular culture?

I also wonder whether the relative decline of dance in black popular culture and the curiously unmourned disappearance of breaking may have been connected to the negative impact of video technologies on expressive forms that had previously been sound-rather than vision-based and which were absolutely inseparable from the dance cultures in which they were embedded? We need to comprehend how the growing marginalisation and possible retreat of dance may have meshed with the privatisation of black vernacular culture: the decay of its precious oppositional public institutions and the growth of those corrosive individualisation effects that mark the novel patterns in which counter-culture becomes something that is consumed rather than simply used. Even in residual form, the conjunction of music and dance characteristic of African expressive cultures orchestrated the relationship between the individual and the group. It nurtured forms of self-consciousness, historicity and sociality even during the extreme conditions of slavery, when basic institutional arrangements like family life could only be maintained with the greatest difficulty.

As the memory of that slavery has grown less attractive as a source of solidarity and a means of collective identification, subaltern sociality and its secret public institutions have changed. They exemplify a decisive move away from the concern to ground sociality in what black bodies do and towards an almost morbid obsession with what they are, what they contain. At its worst, this makes sociality impossible. Sociality cannot be practised. It has to be simulated. Instead of taking our places in the circle of the dance where subordination was ambivalently enacted, transcended and transformed into the compensatory agency that flowed from exer/orcising power in a very limited space, we are invited to consume particularity just like any other commodity. The ring shout gives way to polite applause. Let me put this another way: it is not possible to dance in a car, however large and loud a sound system it may contain.

The appearance of new, culturally-sanctioned settings in which music is heard and enjoyed is only the most obvious example of the changes I am sketching here. Of course the ritual practices involved in showing the world that you have the prestige and wealth that a car represents, and that your car is well-stocked with sound-reproduction equipment, has acquired a public counter-cultural significance of its own in diverse urban locations. However, even when filled with sound and placed on display, I want to suggest that it makes more sense to see the car and the cult around it as another defeat, another capitulation to a system of value that represents the undoing of insurgent black political culture. In this light, the car is an expensive larger-scale equivalent to the personal stereo in the way it transforms community and sociality. BMWs are not Bob Marley wagons, whatever Bob may have said to the contrary.

Hip-hop has changed under these pressures too. It is probably heretical to suggest that music has become far less important to it than it once was. But one can buy in to the hip-hop nation by other means than music. The old feral, democratic spirit has become domesticated in the pursuit of crossover cash, stardom and commercial longevity amidst the relentless contemporaneity of the postmodern. The 'traditional' counter-values forged on the slave plantations, and reactivated in condensed form in those circles that endorsed the mutant offspring of Capoiera and the Caribbean dancehall, have been dissipated. They have been painted over in the sparkling logos of an indifferent corporate appropriation of blackness that would harness the insurgent vitality of the abject and make it into nothing more than an exciting means to dwell in the body. Carefully simulated black subcultures supply an ecstatic but unsyncopated soundtrack for the joyous discipline of Working Out.

The protracted competition between sound and vision to define the conceptual co-ordinates and axiological priorities involved in black sub-sub-culture and its overground offshoots cannot be won by sound. However, there are other catastrophic developments that convey the grim changes in black political culture and its historic patterns of public interaction. For example, the rapid accommodation between hip-hop and the fashion industry conveyed in the rise of avowedly 'pro-black' labels like Phat Farm and Karl Kani is one more chapter in a sorry narrative about the changing power of the black body as a sign of exotic alterity. Authenticity and particularity are conveyed, not by the display of the unclothed body with its mix of vulnerability and erotic charge, but by the way the body is clothed in expensive items of clothing and footwear. Defiance can apparently be reduced to the manner in which the waistband of your Tommy Hilfiger underwear is visible above the belt of your oversize trousers. The parallel vogue among black men and women for marking the body in various ways – elaborate tattoos, shaved heads, piercing, brands, etc. – supplies further clues as to the changed status and value of the body in the recent development of black popular culture where blackness itself, unadorned or unmodified, is felt to be insufficiently potent even as a sign of racial sameness and transgressive, cryptic solidarity. As with the car cult, the liberatory moment in this is harder and harder to locate.

But what of breaking? It faded right out of hip-hop partly because of a

steady long-term decline in the importance of dance post-disco, and secondly because some of its specific formal features – its assertive extremity,
if you like – were incompatible with the packaging and marketing of
hip-hop as just another form of official popular culture. It could not be
transformed into an object for sale, and its disappearance (like the simultaneous loss of double-Dutch skipping; an invigorating component in the
early hip-hop shows that was the first casualty of wild style's corporate
hyper-masculinisation) conveys the secret of hip-hop's fateful transformation. Today the merest traces of those extraordinary innovations in dance
remain an important element in the mythology of hip-hop style and its
contested historicity.

However, the practice of breaking and the precious circular, public spaces
in which it happened have been irretrievably lost to us. They have been
replaced by a different set of spatial and kinetic habits that anticipate and
organise spectatorship in quite different ways and which play a pernicious
role in the simulation of community. The key trope here is basketball, and
though we should not underestimate the significance of the ballcourt as
distinctive public stage for the real-life drama of male bonding, the met-
onymic extension of the team and the game into wholly male representations racial community are especially disquieting. These alternative images
of black vitality appear regularly outside real time and face-to-face interaction. It is only rich men like Spike Lee who can afford the courtside
seats at Knicks games.[1] These sports-oriented alternatives to dance are
circulated by television. Their most important characteristic is revealed in
the way that they have altered the fragile equilibrium between individual
and group, that helped to define the antiphonic relationships that have governed the operations of this hidden public realm from its inception. It bears
repetition that these images of black vitality and physical prowess are increasingly remote from music. Because they derive from team sports, their
favoured forms of movement are always purposive, strongly directional and
precisely goal-oriented. Even when they are encountered live, the time axis
of their distinctive time–space relationships has been determined by the
eccentric demands of television presentation. In appreciating the extent
of these slow but relentless changes, it is also important to consider where
the black body in motion has appeared to mediate the tensions between
what might respectively be termed the performative and essentialised
understandings of black identity – understood here as subjectivity and self-
consciousness. This enquiry might begin by counterposing approaches to
blackness based on the idea that racial particularity is the simple product
of some distinctive supra-individual force, say biology or invariant culture, with those alternative conceptualisations which have emphasised the

possibility that the difference 'race' makes is somehow the effect of contingent historical practices (even those that are imagined to precede it). Accordingly, the latter have placed special attention on the collective, expressive and ritualised cultural practices that mobilise and create solidarity and articulate community.

Divorced from this traditional setting for solidarity-creating and community-precipitating action and interaction, the whole, perfect, exemplary black body has recently become visible in the sports cultures that have been produced to rival and supplant the older representational patterns common to antiphonic practices from worshipping to breaking. Images of the black body in motion now adorn every advertisement for shoes and sportswear aimed at people under the age of 25. The movement they present is always purposive – towards the winning tape, towards the hoop on the ballcourt. It may include elements of dance with or without accompanying music, but any elements of dance it encompasses are not central features of how we are invited to appreciate it. Sports have become an increasingly important alternative to dance, less for the appreciation of kinesics on display – almost always tailored to the possibility of the video replay – but for their value in staging especially heroic types of masculine and masculinist activity.

I want to suggest that the disappearance of breakdancing and the distinctive relationship between music and dance that it celebrated communicates many of the wider changes in black expressive cultures. In particular, I would like to consider whether the very different ways of seeing and, indeed, of enjoying the body in motion that exist in opposition to one another under the headings 'dance' and 'sport' may express and reveal important developments in the organisation of the black public sphere, transformed by the catastrophic state of black urban life in the overdeveloped countries, but nevertheless projected outwards on an unprecedented planetary scale. As the twentieth century draws to a close, the meaning of blackness has become more evasive and less amenable to the certainties of the colonial period. Setting the ongoing struggle against white supremacy aside for a moment, if we want to maintain the democratic core of black political culture and renew its most generous moral and political aspirations, we should be cautious about allowing the racial body to stand by default as the cipher of authentic identity.

Thinking about the politics of performance-centred expressive culture can help to challenge these fashionable views of the body as the repository and confirmation of absolute racial difference. Against those authoritarian hopes, the black body can be affirmed as it emerged from the living arenas of vernacular culture: broken, twisted and vulnerable. In that distinctive light it bears an ironic confirmation of the essential similarity of species being, as well as the still weeping wounds inflicted under colonial subordination. Before we recommend that artists accept the poisoned chalice of a new obligation and undertake the impossible missions involved in communicating a novel, possibly more misanthropic, humanism in their manipulation and display of human similarity embodied on the scale in which dance can be perceived, there is a little more to say about the black body, the patterns of solidarity and identification that it helps to establish and the disruptive processes of epidermalisation that arise to block any new humanism and divert it back into their frozen dialectic of body and world. Frantz Fanon considered exactly this possibility and the crisis it instantiates in a celebrated passage from *Black Skin, White Masks*.

> Then, assailed at various points, the corporeal schema crumbled, its place taken by a racial epidermal schema ... it was no longer a question of being aware of my body in the third person ... I was given not one but two, three places ... It was not that I was finding febrile co-ordinates in the world. I existed triply: I occupied space. I moved toward the other ... and the evanescent other, hostile but not opaque, transparent, not there, disappeared. Nausea .... (Fanon, 1968, p. 112)

Under Fanon's guidance, we should remember, first of all, that the black body does not speak for itself. Secondly, we must question the ways in which the body and the idea of racialised embodiment have emerged as an anchor in the stormy tides of identity politics. There are now racial epidermal schemas that attack the power of white supremacy rather than reproduce it. They also conflict with the 'slow composition of my self as a body in the middle of the spatial and temporal world' that Fanon presented as the corporeal alternative. Their power derives from a situation in which the body has become the means by which individual freedom and racial solidarity can be bound to life itself. The black body is a body that is no longer to be supervised by the soul which was once imagined to outlive it. There is no longer a soul there, it has been banished by the same fatal affirmation of carnal and corporeal vitality. Disturbingly, the enthusiasm with which this has been undertaken recalls something of Fanon's observation about the importance of dreams of bodily potency and activity in the motionless, Manichaean colonial setting:

> The first thing the native learns is to stay in his place, and not to go beyond certain limits. This is why his dreams are always of muscular prowess; his dreams are of action and of aggression. I dream I am jumping, swimming, running, climbing: I dream that I burst out laughing,

that I span a river in one stride, or that I am followed by a flood of motor cars that never catch up with me . . . the native never stops achieving his freedom from nine in the morning until six in the evening. (Fanon, 1968, p. 40)

The image world of contemporary youth culture reveals that these dreams are no longer confined to the natives. Similar fantasies have been solicited, amplified and projected by new technological means through cultural industries that encompass the globe. The leaping native is particularly visible in the corporate versions of multi-culture. That dynamic figure is the linchpin of their premature universalisms. The native's exceptional prowess lends magical qualities to the sale of commodities like sports shoes and clothing which promote complex forms of intimacy and mimicry across the line of colour. A picture of Michael Jordan advertising Nike sneakers can be captioned 'You'll believe a man can fly' without anybody raising an eyebrow.

Similar investments in the magic of black vitality are associated with views of the body as confirmation of racialised particularity that have taken root inside the black communities themselves. This version has much in common with the other types of epidermalism whose damage it strives to repair. It operates comfortably in conjunction with the new genetic and biological determinisms that are being voiced, not only by the Bell Curve ideologues but in comparably pernicious forms by a diverse range of political opinion from within black communities. The occultist presentation of melanin as the fundamental measure of black superiority is the most pressing example here:

What makes BLACK CULTURE? Why do BLACK HUMANS express themselves uniquely and differently from non-BLACK human species? Why do we dance, sing, dress, walk/run, cook, laugh/cry, play the game of football/basketball, think work etc. differently from other races? If you compare BLACK CULTURES around the world, you will become pleasantly aware that BLACK HUMANS are not different! From one end of the globe to the other end of the globe, you will find black humans are Expressive, colourful, creative, industrious, generous, cocky . . . just like your neighbour across the street or across town. All 'Industries' created and designed by the BLACK HUMAN (and from his culture) will be 'RICH' in essence and depth! Even when the BLACK HUMAN is poor, the resources he has to work with may be limited but the produce that he produces will be well prepared and EXPRESSIVE! (Barnes, n.d., p. 53)

To be sure dance comes first in the list of racial practices but this priority feels like an anachronistic gesture. This approach to the ontology of blackness is far more interested in what the body is than in what it does. Its mechanisms work in one direction only, from the outside inwards. I puzzled for a long time over these curious sentences which articulate the yearning for a lost scale of sociality as readily as they convey a taste for the vain alchemy of hyper-similarity and absolute invariance. Work is notably present in this grim utopia from which all difference has been expelled, a utopia that adds veracity to the oldest of racist stereotypes and re-energises a worn-out Victorianism. The tropes of this black 'humanism' are striking too. Less surprisingly, the gendered prowess that gets showcased on the ballcourt and other popular representations of sporting excellence supplies the key figures. Together, they create a climate in which black physical superiority appears plausible compensation for the wrongs of an unjust world skewed by racial typologies. The melanin theory tells us why white men can't jump. These expressive, colourful, creative industrious, generous, cocky, racial selves are nothing but body; 'The negro is only biological' said Fanon (1968). And yet, even among the most ardent 'melanists' the technologies of the racialised self make their inevitable appearance. Even here the force of nature turns out to be insufficient. People have to be induced, taught how to recover and remember the potency of melanin in their bodies, to listen once again for the ways in which their bodies – readily reduced here to the units of their cells – call out to them and to each other the siren song of a collective racial memory which in the new-age versions of Africentrism appear legitimated by appeals to the insight and authority of Jung.

The rate at which one loses tour with melanin's powerful influence on the spiritual self is directly related to the amount of European socialisation and 'education' received ... the avenues to our melanin centres are partially blocked by our adoption of Western diets, environmental pollution, and ways of thinking. Since melanin acts like an antenna or highly-tuned receiver, it will resonate in sympathy with whatever is going on in your environment. So if you surround yourself with negative forces (in your family, workplace, social life, or bad food you consume), they will alter physiologically and neurologically that which acts to preserve your melanin.

The ancient prophecy that there will be war until the colour of a man's skin is of no more significance than the colour of his eyes springs to mind here. Its open plea against the power of phenotype which condemns human beings to interminable and irrational conflict, stands in stark opposition to these more recent approaches to racial biology. They revel in the meat world and defer to bio-social mechanisms, departing sharply from the image of an integral, over-coded body, loaded with the latent superiority that nature has endowed in it. That powerful phrase sets the body against itself in pursuing the project of stripping white supremacy of its rationality. For Bob Marley, the human body was not whole or integral. It could not speak with one voice. Eyes and skin, body components of equivalent status, transmit opposed messages about the material truths of race and their signification. Phenotype has no natural meaning anterior to its mutable historical and cultural codes. The contested process of signification is the only issue. And yet, what might be called the biopolitical impulse to present the body as the essential cipher of identity and a potential guarantor of solidarity is common to a wider range of black political thought than the melanin example suggests. It connects the out and out occultism of those who believe that melanin is the biological proof of black superiority to the less obviously biologistic writings of hipper, more respectable and scholarly folks who might even oppose some of the oddball political positions adopted at the meeting-point of eighteenth-century racial science and Americo-centric nationalisms. The body and its semiosis have come to host a battle royal in which different interests fight for the pleasure of annexing its special communicative powers in their contending representational regimes. This is the background to the growing appeal of theories of racial particularity centred on the idea of common attributes coded into black flesh by means of memory. Memory has the virtue of blurring the line between biology and culture. As with the melanist approach, we are invited to pass through the skin and with it through the destructive stage that Fanon described. We move inside the body so that we can perceive how the calculus of particularity operates on what we can only call a nano-political scale. The skin is our threshold, the new frontier for utopian and fundamentalist hopes. It is not a barrier between ourselves and the world, and our Others. That external surface is the most important expression our inner differences, the outward sign of a difference so profound that we do not need to do anything else except learn to listen to its inarticulate specification. If we are roused from our an-aestheticised state into any sort of political consciousness it is not as a result of righteous moral anger but because common embodied memory demands it of us. So that's all right then.

Contemplating attempts to resolve the crises of racial sameness and solidarity by appealing to the power of the body drew me into a more benevolent attitude towards the subversive profanity of black vernacular culture. Rappers like Eazy E, Snoop, Willie D and their insubordinate peers have adopted a deliberately vulgar and disorderly stance which resists discipline and pushes all the time towards the border zones where the stubborn divisions of region, class, sex and gender reassert themselves and refuse to be translated into invariant, epidermal, cellular or nano-political inscriptions. The boyz and girlz from the hood will resist being drafted into the programme of racial recovery proposed by their betters in the bourgeoisie. In contrast to the transcendent essentialism of hyper-similar cells and racial memory, gangsta consciousness is fiercely territorial. The form of solidarity it favours, if solidarity is recognised at all, is spatialised. The gs locate and adhere to the lived boundaries of community. This agenda assumes an absolute minimum of a-priori racial unity. It prompts our understanding of what solidarity adds up to in a dog-eat-dog world. MC Eiht, besides whom Snoop and Eazy sound tender and tame, put it like this:

> Muthafuckas is successful now, right now. Everybody in this muthafucka got the mentality we don't give a fuck about what nobody say. Nigga gonna make his money, he gonna live like he wanna live. When that day come if a nigga got to die, that's the day. For the community – it always seems to me that everytime a nigga get to a certain level he got to come back to the community and he got to put community centers etc. That justifies him saying, 'Okay, I love the community and I'ma do something for where I'm from.' I ain't dead, muthafucka. That's me. When I was in the muthafuckin neighborhood, I ran with the niggas. Niggas didn't put no money in my pocket, niggas wasn't givin' me no dope. Niggas wasn't doing shit for me except sayin', 'He the homie'. So for my community, I'ma make the music that my niggas like but I ain't gonna sit up here and go build me a child center over here and build me this over there 'cause that's fuckin bullshit. I'm in this shit for me . . . I ain't no political muthafucka. I ain't taikin about muthafuckin' stop the violence. I ain't talkin about the Black movement 'cause that shit ain't going on in the hood. Ain't no muthfucka comin' up with no bean pies standin' on my corner. (*The Source*, 57, 1994, p. 72)

Thus the ghetto-centric individualism of the poor can easily defeat the convenient bio-essentialism of the elite. You choose to be a gangsta and you can renounce the affiliation at any time. Eiht states the consequences of this changed orientation clearly when he derides the black voices raised against gangsta rap in these terms: 'Them color-coated ass – I don't even call them Black, they ain't Niggas to me' (*The Source*, 57, 1994, p. 70).

Similar class divisions have been revealed in equally bitter intra-racial conflicts arising from vernacular discourse on sex. The body figures here too. But again, it is not presented whole, as an organic vehicle for common racial memory. Like the dog and the bitch, the gangsta is driven by instinct – a pre-conscious form of memory not susceptible to regulation.

In capitulating to it, Snoop laments the fact that he cannot help but chase that cat. Nature is not the friend, guide or ally that it appears to be in the memorialising discourse of the pseudo-scientists, melanists and epidermalisers. Nature is a curse, another indefinitely suspended sentence, just like life.

Moving in a similar direction to Marley's suggestive distinction between eyes and skin, the body is fragmented, its truths dispersed. This time however, particular parts are prized. Selected zones are affirmed and celebrated because the space over which power can be exercised just keeps on shrinking and because they are close to the disguised animal dimensions of vitality. Here we should consider the way that the dog thaang lowers the black body's centre of gravity, taking it closer to the low-down and dirty. For example, it involves encountering your sexual partner nose to tail. The body responds to the summons that Blackstreet have eulogised as a 'booti call'. This is not only a restatement of the traditional hedonism articulated in previous vulgar reclamations of the black body from the troubled worlds of work and labour, or its celebration as a locus of resistance, pleasure and desire. It is something more potent that reorders the hierarchy of body zones and organs in a pattern that moves decisively beyond the old oscillations between sex and violence which James Baldwin once identified as alternate fillings for the shell of black cultural expression.

The re-evaluation of the booti/butt/batty is one element in the same desperate quest, firstly to centre black particularity in the body. bell hooks (1992) and Carolyn Cooper (1993) have pointed out that in different locations, the butt cult encompasses bids to revalorise the abject bodies of black women. These operations are centred on the dance-hall, which as we have already seen, is no longer monopolised by men, many of whom have migrated to the ballcourt and its equivalents in pursuit of their favoured forms of homophiliac association. DJ Shabba Ranks, whose fundamentalist pronouncements in the area of sexual morality go beyond homophobia into a more complicated realm of ambivalence, shows how taboos regulating sexual practice can come to specify the limits of the racial collectivity in the most unexpected ways: 'I don't care what they want to say about me, so long as no one can say that I suck a pussy or fuck a batty' (Kenner, 1994, p. 76). This anxiety underscores the mutability and multi-accentuality of the body as a material/semiotic actor. In Shabba's vernacular, blackness has not been written into or even on to the body, for the body is not stable or still long enough to permit that act of inscription. It is not what the body is or carries inside it that counts but rather what the body does in its relationship to other bodies. The mind/body dualism is not being covertly reinstated through appeals to memory over which a guilty, privileged 'colonial' elite can preside. Blackness emerges, then, as more behavioural, dare I say cultural, attribute? It can be announced by indicative sexual habits and bodily gestures. Under some circumstances, it can even be acquired in simple economic processes. You can buy it. Identity as sameness and solidarity is definitely not being essentialised. Items can be purchased that lend an eloquent uniformity to the mute body on a temporary, accidental basis. This is not an inward journey after all but a journey to the shops, preferably undertaken in an appropriately ostentatious form of transport.

Style and fashion offer something of the same forms of mechanical solidarity conferred by the uniform of the bourgeois male which works a different racialising magic for the Nation of Islam. It bears repetition that in both cases, the unclothed body is not considered sufficient to confer either authenticity or identity. Clothing, objects, things, commodities provide the only entry ticket into stylish solidarities powerful enough to foster the novel forms of nationality found in collectivities like the Gangsta Nation, the hip-hop Nation and of course, The Nation of Islam.

Let me try to draw these speculative strands together. Inside the black communities, as old certainties about the fixed limits of racial identity have lost their power to convince or even make sense of the extreme divisions produced by deindustrialisation, an ontological security capable of answering a radically reduced sense of the value of black life has been sought in the naturalising powers of the body: clothed and unclothed, fragmented or whole. The old compensatory themes that answered black powerlessness – sex and gender – have been transformed by the rise of a body-centred nano-politics. The freaky programme of sexual play and recreation celebrated by artists like R. Kelly, Patra, Aaron Hall and Wayne Marshall appears as a ludic alternative to the mechanical solidarity of race, whether this is articulated through the austerity of the Nation and its surrogates, or the fantasy of masculine hyper-similarity projected through the culture of black sporting excellence, and the heroism cultivated there by marketing men and women who want to sell shoes and sportswear to white teenagers. Sex is more disorderly and unstable than the conventional images of black vitality that have been complicit for so long with the core of white supremacy. Shabba's example reveals exactly how sex has to be trained, domesticated, diverted and technologised into appropriate channels in order to ground the family and thus the nation.

The body emerges in the double role of actor and contested object. It is being claimed by various regimes of representation and desire which create distinct forms of identification and usher in widely differing political possibilities that are not so conveniently arranged as to be mutually exclusive. Fashion spills over into the sports cult which bleeds into the dreams of chemically-programmed black superiority. Items of clothing are trafficked between the public, crossover world and its hidden black counterparts. The discourses playing on coding, materialising black flesh promise power but can readily revert to simple racist type, especially where excessive physical strength banishes cognitive capacities and wanton, equally excessive sexuality supposedly defines us outside the official syntax of gender. These dangers are not confined to the effect they may have on white spectators but can also be felt where blacks begin to live, not with, but through them and the doubtful forms of empowerment they can offer.

An emergent trans-local culture is giving the black body a makeover. We are witnessing a series of struggles over the meaning of that body which intermittently emerges as a signifier of prestige, autonomy, transgression and power in a supra-national economy of signs that is not reducible to the old-style logics of white supremacy. Faced with that and with deindustrialisation, the proliferation of intra-communal divisions based upon wealth and money, sexuality and gender, the black elite may find it expedient to fall back on exceptionalist narratives and essential identities. It may even reconstruct them through a variety of political languages: melanin, memory, authoritarian nationhood and Afro-centrism, or a combination of them all. I comprehend those responses but I wonder how much they are about a privileged group mystifying its own increasing remoteness from the lives of most black people whose priorities, habits and tastes can no longer be considered as self-legitimating indicators of racial integrity. The body is being used to restore that fading integrity in ways that abrogate the historic responsibility of intellectuals (not academics) to make it communicate the precious, fragile and contingent truths of black sociality. In the face of reborn bio-powers, is it possible to articulate an alternative, post-anthropological understanding of culture that has anything like the same explanatory power? What role might thinking about vernacular dance traditions play in that? We must be quick before they disappear.

NOTE

1.   A recent interview with Lee in *The Source* revealed that the price of these seats has recently tripled from $300 to $1000. '"Don't worry, I'll still be there," he says with a Cheshire grin' (*The Source*, 73, October 1995, p. 70).

REFERENCES

C. Barnes, *Melanin: The Chemical Key To Black Greatness* (Houston, TX: C. B. Publishers, n.d.), p. 53.

C. Cooper, *Noises in the Blood* (London: Macmillan, 1993).

F. Fanon, *Black Skin, White Masks* (London: McGibbon & Kee, 1968).

'Gangsta Rap Summit: "Reality Check"', *The Source*, 57 (June 1994), p. 72.

b. hooks, *Black Looks: Race and Representation* (Boston, MA: Southend Press, 1992).

R. Kenner, 'Top Rankin'', *Vibe* (October 1994), p. 76.

G. Peart, 'More Than The Colour of My Skin', Science Focus, *The Alarm*, 9 (November 1994), p. 25.

3 'Keep Your Great City Paris!' – The Lament of the Empress and other Women

Valerie A. Briginshaw

This chapter investigates the use of cities as settings in seven dance films and videos. It is based on the premise that space, and the related concepts of travel and mapping, are constructions which are gendered and consequently invested with power (Briginshaw, 1995).[1] Since cities are particular kinds of constructed spaces, the ways in which they are gendered and invested with power have implications for the interpretations of dances set in them. The treatment of city spaces by the choreography and filming in these dance texts is examined to determine the extent to which the cities are positioned as 'natural' or constructed; hiding or revealing key constituents of that construction, such as gender.

The postmodern city, like the postmodern subject, is fractured and fragmented, it is falling apart and full of contradictions. It is utopian and dystopian, attracting and alienating. It is constructed as labyrinthine, free-flowing and uncontrollable, but also as containing and trapping. The first half of the chapter examines ways in which the choreography and filming in the dance texts contribute to the construction of some of these connotations associated with the postmodern city. Constructions of the city are inextricably bound up with constructions of subjectivity. Consequently in the analysis of the dance texts, particular attention is paid to the ways in which the dancers' interactions with the urban environments contribute to these construction processes and the role gender plays. In some of the dance films examined the male or masculine gaze contributes to the construction of cities and subjects, and so the implications of this for the gendering of these sites of meaning are also outlined.

Metaphors of travel and mapping have been employed in postmodern discourse to reposition or orientate fragmented, displaced subjects (Briginshaw, 1995). The second part of the chapter examines the roles travel and mapping play in the construction of subjects and cities in the dance texts.

Reappropriations of these metaphors are suggested to illustrate the ways in which some of the texts reveal and explore the constructed and gendered nature of cities and subjects, whilst others use the city as a backdrop for dance, without paying attention to the 'complex web of power, space and difference' within which the 'public spaces of the city and the private lives of its inhabitants must be understood' (Bell & Valentine, 1995, p. 113).

CONSTRUCTIONS OF CITIES AND SUBJECTS – INSCRIPTION AND INTERFACES

One of the attractions of the postmodern city is that because 'it is mainly about the production of signs and images' it provides an exciting arena for representations. It has been likened to 'a theatre, a series of stages upon which individuals could work their own distinctive magic while performing a multiplicity of roles' (Harvey, 1989, p. 5). The city's plasticity allows and invites interactions of many kinds which can open up possibilities for a shifting kaleidoscope of identities. It is perhaps not surprising that this 'soft city of illusion, myth, aspiration, nightmare' (Raban, 1974, quoted in Harvey, 1989, p. 5), which fires the imagination, has become a favoured setting for recent dance texts.[2]

The particular ways in which cities and subjects 'mutually define' each other are evident when interactions of dancers with urban landscapes are examined. Bodies and cities can be seen to 'inscribe' each other; 'there is a two-way linkage that could be defined as an *interface*' (Grosz, 1995, p. 108). This 'interface' provides a space in which identities can be discovered, forged and played with. 'In learning a city (as "city") we learn ourselves' (Preziosi, 1990, p. 262).

'Cities' and 'ourselves', whose identities are forged, played with and constructed in this sense are not therefore neutral or 'natural'. Rather, they are traversed by a complex web of power relations, determined by the ways in which the world is seen and conceived, and one strand of this conception and construction is gender. Space tends to be feminised deriving from Plato's notions of the female *chora*. The associations that result have similarities with descriptions of the soft, postmodern city (Raban, 1974, in Harvey, 1989). In Plato's view space is conceptualised as 'a bounded entity', 'a sort of container' associated with the female body, particularly with that of the mother (Best, 1995, p. 182). He states 'it [the receptacle/ space] . . . is a kind of . . . plastic material on which changing impressions are stamped by the things which enter it making it appear different at different times . . . . We may use the metaphor of birth and compare the receptacle to the mother' (quoted in Best, 1995, p. 184). These conceptions of space as feminine, containing and bounded are particularly relevant where cities are concerned and in the dance texts that are examined.

Surfaces in Contact/Connotations of Containment

In two of the dance texts the interface between bodies and cities is particularly marked because there is considerable contact between the surfaces of both. The bodies of the dancers literally brush up against and collide with walls, floors and pavements of the city. Its architecture and buildings are clearly seen to contain, even to trap and impound the performers.

In *Step in Time Girls* (1988), choreographed by Yolande Snaith and filmed by Terry Braun, three women from different periods; 'contemporary', 'wartime' and 'Victorian', are seen inhabiting and coming and going from the same London flat. Frustration with the environment and situation are evident when the women repeatedly rock back and forth in chairs, run and jump up against walls and windowsills and stride back and forth along table and windowsill. Their containment and alienation are emphasised because they are often seen in relation to the windows; their link with the outside world. They look out of them, pace up and down in front of them and dance on the windowsill. They are also viewed from outside; as the camera recedes, minute pictures of private lives are glimpsed, framed by the numerous identical cell-like windows of a block of flats. The space of the flat is coded 'domestic' by aspects of the choreography; the dogged repetition of tasks that the women perform, such as opening cupboards and drawers, returning a baby's spoon to its high-chair tray and running up and down stairs. The choreography abstracts and emphasises the movements through development, exaggeration and particularly, repetition. Different parts of the body, such as shoulders, backs and feet, contact the furniture and walls and repetitive rhythms are often built up, giving impressions of obsession and frustration. Thus the choreography and filming of *Step in Time Girls*, by revealing ways in which urban spaces contain and trap, gender them traditionally feminine and render the inhabitants, also gendered feminine, powerless to a certain extent.

Surfaces of the body and of the city also meet in *Muurwerk* (1987), a female solo set in a Brussels alleyway, choreographed and performed by Roxane Huilmand and directed by Wolfgang Kolb. There are very few moments when one or other part of Huilmand's body is *not* in contact with the walls or ground. Repetitive phrases of rolling and spinning along the walls and floor of the alley are interspersed with Huilmand, for example, circling round on the ground, from sitting to rolling on to hands and feet.

This literal inscription of body and city is emphasised through camera close-ups, choreographically through persistent repetition and dynamic contrasts of speed and body tension, and aurally in the soundtrack where the brushing, scraping and hitting of body on walls and ground is heard. Although Huilmand is clearly contained and bound by the sides, floor and end of the alley, she does not appear trapped. The space as container is gendered feminine, but it is not totally restrictive. The choreography and filming open up possibilities for change in the interface between the subject and the city. Huilmand seems at least partly able to create her own labyrinth and through this discover new movement and identity possibilities and the potential of new relationships with the city and its spaces.

Foregrounded Constructions

Other examples where the interface between bodies and cities is opened up occur in *The Lament of the Empress (Die Klage der Kaiserin)* (1989), a film partly set in the German city of Wuppertal and choreographed and directed by Pina Bausch. Although the film is not set entirely in an urban environment, there are scenes in busy traffic, where performers appear to be inscribed on the city. At a major intersection a woman sits in an armchair nonchalantly smoking a cigarette, seemingly oblivious of the passing traffic. Her minimal choreography consists of the occasional turn of the head or slight adjustment of her sitting position. In another scene a male performer crouches in the gutter of a very wet street assiduously attempting to shave. He is repeatedly soaked by the spray of passing cars. Here dancers are not simply presented against the background of a city in a transparent manner that conceals the constructed and gendered nature of cities and subjects. By putting her performers in extreme situations, Bausch succeeds in drawing out exceptional qualities of projection from them. Her choreography and direction, including the careful placing of the performers, render them so *out* of place in the urban landscape that any 'natural' interface between subjects and cities is questioned. As Sanchez-Colberg (1993, p. 224) states: 'the work treats the relationship between body and space intertextually'. By radically juxtaposing performers, choreography and environment, Bausch questions the 'natural' relations assumed between bodies and space and 'the sign/signifier relationship of the individual elements (whether the space or the behaviour) is broken' (*ibid.*). In this way the mutual definition of cities and subjects and the fact that they are constructed and not 'natural', are foregrounded self-reflexively in the performance and filming.

Contradictions and Ambiguities/Fragmented Cities and Subjects

In *Dark Hours and Finer Moments* (1994), as in *Freefall* (1988), both choreographed by Gabi Agis and filmed respectively by Douglas Hart and Bob Bentley, there seems to be some ambiguity concerning the interface of the women dancers' bodies with cities. Hints of the excitement, promise and temptation of the city that rest on desire and its satisfaction appear and reappear throughout both pieces, but there are also suggestions of vulnerability, alienation and fragmented subjectivity. Cities are often portrayed as labyrinths in which people lose themselves and as sites of 'inexplicable violence' (Harvey, 1989, p. 6). As Raban (1974) states: 'the very plastic qualities which make the great city the liberator of human identity also cause it to be especially vulnerable to psychosis and totalitarian nightmare' (quoted in Harvey, 1989, p. 6).

In *Freefall* and *Dark Hours* there are both moments of power and of vulnerability and 'the sexual *frisson* of the metropolis' (Best, 1995, p. 152) is suggested. Near the end of *Freefall* five female dancers in brightly-coloured, flying silk dresses are seen in a dark, wet street under arcade arches and massive stone pillars. The choreography, which includes women loitering by and appearing from behind the pillars and running and leaping across the space, hints at the kind of vulnerability associated with women alone in cities at night. Is the image projected one of vulnerability or one of power, are these women perhaps 'reclaiming the night'?

In *Dark Hours* playful cross-dressing might also suggest gender ambiguity. Four women dressed in men's trench-coats and wearing ludicrously false beards are spread across a street in line, dancing seductively in unison and then in pairs. As they leap through the air their coats fly open, revealing glimpses of knickers. The final shot is of the performers lined up across the road facing away from us, slowly slipping their coats down to their waists, revealing their naked backs wearing only bras – each one a different colour. This is ambiguous – is the cross-dressing empowering and playful, parodying flashers, and the stripping and coloured bras, parodying prostitutes? Does the androgyny suggest a refusal to conform to and thus, liberation from, discourses of gendered heterosexuality? Or does this scene leave itself open to other readings informed by a voyeuristic and possessive male gaze? The contradictions and ambiguities evident in the readings of these two films compound and mask the gendering of subjects and space and point up the fractures, fissures, utopias and dystopias of the postmodern city.

Hints of the fractured identities of postmodern cities and subjects become apparent when extracts from *Freefall* and *Circumnavigation* (1992), a film

in four parts, each set in a different city, choreographed and directed by
Norbert and Nicole Corsino, are examined. In the Trieste section of *Circumnavigation*, there is a scene where classical pillars surround a marble
floor, creating a similar setting to the arcade and pillars in *Freefall* described
above. In both cases the geometry and scale of the historic, classical buildings suggest might and power. This is further emphasised by the contrast
of female dancers, spreading their arms, spinning and turning in these
spaces. However, the gendered nature of both subjects and space is concealed to a certain extent by the aesthetic that prevails. The juxtaposition
of dancers and setting, particularly in *Circumnavigation*, begins to appear
'natural' because throughout the film the same performers have been seen
dancing similar choreography against a range of different city backdrops.
To a lesser extent this is also the case in *Freefall*. The style of the choreography provides a thread through the films that masks the significance of
the inscriptions of bodies on cities, rendering them transparent. When the
gendered constructions of subjects and spaces are considered, fractured
rather than uniform identities are revealed. The containment of the space
could be seen as a feminine characteristic, but the vertical grandeur of the
architecture, when contrasted with the performers, gendered feminine by
the choreography, appears decidedly masculine.

This is particularly evident in the *Circumnavigation* extract, which is set
in the foyer of a grand building. After a short female solo, two men enter
in turn; the first looks down at the soloist, she pauses briefly then continues
her revolving choreography, occasionally stretching her arms upwards and
outwards; the second puts his hand on her elbow as if to restrain her. As
she dances away the two men remain standing, each vertically aligned
with a pillar in the camera shot. The choreography and filming subject the
bodies of the male dancers to the structures of the building, suggesting
comparisons.

The Gaze and the City

In these extracts just discussed the dancers are partly gendered by the
ways in which the performers look at each other. Theories of the 'look'
or the 'gaze' and the ways in which looking is gendered are prevalent in
feminist scholarship from Berger's (1973) statement that 'men look' whilst
'women appear' and connote 'to-be-looked-at-ness' to Mulvey's (1975)
theory of the male gaze at work in Hollywood cinema. There is much
evidence of the ways in which the male or masculine gaze objectifies,
masters and controls, and of its contribution to the gendering of space
(Briginshaw, 1995).

When this masculine gaze is turned on the city it could be said to have its origins in the concept of the late nineteenth-century *flâneur*, associated with the writings of the Parisian poet, Baudelaire, by the critic, Walter Benjamin. The *flâneur* was the hero of the modern city, enjoying the freedom to stroll in the boulevards and arcades, visit the cafés and department stores, get lost in the crowds but, importantly, 'observe and be observed' (Wolff, 1990). The objects of his gaze were women and the spectacle of the city. Remnants of this nineteenth-century phenomenon still exist today: Deutsche (1990, p. 136) writes of urban discourse constructing space as 'a feminized object surveyed by mastering subjects'. In the extracts of the dance texts analysed so far, it has been suggested that, at times, the city, through its associations with containment, has been constructed as feminine. However, the implications of the masculine gaze objectifying and mastering cities and subjects, although mentioned with reference to the cross-dressed female 'flashers' in *Dark Hours*, have yet to be investigated.

In *Circumnavigation* the female dancer, who features prominently in all four sections, appears to be on display; she and her dancing are frequently foregrounded, she is filmed and choreographed, for the most part, to be looked at rather than to look. This is stated clearly at the outset, in the first section set in Marseilles, when one of the male performers takes photographs of her and the camera shots are framed and frozen to look like polaroid photos; she is seen through the eyes of her male partner through the lens of his camera. There are occasional 'photo shots' of him and the other male performer also, but most are of her. Throughout the piece the gaze is at work; her two male partners together, and in turn, gaze at her and at times extend this 'looking power' or visual control into physical control by restraining her dancing. The choreography also contributes to this 'geography of gender power' (Tagg, 1990) by giving her expansive, expressive and varied dance movements, which attract attention to her, while the men's mainly pedestrian movements; walking, running, standing or sitting watching, allow them to remain detached. She tends to be controlled and objectified by the gaze; the men, at times, could be regarded as *flâneurs*.

TRAVEL AND MAPS

I have considered elsewhere (Briginshaw 1995) the importance of mapping and travel metaphors in postmodern dance and discourse. Reasons for their presence, I suggested, include the context of an increasingly accessible world, where distances in space and time are shrinking, resulting in an increase in cultural flows of information as well as people. Concepts of a 'fragmented subject' or 'nomadic subjectivity', which illustrate the instability of subjects, identities and notions of 'meaning' and 'truth', have led to the employment of metaphors of mapping and travel, such as 'cognitive mapping' introduced by Jameson (1988) (Briginshaw, 1995). I also suggested that travel tends to be gendered masculine. In Italo Calvino's poetic collection of city vignettes, *Invisible Cities* (1974), the masculine traveller, Marco Polo, observes, objectifies and penetrates each of the cities, all of which have feminine names: Olivia, Zora, Dorothea, for example.

Travel is suggested in the title and concept of the dance film, *Circumnavigation*, which maps a journey through the four ports of Marseilles, Trieste, Rotterdam and Riga. *Dark Hours and Finer Moments* also contains several travel references. It begins at an airport where a young woman addresses the camera 'I arrive by air' and, after a brief statement about time-zones crossed, she says 'I prefer travelling on my own.' A 'travel leitmotif' characterises her intermittent appearances. She is next seen unpacking in a hotel room, where she comments about the challenge of travelling alone. Towards the end of the piece she says 'if I could find a country to settle down in, I would', giving the impression of the permanent traveller or nomad; a fragmented subject lost in the maelstrom and chaos of the multiple signs and symbols of the postmodern city.

Maps and mapping can be seen as an extension of the gaze; they also order, bound, survey, colonise, possess and control.[3] Like the masculine gaze their visualisation of space depends crucially on a particular perspective and point of view, which is not neutral. Like space, maps and mapping are invested with power; they position and control 'the other', which includes the feminine (Briginshaw, 1995).

Moments in the Rotterdam and Riga sections of *Circumnavigation* make references to mapping. In *Rotterdam* a maze about six inches high, or parterre, is featured; first a map of the area is seen, then the parterre itself, filmed from above, with the female performer dancing in it. The dancer is alternately shot from above and in close-up at ground level. Another rather different example of a mapping metaphor is possibly suggested at the end of the Riga section of *Circumnavigation*, where a snow covered quayside is dotted with people. They are all walking in straight lines in one direction or the other, in effect marking out a simple grid or pattern on the plain white ground. This view of space and people appears transparent, but it is in fact carefully constructed by the filming, which places the audience in the position of surveyor. There are other examples in *Circumnavigation*, and also in *Step in Time Girls*, of the camera carefully composing, framing and controlling the shots of dancers and urban environments, so that they are seen from a particular perspective, mapped, objectified and feminised by a masculine gaze.

Another example of mapping occurs in the opening moments of *Freefall* when Gabi Agis is seen tracing a pathway on paper with a red pen; this is followed by a shot of a dancer seen from above on a rooftop apparently tracing a similar pathway. Juxtaposing these two shots suggests that the camera, and by implication the audience, when viewing the dancer from overhead, are positioned as surveyors, seeing the space and the female dancer with a masculine gaze.

REAPPROPRIATION OF TRAVEL AS MOVEMENT

Movement *through* the city; travel from one part to another, can be empowering. The extracts from the dance texts cited so far have included references to travel, and movement in the sense of dance performance, but they have not included movement *through* the city. Yet, as Munt (1995, p. 125) has stated with reference to the construction of lesbian subjectivity (and the statement might equally apply to any subject): 'lesbian identity is constructed in the ... mobilisation of space, ... as we move *through* space we imprint utopian and dystopian moments upon urban life'.

The implication is that movement through space plays an important role in the mutual definition of subjects and cities; that the movement by leaving its trace on the city partly constructs it empowering the subject. De Certeau (1984, p. 97) writes of pedestrian movements forming real systems whose 'existence ... makes up the city'. Movements become part of the city's identity, they say something about the city. The act of walking through the city, according to de Certeau (1984, p. 98), creates a 'space of enunciation'. Movement through the city in this sense is a kind of voice. The soft plasticity of the postmodern city makes these 'spaces of enunciation' possible. At the same time the fluid and fragmentary nature of the city makes it difficult to map in the traditional sense. 'The very idea of a map, with its implicit dependence upon the survey of a stable terrain, fixed referents and measurement, seems to contradict the palpable flux and fluidity of metropolitan life and cosmopolitan movement' (Chambers, 1994, p. 92). Similarly journeys through the postmodern city cannot be mapped. De Certeau (1984, p. 122) suggests that a tour; a description of a journey or place made up of operations and movements, a story that 'tells us what ... [we] can do in ... and make out of [space]' is more appropriate. These stories of movement through the city are 'treatments of space' (*ibid.*, p. 122). 'Walkers' ... bodies follow the thicks and thins of an urban "text" they write' (*ibid.*, p. 93). The act of walking through the city describes, inscribes and constructs the journey which is part of the city and the subject.

This kind of movement through city space is captured in *Topic II* (1992), a film directed by Pascal Baes and choreographed by Sarah Denizot. It is composed of hundreds of single-frame shots of two women taken by a camera that is moved through the streets of Prague. A strange skating effect is created as the dancers are moved over bridges, under lamps, up and down flights of steps, cobbled streets and under arches. The audience is taken on a tour of the city. The varied spaces of the city are explored as the dancers' bodies 'follow the thicks and thins of [the] urban "text" they write'. Through their intimacy with the nooks and crannies of their city, the performers 'tell us what . . . [we] can do in . . . and make out of [space]' (de Certeau, 1984, p. 122). The small, simple movements the dancers make, such as raising a leg or an arm slightly, turning to face another direction, or crouching down briefly, in no way position them as objects of a controlling gaze. Despite the fact that they sometimes appear to take up, fleetingly, poses of fashion models, because these are only ever held for a fraction of a second, the effect is one of movement through the city rather than posing against it or becoming inscribed on it. The dancers do not appear on display or under the control of a gaze. The city and the power are theirs as they tell their 'spatial story', write their 'urban "text"' (*ibid.*, p. 93).

This sort of representation of movement through the city is liberatory precisely because the movement cannot be mapped, constrained or con- trolled in any simple, straightforward sense. As de Certeau (1984, p. 99) states, 'these enunciatory operations are of an unlimited diversity. They therefore cannot be reduced to their graphic trail'. The multiplicity of imagined stories of the city that might be released precludes the kinds of reinscription and mapping that fix images and journeys. 'The fluctuating contexts of languages and desires pierce the logic of cartography and spill over the borders of its tabular, taxonomic space' (Chambers, 1994, p. 92). Images of overflow are sometimes associated with the space of the city, not- ably when this space is conceived as feminine and uncontrollable (Knopp, 1995). What is needed possibly is a re-appropriation of such imagery and of some of the empowering elements of it and of mapping.

In her essay entitled 'The Lesbian *Flâneur*' Sally Munt (1995) proposes a reappropriation of the role of the *flâneur* to address these issues. She states, 'the familiar construction of woman as excess has radical potential when appropriated by the lesbian *flâneur*' (Munt, 1995, p. 121). Recognis- ing the power inherent in the movement through the city that belonged to the *flâneur*, she asserts, 'within the labyrinth [of the city], the process of making up meaning in movement becomes the point, and perversely too the pleasure, as we become lost among the flowing images' (*ibid.*, p. 116). This could describe the movement of the dancers in *Topic II* and also the opening moments of *Freefall*. Here, shots of Agis dressing up to go out are intercut with shots of the hand that traces a 'map' in red pen. Close-ups of Agis doing up buttons, putting on a belt, lacing up boots and running her fingers through her hair, whilst looking in the mirror, suggest intertextual references with films such as *Saturday Night Fever* (1977) and *American Gigolo* (1980). The lead characters played in these films, by Travolta and Gere respectively, can be likened to *flâneurs*; they enjoy strolling and driving through the city, observing and being observed. Agis is seen going out into the urban spaces enjoying her own mobility, she runs down an alley and then up stairs and steps until she emerges on a rooftop and looks out at the cityscape spread before her. There is a sense in which all the movements that make up this part of her performance are important because for her, as for the 'lesbian *flâneur*', 'motion continually stamps new ground with a symbol of ownership' (Munt, 1995, p. 120).

REAPPROPRIATION OF MAPPING AND INSCRIPTION

Mapping, as well as surveying and controlling, can also empower through providing information, showing the way. If these positive attributes of the concept are adopted then the movement of the 'lesbian *flâneur*' could be seen as a new kind of mapping. Through moving she is mapping; weaving her own labyrinthine map which is empowering. This sort of movement evades the constraints, limits and controls of the gaze and traditional mapping because she (the lesbian *flâneur*) is able to take on a fluid identity. 'She breaks down the boundary between Self and Other . . . . She collapses the distinction between masculinity and femininity . . . [and] she slips between, beyond and around the linear landscape' (Munt, 1995, p. 121). The lesbian *flâneur's* mobility and performativity challenges oppressive power relations. 'The physiology of this *flâneur's* city is a woman's body constantly in motion' (*ibid.*, p. 121). In this sense the notion of inscription of bodies and city spaces has the potential for reappropriation.

Inscription of bodies and cities involves gender. If this element of the mutual definition and construction of cities and subjects is concealed and appears 'natural' and unproblematic, then the potential for change is limited. A reappropriation of mapping as suggested above, and of inscription, which would reveal rather than conceal elements of the construction, could open up possibilities of new interpretations, thereby providing opportunities for change.

In *Muurwerk* the solo female performer's bodily brushes with the fabric of the Brussels alley are unremittingly hurled in the audience's face. Perhaps this indicates an alternative to the possibly expected reading of the bare facts of the situation; a young woman, dressed in a sleeveless, low-backed, short-skirted frock, alone in a deserted alley, often literally pinned to the walls or floor. The insistent repetition of what appear to be sometimes angry, sometime mesmeric, caresses and collisions with concrete in *Muurwerk* flies in the face of any suggestion of vulnerability, which rather looks like it's being worked out of her system cathartically. When Huilmand rolls into the gutter and her skirt flies up revealing substantial plain white knickers, she seems to be defiantly saying 'so what!' Her apparently fearless performance of a limited but thoroughly known and worked-through vocabulary seems at times brazenly confident and at others subtly playful. There is also a sense that, as Huilmand slowly rolls across a wall's surface leaving the audience with a shot of the recently traversed stone, her imprint or mark remains there. Grosz (1995, pp. 108–9), in her discussion of the mutual definition of bodies and cities, states 'in turn, the body (as cultural product) transforms [and] reinscribes the urban landscape'. The inscription in *Muurwerk*, it might be argued, is an attempt to come to terms with aspects of the alienating urban environment and, by putting a stamp on it, take control and own it. Huilmand could be said to be reappropriating inscription in an empowering manner.

THE LAMENT OF THE EMPRESS

Inscriptions of bodies on cities are reappropriated in a different way in *The Lament of the Empress*. The penultimate image in the film is of a woman sitting alone in a constantly circling monorail car. Whilst travelling round the city, she utters her lament in German in a growling, drunken, witch-like voice. Its translation is: 'If the king were to give me his great city Paris' – 'If only I would abandon my love, my beloved' – 'I know I would say to the king "Keep your great city Paris!"' One critic has suggested that the film's leitmotif of loneliness and the absence of love becomes clear at this point. I think this is only part of the story. The rejection of the gift of Paris might be the rejection of the modern world – many of the images in the film are melancholic and some display brutality to the environment, animals, children and people. This modern world is one which is exemplified at its height in the model of the modern city (Williams, cited in

Chambers, 1994, p. 27). The city, constructed and enmeshed in a complex web of power relations, traversed by the tracks of the male *flâneur*, albeit in different guises, objectified and feminised by his gaze, is being rejected by this 'empress'. Images and ideas of this city collude in the construction of unequal power relations based on difference. By exposing the contradictions and inequalities of such a world, Bausch opens up a space for something else; Munt's (1995) lesbian *flâneur*, perhaps, who through her mobility and performativity challenges entrenched, oppressive power relations.

The final image in *The Lament of the Empress* is of an old woman dancing alone 'simply entrancingly – to sounds from a juke-box' (Rosiny, 1990, p. 74). An image of loneliness and absence of love? Not from the evidence presented; the expression on the woman's face suggests total absorption and involvement, also glimpsed in her shimmying shoulders picking up the beat of the music and occasional little lifts of her skirt.

As Chambers (1994, p. 95) states:

> The labyrinthine and contaminated quality of metropolitan life . . . leads to new cultural connections . . . [and] undermines the presumed purity of thought . . . . To travel in this zone without maps and charts, is to experience the dis-location of the intellectual subject and his – the gender is deliberate – mastery of the word/world.

There is a suggestion here of the potential of the postmodern city for 'new cultural connections' and 'the dis-location of the [masculine] intellectual subject ['s] . . . mastery of the word/world'. Some of the postmodern dance films and videos examined here exhibit a similar potential. Whereas some of the texts largely appear to substantiate claims made about bodies, subjects and cities, the potential of the postmodern city that Chambers (1994) hints at, is evident in those dance films and videos which challenge various claims. For the most part *Circumnavigation* supports many of the claims made about the ways in which cities and bodies mutually define and inscribe each other with unequal power relations based on difference, explored here in terms of gender. *Step in Time Girls, Muurwerk, Freefall* and *Dark Hours and Finer Moments*, are more ambiguous; they present possibilities for subversion and questioning of received ideas about the ways in which cities and bodies mutually define each other in terms of gender. *Topic II* and *The Lament of the Empress*, however, in very different ways, open up new spaces in the city. The possibilities of power in movement through the city are evident in *Topic II*, where the combination of choreography and filming precludes any suggestions of transparent inscription and mutual definition that is disempowering. In *The Lament of the Empress* the intertextual treatment of bodies and city spaces opens up the interface between them, challenging and problematising the ways in which space and subjects can be mapped into asymmetric power relations because of difference. These asymmetric power relations are largely a legacy of the modern metropolis exemplified in nineteenth-century Paris, so in order to open up new cultural connections and dis-locate the [masculine] intellectual subject's mastery of the word/world, the lament of the empress needs perhaps to be the metaphoric battle cry of all.[4]

NOTES

1. The focus in this chapter is on gender, but it is important to recognise that the power invested in space, travel and mapping discriminates in different ways and that race, class, sexuality, age and other factors all also play a part.
2. Other examples of dance texts that use cities as settings or inspirations include *Palermo, Palermo* (1990; choreographer: P. Bausch); *49 bis* (1992; choreographer: S. Denizot) and *Duets with Automobiles* (1994; choreographer: S. Jeyasingh).
3. It is important to point out that I am not using 'mapping' in the sense used by Deleuze and Guattari (1988), who state:

    what distinguishes the map from the tracing is that it is entirely oriented towards an experimentation in contact with the real. The map does not reproduce an unconscious closed in upon itself; it constructs the unconscious . . . . The map is open and connectable in all of its dimensions; . . . [it] has to do with performance, whereas the tracing always involves an alleged 'competence' (p. 12).

    My use of what I term 'traditional mapping', which surveys, controls and colonises, has affinities with their 'tracing'. My proposed *reappropriation* of mapping to describe the movement of the 'lesbian *flâneur*' (see pp. 45–6) has more affiliations with their concept of mapping.
4. I should like to thank Ramsay Burt, Geoff Seale and Virginia Taylor for reading and commenting on an earlier draft of this chapter. However, I take full responsibility for this final version.

REFERENCES

D. Bell & G. Valentine (eds), *Mapping Desire* (London: Routledge, 1995).
J. Berger, *Ways of Seeing* (London: BBC Books, 1973).

S. Best, 'Sexualising Space' in E. Grosz and E. Probyn (eds), *Sexy Bodies* (London: Routledge, 1995).

V. A. Briginshaw, 'Metaphors of travel and mapping in postmodern dance and discourse' in C. Jones and J. Lansdale (eds), *Border Tensions: Dance and Discourse* (Guildford: University of Surrey, 1995).

I. Calvino, *Invisible Cities* (London: Secker & Warburg, 1974).

I. Chambers, *Migrancy, Culture, Identity* (London: Routledge, 1994).

M. de Certeau, *The Practice of Everyday Life* (Berkeley and Los Angeles: University of California Press, 1984).

G. Deleuze and F. Guattari, *A Thousand Plateaus: Capitalism and Schizophrenia*, 1st pub. 1987 (London and Minneapolis, MN: Athlone and University of Minnesota Press, 1988).

R. Deutsche, 'Men in Space', *Strategies*, 3 (1990), pp. 130–7.

E. Grosz, *Space, Time and Perversion* (London: Routledge, 1995).

D. Harvey, *The Condition of Postmodernity* (Oxford: Blackwell, 1989).

F. Jameson, 'Cognitive Mapping' in Cary Nelson and Lawrence Grossberg (eds), *Marxism and the Interpretation of Culture* (Urbana, IL and Chicago: University of Illinois Press, 1988).

L. Knopp, 'Sexuality and Urban Space' in D. Bell and G. Valentine (eds), *Mapping Desire* (London: Routledge, 1995).

L. Mulvey, 'Visual Pleasure and Narrative Cinema', *Screen*, 16, 3 (1975), pp. 6–18.

S. Munt, 'The Lesbian *Flâneur*' in D. Bell and G. Valentine (eds), *Mapping Desire* (London: Routledge, 1995).

D. Preziosi, 'Oublier La Città', *Strategies*, No. 3 (1990), pp. 260–7.

C. Rosiny, 'Film Review: Pina Bausch, "The Lament of the Express"', *Ballett International*, 6/7 (1990), p. 74.

A. Sanchez-Colberg, 'You can see it like this or like that' in S. Jordan and D. Allen (eds), *Parallel Lines* (London: John Libbey, 1993).

J. Tagg, 'The Discontinuous City: Picturing and the Discursive Field', *Strategies*, No. 3 (1990), pp. 138–58.

J. Wolff, *Feminine Sentences* (Cambridge: Polity Press, 1990).

4 The Beat Goes On: Trance, Dance and Tribalism in Rave Culture

Georgiana Gore

Rave
Specifically a one-off gathering for late night consumption of pre-recorded dance music, a musical definition of rave is more problematic. Descending from the acid house sound and ethos, the main fare tends to be fast techno and hardcore records, pitched between 125 and 140 bpm and often released on tiny independent labels with little background information.

(Ogg, in Larkin, 1994, p. 302)

INTRODUCTION

Universe's Tribal Gathering 1994, second of its kind, brought together some 25 000 people in a disused 1930s airport outside Munich. Ravers had come from all over the world to dance all night to the sounds of 'superstar' DJs, each with expertise in a particular house dance-music idiom: Carl Cox, British stalwart of European techno and house, Laurent Garnier, France's finest techno spinner, Holland's Miss Djax, whose dialect is hard acid, etc. At an early stage in the event 'a most spectacular occurrence [was] witnessed: a melting together of 8,000 to 10,000 bodies all with hands held in the air' (Koehler, 1994, p. 50).

To characterise rave culture in the mid-1990s is no easy task, as it has grown into an international, predominantly European network of dance-music events at which the participants move to the sounds of techno, hardcore, acid house, trance, gabba, jungle and other variants of house music. These events include festivals (indoor and outdoor, commercial/licensed and free/unlicensed), free 'warehouse' parties (often held in abandoned industrial urban spaces, including factories and warehouses, but also on beaches or common land) and club nights (either one-off events or regular weekly or monthly spots). Some would say that in Britain the rave is dead, killed off by media hype and commercialisation as well as the state's systematic criminalisation of ravers, others believe that it has gone underground, and still others that it has mutated abroad, with Germany and Holland competing for status as European rave mecca in the north, and Spain and Italy in the south. Perhaps the rave should be compared to the mythological many-headed Hydra, a creature which captivated and entranced, only to make disappear, all those who beheld it, and which mutated inexorably, by growing new heads, when its protagonists attempted to destroy it.

Lack of consistency, of coherence, of veracity characterise representations of rave culture. There are competing versions of many of its landmarks, not only because of differences in personal, political or professional perspectives, but also because of the fluid, slippery and unstable 'nature' of this dance-music movement, which allows no unified perspective and resists definition. It has been difficult therefore to map, with accuracy, its history (even a history of discontinuities and ruptures), especially as I have not been immersed in it as I was in hippie culture of the late 1960s and early 1970s, but have only participated sporadically. What follows therefore is necessarily a partial and provisional analytical account of some aspects of raving. For those with some familiarity with the topic, this should come as no surprise.

Rave culture may be conceived as a microcosm of the contemporary metropolis, which has itself been proposed as a metaphor for postmodernity, that 'condition' which celebrates fragmentation, deconstruction, dispersal, discontinuity, rupture, asubjectivity, ephemerality, superficiality, depthlessness, flatness, meaninglessness, hyperreality, etc. Therefore if rave culture resists definition and analysis using conventional theoretical tools drawn from the human and social sciences, as Redhead suggests (1993, pp. 1–6, 23–4), this is logical, since no totalising meta-narrative can adequately account for something as fragmented, as elusive and as dispersed, yet as apparently indestructible. To describe raving as a ritual of resistance and rebellion is to ignore the explicitly apolitical stance of many of its participants; to analyse it within the conventional dualistic categories of social control/liberation, of individual/collective action, is necessarily to reduce its multiplicity.

The following conception of the metropolis may therefore provide a line of entry into raving: 'a system of anarchic and archaic signs and symbols [and practices] that is constantly and independently self-renewing' (Klotz in Harvey, 1989, p. 83). For definitions of the 'rave' (an expression also used in the 1960s to describe psychedelic partying and which may be outdated, as Saunders [1995, p. 3] suggests), see, for example, Jordan (1995, pp. 128–9) and Rietveld (1993, p. 41).

In this chapter I will explore a number of related issues: the possible connections between hippie culture of the 1960s and rave culture both conceived as forms of 'neo-tribalism'; the transformation (and commercialisation) of 1980s rave culture from a form of cultural nomadism into a form of settled urban tribalism, and the possible effects on dance 'style' or performance; the role of the disc jockey (DJ) as shamanistic figure with star status and 'magical' powers to induce trance through the manipulation of the musical materials.

THINGS RITUAL AND THINGS TRIBAL: THE HAPPENING AND THE RAVE

Dancing, and especially continuous dancing for prolonged periods of time, is the single most important element, if not the *raison d'être*, of rave culture. This, amongst other things, distinguishes it from its psychedelic counterpart, hippie culture of the 1960s and early 1970s. In the latter, dancing was but one expressive activity in the panoply of liberatory practices, which included radical therapies (such as Reichian vegetotherapy and Laingian psychiatry), meditation, listening to music and the imbibing of hallucinogenic drugs (especially marijuana and LSD [lysergic acid diethylamide], but also peyote and mescaline). Amongst the aims of these practices were getting 'stoned' or 'high', inducing altered states of consciousness (as in 'tripping out on acid') and thereafter transforming socio-cultural realities. Getting 'happy' (symbolised in the late 1980s by the Smiley logo on tee-shirts), with its concomitant feeling of social empathy, is generally the avowed aim of raving. The drug Ecstasy (MDMA or methylenedioxymethamphetamine),which is referred to by law as a psychedelic amphetamine, but which in fact contains no amphetamine (Saunders, 1995, p. 148), despite its energising effects, is, along with dancing, crucial to inducing these feelings of well-being, sociability and gregariousness. (Saunders's carefully researched book *Ecstasy and the Dance Culture* [1995] provides detailed information on Ecstasy and other dance drugs, and on their effects in diverse contexts.)

There is no doubt that the 'feel-good factor' was important in hippie culture, but equally valued was experimentation, artistic, social, sexual and political, which carried with it the possibility of failure as well as success. Rave culture also incorporates elements of experimentation, especially artistic but also socio-political, the aim of which is not however direct counter-cultural contestation, but rather the celebration of values seen as alternative to those of the 'right-wing *"realpolitik"* of the 1980s' (Rubin, 1995). An example of this is Berlin's annual Love Parade, held along the Kurfurstendamn (the equivalent of Oxford Street) every first weekend of July since 1989, when DJ Dr Motte, the parade's organiser, staged the first event with 'just one hundred and fifty participants on three little trucks' (Motte, 1995). Since its inception, the parade has been a 'registered demonstration for "peace, love and unity"' (*ibid.*). By 1995, this techno street-party demonstration had mobilised some 250 000 ravers dancing for 'hedonism' and 'Peace on Earth', the motto of this year's parade, which called for an immediate cease-fire in Bosnia, Chechnya and Mexico (Koehler, 1995, p. 92)!

A number of further connections shall be made between these two sociocultural movements. For a more thorough comparative analysis, however, Russell's contribution to *Rave Off* (Redhead, 1993, pp. 91–174) is useful, although I do not entirely concur with his account of the 1960s as I believe that he undervalues the significance and scale of the movement in Britain.

Drug-taking is undeniably central and, in both cases, has clearly precipitated the media furore, as this illegal activity symbolises the absolute otherness and eccentricity of the two cultures to the Establishment of the time. It is, nonetheless, short-sighted to conceive of the drugs as the uniquely psychedelic elements of raving and hippiedom, since dancing, meditation and listening to music are also known to alter the chemistry of the brain and to transform consciousness. Rather it is the combination of elements, their synergy and synchrony, which constitute freaking out and raving, or the rave 'machine assemblage', to borrow from Deleuze and Guattari (1981, p. 50). And the simultaneous bombardment of all the senses, through lightshows, music, drug-taking and dancing *en masse*, instigates what has been analysed, incorrectly perhaps, as a process of 'implosion', a 'mode' or 'ritual of disappearance' (Melechi, 1993, p. 34, 38; Rietveld, 1993, p. 41). For if the postmodern subject is constituted as surface, without depth, as a 'body without organs', then there can be neither implosion nor explosion, only a sliding, a shifting of intensities, which, on reaching a certain degree, transform the quality of the terrain, of that body without organs. Lines of flight are opened up and a process of deterritorialisation set in motion which may lead to a deconstruction of subjectivity, experienced as feelings of dizziness, vertigo, disappearance or loss of self – in other words, to trance. It is not, therefore, the fact of taking Ecstasy which ensures the 'happy' outcome in raving. Rather it is the *repetition* of the same formula on each occasion, the *ritualisation*.

The most striking conclusion was that there was no difference in the happiness level of regular clubbers on drugs and those who weren't. The real difference was between regular and occasional clubbers. Regulars were nearly twice as happy, whether on drugs or not. So the key to enjoying a rave doesn't seem to be the drugs, but how often you go. You learn to like it, and the way you do that is by going again, and again. (*Rave New World*, 1994, p. 13)

To the rave of the 1980s and 1990s may be juxtaposed the multimedia participatory event of the 1960s, the happening. The happening was a controlled environment for creative experimentation, constituted of disparate artistic elements including light-shows, painted backdrops, live and recorded music, dancing bodies decorated with paint, diaphanous materials, beads and bangles, etc., as well as of impromptu performances and unforeseen events. Within the love and peace ethos of the 1960s, everything was permissible at a 'happening', whence the name which connotes both a notion of process as well as of the unexpected. These events encouraged spontaneity, communication and sensuousness, and were sometimes imbued with an aura of eroticism which stimulated sensuality and sexual exploration. Body contact, hugging and feelings of togetherness formed part of the ideological backdrop, as in raving. The happening too was ritualistic in the way that it combined and orchestrated multimedia elements, but not, perhaps, ritualised. Because it encouraged individual creativity and expression within an ethos of group communication, each event was unique even if the combination of elements was familiar.

While dance may not have been central to hippiedom, it is interesting to note that, in common with trance dancing which characterises raving, 'freaking out' to music usually required dancing alone in order to focus on subjective experience and the feelings (or 'high') induced by the combination of dance, music, drugs and environment. Both dance forms entail sinuous on-the-spot body movements with a focus on spinal vibrations or torso and pelvic contractions (which connect with the rhythm of breathing), while the arms are held aloft and perform wavy movements during moments of trance. In this 'ecstatic syntony' (Schutz in Maffesoli, 1991, pp. 112–14 and 1995, pp. 151–2) which is raving, is celebrated an infinite present, which abnegates the demarcation or segmentation of time characteristic of other modes of dancing, which privilege leg movements and where rhythm becomes a form of spatialisation, as in stepping, walking or running.

The happening, however, unlike the rave for 1990s dance-club culture, was not the focal event of 1960s hippiedom, but, I propose, its symbol. Nonetheless both multimedia events articulate materially an ideology of 'neo-tribalism', which characterises the two cultures. This 'neo-tribalism' is constituted of several strands. There is on the one hand a discourse of nostalgia, which evokes cultures which are seen as ecologically and socially less exploitative and fragmented. This was epitomised in the hippie idealisation of the commune as the optimum *modus vivendi* and experimentation with a variety of such living arrangements. Rave culture, in turn, recreates elements of hippiedom, which, to a generation raised on Thatcherite individualism and entrepreneurship, represents a paradisiac past, worthy of emulation. Moreover, through the staging of events which bring into play diverse artistic/cultural elements, especially music and dance, both movements replicate liminal rituals in non-Western cultures, the aim of which is also collective celebration and/or trance. I am not suggesting that this is necessarily a conscious process of recuperation and replication, although certainly in both movements there exists a strong and vocal constituency which advocates consciousness transformation through ritualistic practices and drug-taking.

Moreover, if, as the French sociologist Maffesoli (1991 and 1995) suggests, the world is undergoing a form of 'tribalisation', not only along ethnically constituted lines but also through cultural or religious affinities, then rave culture today conforms to, as hippie culture prefigured, this tendency towards the crystallisation of 'sociality' (Maffesoli, 1991, pp. 117, 125) into apolitical associative networks based on affiliation through sentiment and shared interests. Common to these 'tribes' is a certain religiosity, to be taken in its etymological sense of a binding together, an inter-reliance. This concern with fusion and empathy (Turner's 'communitas' [1977, p. 96], perhaps?) as modes of interaction, Maffesoli, after Durkheim, calls an 'organic solidarity' (1995, p. 19), or 'adhesiveness' (1995, p. 174). Concomitant with this postmodern and anti-individualistic form of social aggregation is a rejection of rationality and bourgeois modernist politics based on the notion of the social contract and the law, and of the unified subject of representation. The subject is to be construed as multiple, and as constituted in and through relations, not as actor or author, but as one who is thought or moved, or, perhaps I should say, danced.

Maffesoli (1993 and 1995) privileges the aesthetic, as does Eagleton (1990) with greater circumspection, and proposes the 'aestheticisation' of the social as the *sine qua non* of the postmodern 'tribal' condition, since aesthetics refer to the non-utilitarian, the corporeal and sensate as well as to the collective. To quote Eagleton:

Aesthetics is born as a discourse of the body. In its original [eighteenth century] formulation . . . the term refers not in the first place to art, but, as the Greek *aisthesis* would suggest, to the whole region of human perception and sensation, in contrast to the more rarefied domain of conceptual thought . . . . That territory is nothing less than the whole of our sensate life together – the business of affections and versions, of how the world strikes the body on its sensory surfaces, of that which takes root in the gaze and the guts and all that arises from our most banal, biological insertion into the world . . . . It is thus the first stirrings of a primitive materialism – of the body's long inarticulate rebellion against the tyranny of the theoretical. (Eagleton, 1990, p. 13)

Neo-tribalism also entails relations of tactility, of body to body, and the privileging of collective sentiment as the 'glue' which binds people together, not however into a 'union of fullness, a union around a project', but into 'a union of lack, of emptiness; a communion of solitudes' (Maffesoli, 1995, p. 224). These 'viscous' communities (like Deleuze and Guattari's 'multiplicities' [1980, pp. 305–7]) are heterogeneous, unstable, precarious, subject to the inconstancy of passion and emotion. Friction between competing groups is inevitable, and the non-violent resolution of those conflicts through negotiation and other strategies desirable, but not inevitable. Rave culture, as we shall see, is by no means a homogeneous sub-culture. It is a network of competing assemblages, which despite their diversity have, except for a brief period in the late 1980s (see Jordan, 1995, p. 131; Redhead, 1993, pp. 14–20; Russell, 1993, pp. 130–1) when it seemed more a matter of 'war' between the rave machine and the drug machine, eschewed violent confrontation, though they are not without their casualties of death through overdose and/or bodily overheating.

I therefore use the term 'tribalism' in the above senses, because, simultaneously, it evokes the kinds of loose and informal, yet socially (and compulsively) binding networks constituting rave culture, because it articulates elements in the discourse of rave culture and also typifies the rivalry generated between different rave milieux in the mid-1990s.

FROM ACID HOUSE TO 1990S RAVING

For the collective (British) imagination the rave is epitomised by the following 1988 media images: Dionysian revellers high on the recreational drug Ecstasy dancing relentlessly to pounding synthesised music; carloads of young people hovering around telephone boxes at motorway service stations, while they wait for the tip-off indicating the location of a clandestine dance event; police roadblocks, raids and chases through the night to curtail these nocturnal revels. While not inaccurate, these are sensationalist fragments of the history of raving, and fragments which effectively depict, if not construct, the process of the criminalisation of raving, which has led, during the 1990s, to its attempted containment (in the Foucauldian sense) within the confines of conventional clubland. (See Haines in Saunders, 1995, p. 21; Redhead, 1993, pp. 20–1; Rietveld, 1993, pp. 47–50; Saunders, 1995, pp. 102–3 on the criminalisation of raving.)

The climax of this process was the passing of the 1994 Criminal Justice Bill, which explicitly targeted rave events.

> The term 'rave' is even used in the headings in the [Criminal Justice and Public Order] Act [1994]. As defined in the Act, a rave is 'a gathering on land in the open air (including a place partly open to the air) of 100 or more persons (whether or not trespassers) at which amplified music is played during the night (with or without intermissions) and is such as, by reasons of its loudness and duration at the time at which it is played, is likely to cause serious distress to the inhabitants of the locality . . . .' If there is an entertainment licence the definition of rave does not apply. (Banks in Saunders, 1995, p. 103)

The CJA has certainly curtailed the number and scale of unlicensed free parties (*vide* the August 1995 *Mixmag* item: 'Police Use Criminal Justice Act to Crush Free Festival' [Petridis, 1995, p. 13], the biggest event of its kind attempted for three years), except where there exists a benevolent police force to turn a blind eye to an ongoing underground network. For example, between February and May 1995, Sunnyside staged four 'free parties' attended by between 12 000 and 15 000 'happy campers' in an abandoned West Country city warehouse near Bristol ('Diplo', 1995, pp. 14–15)! But raving is, as Jordan (1995) elaborates, a 'desiring machine', a machine assemblage, a multiplicity. Therefore it is rhizomatic (Deleuze and Guattari, 1981) and cannot be killed off; its stems will inevitably proliferate despite pruning. 'A rhizome can be broken, snapped off at any point, it shoots out again along one or other of its lines, old or new' (*ibid.*, p. 55). And so with raving!

Indeed it was towards the end of the 1988 'Second Summer of Love' (the first being the hippie summer of 1967) that raving or 'acid house', as this newly popularised youth culture was then called, took to the countryside. Events were staged in empty fields or post-industrial wastelands in a bid to evade the police crackdowns, which were being made increasingly on licensed and above all unlicensed acid-house parties, which had been taking place since the mid-1980s. (See Rietveld, 1993, pp. 45–50; Russell, 1993, p. 100; Staines in Saunders, 1995, pp. 19–21 for further details.) Since 1985–86 or thereabouts acid house had been an underground, predominantly urban, club dance-music scene, which, with its neo-1960s ethos of love and peace, apparently posed no political threat to anyone, although, through the party scene, it had connections with the squatters' and New Age travellers' movements. It was only when it exploded on to the front pages of the tabloid press that the 'witch-hunts' began and that ravers became nomadic outlaws, pitching tents to party in ever less accessible areas of Britain, such as Blackburn, and later, by 1990 in Leeds and Shropshire (Rietveld, 1993, pp. 48–9), one-time haven of a number of hippie communes. Media hysteria and increasing criminalisation actually precipitated the popularisation of raving as ever greater numbers joined the 'acid-house trail', in quest of all-night unlicensed dance marathons. The summers of 1989 and 1990 may not have been, for the purists, 'authentic' 'summers of love' (but neither were those of 1968, 1969 or 1970 when hippiedom took root); they did however mark the explosion of an unprecedented dance craze, which embraced all comers irrespective of creed, colour, class, gender or age.

The term 'acid house' is shrouded in a number of myths of origin, some attributing to it British, and others American, pedigree. One version (Ogg, in Larkin, 1994, pp. 176, 212) proposes that it descends from the Chicago-based musical movement of the same name, although, in DJs' accounts of that era, I have only found one reference to American *acid* house in the mid-1980s (DJ Pierre in Fleming, 1995, p. 208). Moreover, it is generally agreed that British acid-house dance music combines elements from Chicago house, such as the characteristic kick drum-beat, and from Detroit techno, such as the latter's minimalism and relentless metronomic 4/4 beat, with the peculiar sound of the '303'. That it is a derivative of house music, which emerged in the early 1980s apparently in Chicago, and perhaps also in New York, goes unchallenged. But whether it was initiated by DJ Pierre in 1986 when he discovered the characteristic 'acid squelch' sound while experimenting with a bass synthesiser called the Roland TB 303, which enabled the bass line to be warped and twisted, or by Marshall Jefferson when undertaking similar musical experiments, remains an open question (Ogg in Larkin, 1994, pp. 212, 249). The British tabloid press are cited, in another version of the myth, as being those who attributed the label 'acid house' to raving, the former being a type of music which apparently drove party-goers into a state of frenzy (Rietveld, 1993, p. 45). In a further, and oft-repeated, version the term 'acid' or 'acid burn' is said to be Chicago slang meaning to steal, and by extension to steal musical ideas as in sampling, whence the name for acid house music (Reynolds, 1990, p. 177; Russell, 1993, p. 122). But it is surely Paul Staines (in Saunders, 1995, pp. 18–19) who must, for the time being, have the last word on this search for origins. He claims to have invented this latter story, which even made it into *Hansard*, the official record of debates in the House of Commons (and House of Lords), in order to placate the British Establishment and discourage anti-party legislation, when he launched the 'Freedom to Party' campaign at the 1989 Conservative Party conference! For indeed as many suspected, the term 'acid' in 'acid-house party' referred initially to the colloquial 1960s expression for LSD, since its use was widespread in the early days of the house dance-music scene in Britain (and America?) before the dissemination of Ecstasy around 1987.

With the demise of the British *underground* acid-house movement towards the end of 1988 and the popularisation and commercialisation of the rave (Melechi, 1993, p. 35; Russell, 1993, pp. 130–1), acid-house music knew a brief period of commercial success before it returned underground when the rave scene dispersed into the partisanship of disparate musical enclaves. However, with the revival of the '303' sound in recent trance music brought back from the Indian hippie mecca of Goa, it has apparently been making a comeback in the mid-1990s but only as a genre amongst many. On the dance-floor acid house has been superseded in popularity since the early 1990s by techno and 'four to the floor' hardcore, the staple fare of hard ravers. More recently 'cheesy' happy hardcore has emerged as the favourite of the under-21s, with jungle being hailed as the potential unifying force to equal acid house, although it is often not considered 'rave' music, due to its connections with reggae, hip-hop and drum 'n' bass.

The explosion into the rave movement of 1988 (to continue until around 1992 with the great 'festi-raves' of Castlemorton and Lechdale) appears to derive from the collision of a number of factors, and to mark a rupture with this previously confined underground (and elitist?) movement. Nascent British dance-club culture was confronted with Balearic all-night revelling, brought back to Britain from the Spanish islands, and especially from Ibiza (Melechi, 1993, pp. 30–3). This had been, with Crete and Kos, the Mediterranean haven of hippie tribalism and drug-taking in the 1960s and early 1970s. A lively holiday dance-club scene flourished there in the mid-1980s due to unrestricted licensing hours, the relaxed gregarious Mediterranean socialising which never begins until 11.00 p.m. with dinner and continues with partying all night, and the easy availability of drugs, especially the newly-arrived Ecstasy. Balearic music was (and still is) characterised by an eclectic sampling of a range of dance-music styles including house, Latin, hip-hop, etc., which contrasted with other dance-music forms in the late mid-1980s, since the latter maintained a certain homogeneity, if only in terms of rhythmic structure. The confrontation, therefore, of Balearic musical eclecticism and of the Mediterranean 'feel-good' factor with the more puritanical and sectarian intensity of dance-music culture, the British manufacturing and availability of Ecstasy, the proliferation of free house-parties in squats (inspired by Thatcherite pauperisation of Britain's youth) and of warehouse parties, along with an entrenched recession, created the conditions for the explosion of a new youth movement. That it should be a 'dance craze' is no wonder when the cult of the body (as efficient machine and beautiful model) had been under way for some twenty years and was reaching new heights of intensification. Indeed if acid house and raving may be seen as deterritorialisation or even disappearance, it is not only into the nothingness of asubjectivity and the atopia of the postmodern present (Gore, 1995, pp. 137–8; Melechi, 1993, p. 38; Rietveld, 1993, p. 63), rather it is into the infinity of the corporeal surface, the Möbius-like materiality which connects the body and the social, beyond any signification (Deleuze and Guattari's 'body without organs' [1980, pp. 185–204]), 'a place where nobody is, but everybody belongs' (Melechi, 1993, p. 37).

Furthermore I wonder what connections, if any, may be made between this explosion of raving on to the British cultural scene in the summer of 1988 and the financial crash of October 1987, when 'someone peeked behind the reflecting mirrors of US economic policy and, frightened at what they saw there, plunged the world's stock markets into such a fearful crash that nearly a third of the paper value of assets worldwide was written off within a few days' (Harvey, 1989, p. 356). Did the realisation of the factitiousness of paper money produce a devil-may-care attitude amongst the young and disenchanted? Did those who had lost their jobs on the money market decide that one final 'end-of-the-century party' was in order before the slow slide into the oblivion of the year 2000? Or are both these events a function and foretaste of some larger postmodern machine assemblage, a cybernation of the planet? The cyber-rave in which the body which twitches in a techno trance at the outer reaches of danceability at 160–220 bpm is corporeity 'technologised'? 'Perhaps there's a kind of "liberation" in submitting to the mechanics of instinct, soldering the circuitry of desire to the circuitry of the sequencer programmes' (Reynolds with Oldfield, in Reynolds, 1990, p. 177).

By 1989 raving had become popularised, and with it came increasing commercialisation, not only as regards the staging of the event but in terms of the array of accompanying services and merchandising. The popularity of raving produced ever larger one-off events (all-night licensed and unlicensed 'parties') and a mushrooming of clubs (weekly or monthly 'parties' held in the same venue) to cater for increasing demand. From a handful of clubs, such as Delirium, Future, Hedonism, Jungle, the Haçienda's

'Nude' nights, Pyramid, Shoom, Spectrum, Stallions, The Garage and The Project, which introduced house and acid-house music to British youth between 1986 and early 1988, have emerged in the 1990s round-the-week nightly clubs all over Britain to cater to the increasingly fragmented, but hegemonic, dance-music club-culture scene. Not only have the promoters benefited financially from this dance explosion, so too have the DJs. With the acquisition of cult status, they have attained financial and professional security if they make it to the top, for it is upon these 'record spinners' that the success of a rave event depends. And while acid house may have all but died a death, its popularisation of rave culture with its non-violent, anti-individualistic ethos of non-competitive dancing has precipitated a global dance explosion since the early 1990s. Indeed some believe that this global dance-music culture will revolutionise the broader socio-cultural environment, providing a 'human face' to planetary cybernation.

TRANCE, DANCE, MUSIC AND THE DJ AS SHAMAN

As we hurtle toward the 21st century every aspect of culture is being transmut[at]ed, the old systems are breaking down and new ones are being spawned.

A new generation of empowered youth is rising, who have experienced a blueprint for the next level of human interaction. In the right environment under the guide of the DJ shaman the collective consciousness is elevated to a higher level: a level that is beyond culture, race, gender or class. A level where you let go your own ego, a level where you experience ultimate freedom. (Betz, 1995)

One of the peculiarities of the acid-house phenomenon (and of the current underground acid–techno-trance scene) was the anonymity conferred on *all* aspects of this dance-music club culture, from its production in 'cottage industry conditions' (Reynolds, 1990, p. 173) to its consumption in ever-changing clubs, publicised by word of mouth. In sharp contrast to the rock music industry, there was no star system. What counted for the participants was only the music (Reynolds, 1990, p. 179; Russell, 1993, p. 129) and its 'danceability', not how it was produced, nor by whom. This depersonalisation of musical production has entailed the death of the singer/songwriter, and paradoxically laid the conditions for the emergence in the 1990s of a new cult figure: the DJ as high priest whose instrument is not the drum but the turntable.

This rupture with mainstream pop was made possible initially by the appropriation of electronic music technology by house DJs. The accessibility of cheap music synthesisers such as drum and bass machines, developments in MIDI (Musical Instrument Digital Interface) equipment enabling synthesisers to interact, and the increasing sophistication of musical composition and production techniques such as seamless mixing, the layering of sounds and above all sampling have, in the spirit of precursors such as Stockhausen and Souster, revolutionised (and democratised) musical production. American hardhouse DJ Todd Terry, 'the self-proclaimed sample king' (Swanton, 1995, p. 50), has raised this form of musical piracy to a high art by recycling virtually only his own work.

Technology has also enabled DJs to count the number of beats per minute (bpm) in a sample, and therefore to monitor the effects of rhythmic output on consumers and to manipulate 'scientifically' movement on the dance-floor by varying the tempo of the music. Their aim is to create plateaux of intensity, emotional, physical and social, by carrying participants on a journey with danced music. Correlations are made, by ravers and DJs alike, between heartbeat and musical rhythm, measured in bpm, the ideal for inducing trance and for dancing with whole body movement being between 120 and 130 bpm (Macon, personal communication; Orridge, in Reynolds, 1990, p. 184). By alternating sequences of rhythmic intensity, which build towards a climax which is never fully reached, with breaks into chilling electronic ambient, the rushes and ebbs of orgasm are reproduced. Indeed this rhythmic manipulation and the judicious juxtaposition of different musical textures is at the heart of shamanistic techniques of ecstasy which aim to create a dance/music terrain favourable to the induction of trance. The DJ, like the chief priest or shaman, is an expert in a particular dance-music idiom, and it is around these mediators between the realms of the material and the spiritual, of the individual and social that a cult following builds.

In the same way that in the Nigerian Bini pantheon each deity is associated with characteristic musical rhythms and dance steps, songs, costumes and colours (Gore, 1995, p. 137), so in the fragmented dance-music scene of the 1990s, each rave milieu is associated with a musical genre often characterised by its bpm, as well as by the age/social origins of its participants, the emotional impact of the music, dress codes, etc. Thus house, the progenitor of rave music, is an eclectic uplifting mix at 120–126 bpm with a strong 4/4 kick drum sound, often with vocals; it appeals to a broad constituency with support from an older, more 'sophisticated' crowd, as well as from less urbane 'handbag' club-goers of the provinces. Occupying the zone between 120 and 160 bpm is techno, the Detroit counterpart to Chicago house and with connections to European electro-pop and the early German synthesiser groups such as Kraftwerk, Neu and Tangerine Dream. It uses synthesised sound-layering and little sampling. Fast metronomic 4/4 club techno, which reached its heyday around 1993, is mostly the bastion of white males under 21 with a 'focus on sweaty abandon and sometimes aggressively intense rhythmic manifestos' (Bush, 1995, p. 48). A purist and shrinking scene in Britain, it now thrives in Germany and beyond, where it appeals to a wider audience. The antithesis of modern corporate clubbing, the acid–techno-trance scene represents the political wing of techno. The music, 'a glorious collision of sliding analogue synths, gurgling 303s, racing kickdrums and huge, powerful, epic breakdowns' (Jones, 1995, p. 48), unites a free-thinking underground at illegal free and pay parties. Happy hardcore (or 4-beat) is 160-bpm commercial 'overground' teen music and at the heart of contemporary rave culture. 'Often regarded as little more than a joke on the cooler-than-thou techno and house scenes' (Tope, 1995, p. 61), with its piano riffs and female vocals, it sends entranced teenagers, wearing white gloves, waving glow sticks and blowing whistles and horns, into paroxysms of arm-waving. Also with a tempo of 160 bpm (but without its 4/4 beat) is jungle, a British invention, regularly found in the same venues as happy hardcore but with 'roots' in black music such as rap, reggae and hip-hop. The latter two are said to appeal largely to those from urban working-class backgrounds (Measham, in Saunders, 1995, p. 190). While for the 1990s 'skinheads', the dispossessed and angry, underground gabba at 180–200 bpm and above, where techno has become a 'metabolic rate rather than a music' (Cole, 1995, p. 64), challenges the niceness of the rave scene with the violence of hard beats. Not to be excluded is ambient. Although this is not considered rave music because it is traditionally arhythmic, electronic, atmospheric background music, it is intrinsic to rave culture as it graces the chill-out rooms and clubs which have been spawned in the 1990s to provide spaces for cooling out.

Since acid house, anonymity and impersonality also generally dominate on the dance floor, which is no longer a space for spectacle and sexual posturing as in 1980s disco (Gore, 1995, p. 134). The boundaries between dancer and spectator have dissolved and 'there's a kind of terrain, a shifting dance environment without borders or destination' (Reynolds, 1990, p. 173). Participants are no longer constituted as dancing subjects by the gaze of the (male?) spectator/other, since subjectivity collapses through focusing on the intensities created by trance-inducing movement and incorporated sound, and on the deterritorialisation which results, rather than on the dramatic effects produced through performing visually pleasing, 'aesthetic' dance movements in time to a music located outside the body. This may explain why participants are short on verbal commentary to describe the rave experience, since subjectivity and linguistic ability are inextricably linked. (See Lacan's theorising of linguistics and the constitution of suject-ivity in, for example, Lemaire, 1977.) In this deconstruction of subjectivity produced by trance dancing, participants shift into a realm of collective consciousness 'where "now" lasts longer' (Reynolds, 1990, p. 180), that is, where the spatio-temporal and social dimensions of the habitual are suspended. Raving becomes a form of positive escapism from the hum-drum constraints of the quotidian, not into the nihilism of heroin addiction, for example, but into the celebratory depersonalisation characteristic of liminal rituals in non-Western cultures. Here the corporeal, the collective and the polyvocal are privileged in contrast to the image-laden despotism of Western stardom where the 'singer is the song', where musical identity is mapped on to facial identity. (See Deleuze and Guattari, 1980, pp. 205–34 on the politics of the face, on *visagéité* ['faceness'].)

As Marshall Jefferson puts it, 'Dance music is faceless' (in Dene, 1994, p. 29), because it lacks identifiable instrumentalists, as well as a singer/songwriter. And to the facelessness of trance dance music, the body re-sponds with either 'dehumanised' movements of individual body parts (as in air-punching or arm-waving) or with whole body vibrations which allow for no hierarchising or privileging of any given body part, unlike in the projective pelvic gyrations to soul music, for example, in which both music and dance require identification for their impact. In the anonymity of raving, 'there is no performance, no stage, no play of identification and seduction, no otherness – only deterritorialisation and the "massive buzz"' (Gore, 1995, p. 138).

With the growth of the rave machine and the proliferation of specialist clubs, it was inevitable that the complete anonymity of acid house would be lost. For acid house was a 'war machine' (Jordan, 1995, p. 133), deter-ritorialisation of the body social and politic, and as with all such move-ments, it would inevitably be reterritorialised into new configurations. Thus raving was, for the most part, transformed from nomadic journeying to sedentary tribalism as each dance-music genre developed a profile around specific DJs, who like the chief priests, are simultaneously guardians of a musical tradition as well as potential innovators. This interplay between musical continuity and change is manifest in the tension in rave culture between those DJs who aim to please the crowd and create a good atmo-sphere by mixing records which are familiar, and those who want to make a musical statement by imposing their own tastes and thus introduce new elements. The most successful DJs, I propose, are those who combine both approaches in a creative style by which they eventually become known.

This notion of style of mixing marks a return to concepts of identity and individual production, of 'authorship', characteristic of the commercial music industry. Moreover the power of the DJ is magnified by the fact that most records have limited distribution in that they are produced only in hundreds of copies each with a 'shelf-life' of around three weeks. The DJ therefore has privileged access to musical knowledge and accrues a musical capital which renders him unique, such that 'every DJ is a sub-genre' (Sasha in Saunders, 1995, p. 207).

It is thus that identity has penetrated the scene of rave culture, as temporary, shifting though partisan alliances are formed around diverse dance-music genres spearheaded by the new star performers. This identificatory process is further manifested by the loyalty demonstrated by participants to a particular dance-music genre, as well as by such obvious markers as appropriate fashion, idiomatic language and other sub-cultural codes. And with this return has come, in certain quarters of corporate clubbing, a renewed interest in structured dance movements which require projection to an audience for their effectivity. On the other hand, an underground rave culture thrives; it remains immune to the commercialisation of dance music and to the professionalisation of DJs, and continues to foster the hedonistic parties and abandoned dancing which have made raving internationally famous.

Rave culture is multiple. It connects elements from the commercial music industry with those of underground rave culture; it creates spaces for deterritorialisation, for the transcendence of identity, for the celebration of communitas; it also confines and pens in, reterritorialising energies released on the dance floor into identification with a musical genre or a mixing style; it bridles the body to its metronomic beats only to produce a collective body without organs; it is rebellion and release, control and containment. And above all it is here to stay, because in the turmoil of the inner city it represents a safe zone for recreational drug-taking and dancing, and because, 'in all its forms, [it] is now as English as fish and chips or football' (Marcus, 1995, p. 46).

NOTE

I dedicate this chapter to the late Tim Souster, music composer and friend, who first introduced me to the wonders of electronic music. I wish to thank the following for their help: *Eternity*, 'the controversial dance magazine', and its German correspondent, Oliver Koehler; the magazines *Generator, Mix Mag* and *Muzik*; DJ Dominic Macon of Zoom Records; and friends Chas Comyn, Simon Grant, Josephine Leaske and Ruth Trueman, who first set me on the right track.

REFERENCES

M. Betz, 'Shoot/Anarchic' in R. Klanten *et al.* (eds), *Localizer 1.0. The Techno House Book* (Berlin: Die Gestalten Verlag, 1995), pp. LOC/1.0/FAS/4.3/SHO.

C. Bush, 'Techno – The Final Frontier?', *Muzik*, No. 4 (September 1995), pp. 48–50.

B. Cole, 'Trip Hop. Where Now?', *Mixmag*, II, 51 (August 1995), pp. 62–6.

The Concise Oxford Dictionary of Current English, 8th edn (Oxford: Clarendon Press, 1990).

G. Deleuze and F. Guattari, *Mille Plateaux* (Paris: Les Editions de Minuit, 1980).

G. Deleuze and F. Guattari, 'Rhizome', *I & C*, No. 8 (Spring 1981), pp. 49–71.

L. Dene, 'The Life and Times of Marshall Jefferson', *Generator*, No. 16 (November 1994), pp. 26–30.

'Diplo', 'Sunnyside', *Eternity*, 31 (1995), pp. 14–15.

T. Eagleton, *The Ideology of the Aesthetic* (Oxford: Basil Blackwell, 1990).

J. Fleming, *What Kind of House Party is This? The History of a Music Revolution* (Slough: MIY Publishing, 1995).

G. Gore, 'Rhythm, Representation and Ritual: The Rave and the Religious Cult' in *Border Tensions: Dance and Discourse,* Proceedings of the Fifth Study of Dance Conference (Surrey: Department of Dance Studies, University of Surrey, 1995), pp. 133–9.

D. Harvey, *The Condition of Postmodernity* (Oxford: Basil Blackwell, 1989).

N. Jones, 'The London Trance Underground', *Mixmag*, II, 51 (August 1995), pp. 48–50.

T. Jordan, 'Collective Bodies: Raving and the Politics of Gilles Deleuze and Felix Guattari', *Body & Society*, I, 1 (1995), pp. 125–44.

O. Koehler, 'Universe, the Tribal Gathering, Munich Reim, 1st October 1994', *Eternity*, 23 (1994), pp. 50–1.

O. Koehler, 'The Love Parade, 8th July 1995, Berlin, Germany', *Eternity*, 32 (1995), pp. 92–3.

C. Larkin (ed.), *The Guinness Who's Who of Rap, Dance and Techno* (London: Guinness Publishing, 1994).

A. Lemaire, *Jacques Lacan*, trans. by D. Macey (London: Routledge & Kegan Paul, 1977).

M. Maffesoli, *Le Temps des Tribus: Le Déclin de l'Individualisme dans les Sociétés de Masse* (Paris: Livre de Poche, 1991 [orig. pub. Paris: Méridiens Klincksieck, 1988]).

M. Maffesoli, *Au Creux des Apparences: Pour une Ethique de l'Esthétique* (Paris: Livre de Poche, 1993 [orig. pub. Paris: Plon, 1990]).

M. Maffesoli, *La Transfiguration du Politique: La Tribalisation du Monde* (Paris: Livre de Poche, 1995 [orig. pub. Paris: Grasset & Fasquelle, 1992]).

T. Marcus, 'The War is Over', *Mixmag*, 2, 51 (August 1995), pp. 42–6.

A. Melechi, 'The Ecstasy of Disappearance' in S. Redhead (ed.), *Rave Off: Politics and Deviance in Contemporary Youth Culture* (Aldershot: Avebury, 1993), pp. 29–40.

Dr Motte, 'Love Parade' in R. Klanten *et al.* (eds), *Localizer 1.0. The Techno House Book* (Berlin: Die Gestalten Verlag, 1995), pp. LOC/1.0/CLU/2.1/LOV.

A. Petridis, 'Police Use Criminal Justice Act to Crush Free Festival', *Mixmag*, 2, 51 (August 1995), p. 13.

Rave New World (London: Channel 4 Television, 1994).

S. Redhead, 'The Politics of Ecstasy' in S. Redhead (ed.), *Rave Off: Politics and Deviance in Contemporary Youth Culture* (Aldershot: Avebury, 1993), pp. 7–27.

S. Redhead (ed.), *Rave Off: Politics and Deviance in Contemporary Youth Culture* (Aldershot: Avebury, 1993).

S. Reynolds, *Blissed Out: The Raptures of Rock* (London: Serpent's Tail, 1990).

H. Rietveld, 'Living the Dream' in S. Redhead (ed.), *Rave Off: Politics and Deviance in Contemporary Youth Culture* (Aldershot: Avebury, 1993), pp. 41–89.

P. Rubin, 'Chromapark' in R. Klanten *et al.* (eds), *Localizer 1.0. The Techno House Book* (Berlin: Die Gestalten Verlag, 1995), pp. LOC/1.0/CLU/2.2/CHR.

K. Russell, 'Lysergia Suburbia' in S. Redhead (ed.), *Rave Off: Politics and Deviance in Contemporary Youth Culture* (Aldershot: Avebury, 1993), pp. 91–174.

N. Saunders, *Ecstasy and the Dance Culture* (London: Nicholas Saunders, 1995).

O. Swanton, 'How Much', *Generator*, 2, 7 (August 1995), pp. 50–3.

F. Tope, 'Drink, Drowning and Happy Hardcore', *Mixmag*, 2, 47 (April 1995), pp. 60–2.

V. Turner, *The Ritual Process. Structure and Anti-Structure* (Ithaca, NY: Cornell University Press, 1977 [1966, 1969]).

5 Dirt, Noise, Traffic: Contemporary Indian Dance in the Western City; Modernity, Ethnicity and Hybridity

Sanjoy Roy

> The city, the contemporary metropolis, is for many the chosen metaphor for the experience of the modern world.
>
> (Chambers, 1994, p. 92)

This chapter is about human movement – relocation, travel, migration – and the maps that it crosses. It is also about another type of movement – dance – and how it too crosses those maps. I use 'cross' in both senses of the word: geographically, as in moving through territories; and rhetorically, as in contesting an argument.

To continue the mapping analogy, the chapter will begin with a large-scale view – the place of the city in the modern world – and will progressively narrow its focus of time and place to a smaller scale with higher definition, first through a discussion of ethnicity in post-colonial Britain, and then to a reading of some danceworks seen in London in the 1990s.

DIRT, NOISE, TRAFFIC

Cities are dirty, noisy places, not just in a physical sense, but in a cultural one too. Dirt, in anthropologist Mary Douglas's famous formulation, is matter out of place (Douglas, 1966, p. 40): matter is not intrinsically dirty, but only becomes so when it appears where it doesn't 'belong'. Dirt is therefore an effect of a socially defined system of classification, a symbolic map of what belongs where. Within this formulation, two types of dirt can be distinguished, one simpler and less unsettling than the other. The first is matter that has a place, but is not in it. It is a foreign body, but we

68

nevertheless recognise where it should be: in its native habitat. The second is matter that has no place, an unclassifiable anomaly, something that does not fit into the symbolic map. This second type of dirt is similar to what in cybernetics is called 'noise'. Noise is an interference in the communication of information, a disturbance, something that cannot be placed into a recognised pattern. For example, whereas our own language is one in which we perceive order in its streams of sound, and thus imbue it with meaning, a foreign language is noise, sounds without meaning; we don't recognise a pattern in it. Dirt and noise are, therefore, not things in themselves, but relative terms, disorders that are recognised only through a system of order, types of 'otherness'.

The city is dirty and noisy because it teems with traffic – physical, economic and cultural. It is a place where a profusion of peoples, goods, histories and languages circulate, intermingle and interfere. A multiplicity of nationalities and ethnicities inhabit and traverse it. The extent of this plurality suggests that ideas of dirt and noise need to be loosened, made more mobile, because

> the very idea of a map, with its implicit dependence upon the survey of a stable terrain, fixed referents and measurement, seems to contradict the palpable flux and fluidity of metropolitan life and cosmopolitan movement. . . . The fluctuating contexts of languages and desires pierce the logic of cartography and spill over the borders of its tabular, taxonomic, space. (Chambers, 1994, p. 92)

Anthropological dirt and cybernetic noise are defined in relation to a single symbolic map – what in anthropology is called a cosmology: a world order, 'the way things are'. But the 'flux and fluidity of metropolitan life' undermines this singularity: whose map is definitive? What is a foreign language in the babble, the Babel, of the contemporary metropolis? Dirt and noise are relative not only to an order; orders themselves are relative.

This is not, however, to say that they are equivalent: some may be dominant, others marginal.[1] Rather than a single map or system of representation, it is more useful to think of a *hegemonic* one, a type of common sense that, though dominant, is nevertheless open to negotiation, opposition and transgression from the alternative orders (or disorders) of subcultures and minorities. Cultural order and disorder, purity and pollution, do not form a fixed terrain; they are more like a landscape of shifting sands, the site of contested meanings, of reorientation and disorientation as well as orientation.

HOME AND THE WORLD

Within the somewhat general terms of this discussion, certain words –
map, native, foreign, border, orientation – have been deliberately chosen
to prefigure a narrower focus, on nation, race and ethnicity.

Although the geographical boundaries of the United Kingdom may have
not changed since the Second World War (they are still nearly coterminous
with the British Isles), its relation to the rest of the world has altered con-
siderably. Before the war, as Geoffrey Moorhouse remembers, 'the British
Empire seemed practically interchangeable with the British Isles' (Moorhouse, 1984, p. 11) – well, at least to the British. In atlases, half the world
was coloured pink; Britain was the source of that colour. It was 'the roseate
age of England's precedence' (Rushdie, 1991, p. 129). Since then the pink
territory has contracted almost entirely to the size of Great Britain.[2] More
than that, the pink – perhaps I should say 'white'? – has become inhabited,
largely but not exclusively in its urban centres, by different colours.

Although there is a long history of black people in Britain (see Fryer,
1984; Visram, 1986), the largest-scale migration into the nation came during
the post-war years, when the British government invited – indeed advertised and campaigned for – British subjects from the West Indies and the
Indian subcontinent to fulfil a labour shortage in the post-war reconstruction of the nation. If this reconstruction was envisaged in economic terms,
its effects were also cultural: the geographical boundaries of Empire were
redrawn as cultural boundaries within the map of Britain, creating, in
Salman Rushdie's phrase, a 'new Empire within Britain' (Rushdie, 1991,
p. 129).

Those geographical boundaries had never been simply national ones,
however; they were also racial. Moorhouse recalls that there had been a
racialised distinction between the settler colonies of Australia, New Zea-
land, Canada and South Africa, which were occupied by 'cousins', and the
imperial colonies, which were ruled by Britain but inhabited by 'natives'
(Moorhouse, 1984, pp. 11–12). The difference between the British and
their colonial 'cousins' was relative, a difference of degree, whereas that
between the British and the 'natives' was one of kind. The distinction still
obtained in the post-colonial settlement of Britain, and, against a background of Britain's economic decline, became institutionalised in a series
of laws on immigration, nationality and patriality (Fryer, 1984, pp. 372–
86), which found their ideological counterpart in an idea of cultural difference: what distinguished the blacks from authentic forms of Britishness came to be seen not as a biological difference, but as a cultural one.
Rather than the colonial view of a biological hierarchy of races within the

Empire, the post-colonial version offered a racialised picture of cultural difference within Britain. Though the black settlers were physically inside Britain, culturally they were seen as outside:

> The old racism stressed the ideology of an imperial family of nations. This has been replaced by an ideology of Britain as a nation of families. The old racism said 'keep them out'; the new says 'send them back' instead. The old took an economic *laissez-faire* approach to the issue of black citizenship, whereas the new is premised on the qualification and withdrawal of those rights and entitlements . . . . An idea of blacks as a problem for the national community supplies the continuity between these two different folk theories of race but the definition of that problem varies . . . . [W]e British blacks are now a problem, not because of any biological inferiority, but because of the extent of the cultural differences which divide us from bona fide Brits. (Gilroy, 1993, p. 56)

From this perspective, British blacks are matter out of place; dirt seems not too emotive a term. In this chill climate, the word 'immigrant' becomes almost synonymous with 'black' (as in the self-contradictory but nevertheless taken-for-granted phrase 'second-generation immigrant'), and to be both black and British becomes an implicit contradiction in terms, an impossibly compound identity which is at best an exception to the rule, at worst a violation of it. Gilroy (1987) sums up this rule pithily: 'there ain't no black in the Union Jack'.

There is of course a more benevolent, liberal side to the idea of cultural difference: multiculturalism, in which to belong to another culture does not necessarily imply inferiority or exclusion, merely 'difference'. (Note, however, that the biologistic version – multiracialism – need not imply inferiority either.) There are two problems with this. First, it assigns to different cultures the status described above as 'at best an exception to the rule', leaving the rule itself – who the *bona fide* Brits are – unquestioned. In liberal multiculturalism, 'dirt' is expanded into the less pejorative 'diversity':

> although there is always an entertainment and encouragement of cultural diversity, there is always also a corresponding containment of it. A transparent norm is constituted, a norm which says that 'these other cultures are fine, but we must be able to locate them within our own grid'. That is what I mean by a *creation* of cultural diversity and a *containment* of cultural difference. (Bhabha, 1990, p. 208)[3]

The second, related problem is that the ghettoisation of 'other' cultures into different compartments does not take into account the traffic which crosses the borders between them, both in historical and in social terms.

Historically, the British Empire has produced connections as well as sep-
arations between Britain and its former imperial subjects – language, dress,
food, sport and architecture being obvious examples, but also including
literature, music and art. The recent history of Indian classical dance, for
example – its nineteenth-century decline and twentieth-century rejuvena-
tion – is intimately interwoven with the British presence in India, as well
as the presence of Indian dancers such as Ram Gopal and Uday Shankar
in the West (Jeyasingh, 1990, p. 34; Rubidge, 1996, p. 26). Homi Bhabha,
referring to Rushdie's *The Satanic Verses*, highlights the critical import of
this historical trafficking:

> The Western metropole must confront its postcolonial history, told by
> its influx of postwar immigrants and refugees, as an indigenous or nat-
> ive narrative *internal* to its national identity; and the reason for this is
> made clear in the stammering, drunken words of Mr 'Whisky' Sisodia
> from *The Satanic Verses*: 'The trouble with the Engenglish is that their
> hiss hiss history happened overseas, so they dodo don't know what it
> means.' (Bhabha, 1994, p. 6)

Socially, the distinction is far from clear-cut either: all Britons, black,
white or anything else, are subject to British national culture even while
it positions them differently. The hegemonic mapping of a (white) cultural
identity on to a (British) national one thus produces a more complex experience for those non-whites than the simple idea of cultural difference
suggests. Rather, it is an experience of 'double consciousness'. This is, I
think, rather more than Rubidge suggests – being conscious of two cultures at once (Rubidge, 1996, pp. 12, 40); it is also the paradoxical sense
of being inside and outside at the same time, what I shall call 'inexclusion'.

IMAGINARY HOMELANDS

The contradictory experience of inexclusion is the subject matter of
Burning Skin, a solo by Canadian dancer Roger Sinha performed in London at the 1993 and 1994 Vivarta Festivals. The work is basically a tea
ceremony, in which tea-making is infused into both Indian and Western
contexts. Sinha enters dressed in a red robe, and, like a religious supplic-
ant, he places a bowl of water at the front of the stage, to the accompaniment of oriental-sounding synthesiser music. Then, to the sound of wailing
electric guitars and thumping drumbeats, he dances a distorted version of
Bharata Natyam, jazzing it up with the robotic posturings of the night-club
dance-floor. Moving to one side, he sits at a table. Evoking the gentility

of the European drawing-room, he pours tea from its pot into a china cup, adding milk from its jug, stirring sugar from its bowl. Seemingly anointed by this experience, he waltzes across the floor and performs a series of rising arabesques lifted straight from the classical ballet vocabulary, to the lilting strains of *The Blue Danube*. He then narrates the story of a black boy who thought he could turn his skin white by scalding it with boiling water. Sinha had read this story 'with understanding': his own skin was 'a curse and I wanted to be rid of it ... I wanted to be just like everyone else'. After describing how his own white childhood friend became a racist skinhead, he moves to the back of the stage, where a circle of kettles are gently boiling, the steam gently rising from their spouts like incense in a shrine. Filling the bowl at the front of the stage from the kettles, he takes off his robe and lifts a steaming white shirt from the bowl; puts it on, buttons it up. The audience winces. He proceeds to don a jacket and tie, now dressed in standard Western outfit: black suit, white shirt, black tie.

This resolution is a brutal image of plurality reduced to a black-and-white distinction: amidst the flux of cultural references – Eastern, Western, high and popular culture – emerges a boundary, Sinha's skin, which separates the white from the non-white. Its effect is not simply to confine Sinha to the status of 'other' but to split his identity into two. The scalding white shirt 'inexcludes' him, physically symbolising the psychological pain of becoming incorporated into a culture which simultaneously defines him as an outsider. It embodies the experience of being defined as matter out place by the homeland in which he grows up.

In his essay 'Imaginary Homelands', Salman Rushdie gives two senses to the word 'homeland' (Rushdie, 1991, pp. 9–21). One sense is as a territory to which a group of people are assigned and to which they are confined, as in the South African homelands (counterparts to the aboriginal or Indian reservations of Australia and North America). These are strange inside/outside places: enveloped completely within the national terrain, and defined in relation to it, they form pockets of otherness within it, stains on the map. *Burning Skin* embodies this sense of homeland, and its trauma: the enveloping white shirt both conceals Sinha's skin and brands it. Inevitably, one is reminded of the title of Frantz Fanon's book, *Black Skin, White Masks* (1986); and this is indeed its subject-matter:

It is one thing to position a subject or set of peoples as the Other of a dominant discourse. It is quite another thing to subject them to that 'knowledge', not only as a matter of imposed will and domination, [but] by the power of inner compulsion and subjective con-formation to the norm. That is the lesson – the sombre majesty – of Fanon's insight into the colonising experience in *Black Skin, White Masks.* (Hall, 1990, p. 226)

Hall goes on to add that,

This inner expropriation of cultural identity cripples and deforms. If its silences are not resisted, they produce, in Fanon's vivid phrase, 'individuals without an anchor, without horizon, colourless, stateless, rootless – a race of angels'. (*ibid.*)

One way of resisting this silence is to adopt a different set of co-ordinates in order to fill the vacuum of belonging 'elsewhere' ('without an anchor, without horizon') with a concrete sense of belonging 'somewhere'. This is Rushdie's other sense of the term 'imaginary homeland', and typically involves a rediscovery of the pre-colonial 'motherland' and its heritage. Cultural events and performances form potent symbols for this identification: referring to 'ethnic' music, Martin Stokes writes that 'Place, for migrant communities, is something which is constructed through music with an intensity not found elsewhere in their social lives' (Stokes, 1994, p. 114).

Classical Indian dance may, and often does, also fulfil a 'community' function by providing Indian migrants with a positive sense of belonging, not only by symbolising a valorised heritage to which they can lay claim, but also by providing occasions at which they can meet in an 'Indian' context, where a sense of community and identity can be participated in, constructed and affirmed.

This reorientation is a necessary response to the experience of inexclusion. It opposes the imposed definition of being matter out of place by referring to another area of the map on which to belong. Yet, as both Hall and Rushdie point out, this rediscovery of home and identity can only ever be partial (Hall, 1990, p. 224; Rushdie, 1991, p. 10). Rushdie learnt this in the process of writing his novel *Midnight's Children* (1981), which, though initially envisaged as a Proustian project of remembrance (of India), inevitably became a broken, fragmentary and even 'incorrect' reconstruction of a country that could only exist in his imagination. (Rather than lamenting this as a loss, however, he turned it into the novel's prime virtue.)

The impossibility of a return home forms the theme of Roger Sinha's subsequent dance piece, *Pehla Safar* ('The First Journey'), a duet for Sinha and fellow-Canadian Natasha Bakht (later a dancer with the Shobana Jeyasingh Dance Company) which was performed in Britain at the 1994 Vivarta Festival. It depicts Sinha's problematic return to India (represented by Bakht). Bakht opens the piece as a Bharata Natyam dancer, self-absorbed, raised on a platform and surrounded by mists. Sinha arrives in search of this iconic being. He is carrying a suitcase – rather literally, his 'cultural baggage' – and wearing his black suit, white shirt, black tie. Bakht re-appears at ground level, now wearing a suit too, no longer the ancient traditional creature he had imagined. Their subsequent duet is a series of mismatches in which his demands for affirmation cannot be met. Their moments of unison are fleeting: when she dances in classical style, he imitates with a distorted version; when he follows her, she turns away; when he touches her, she escapes his grasp. When she takes off her jacket and untucks her shirt into a *kurta*, he follows suit. But though he can mimic, he cannot fully identify: she is always either more or less than he expects. The 'India' he seeks and the 'India' he finds are different countries. This is no return of the prodigal son: the piece concludes with Sinha and Bakht in contact, but circling each other, as if Sinha's search cannot be resolved, must remain unfinished. In one striking image in the piece he photographs her, like a tourist – a symbolic snapshot of the whole encounter.

Burning Skin and *Pehla Safar* represent two different senses of imaginary homeland, yet there remains a curious connection between them: in both, Sinha dons the outer garments of cultures to which he cannot completely belong (though in different ways). The first homeland is a negative space inside the West to which Sinha is confined; the second is a positive but necessarily incomplete reorientation towards India. One is a vacuum, the other an attempt to fill it, if only to make it habitable. Both accept the simple definition of 'dirt' described above: matter that has a place but is not in it. So to construct an imaginary homeland in the East (*Pehla Safar*) is different from but not incompatible with being confined to one in the West (*Burning Skin*). Rushdie points out how these two senses of home-land may occupy the same terrain:

> To forget that there is a world beyond the community to which we belong, to confine ourselves within narrowly defined cultural frontiers, would be, I believe, to go voluntarily into that form of internal exile which in South Africa is called the 'homeland'. (Rushdie, 1991, p. 19)

– to which one might add that although this internal exile may be a necessary response to the experience of 'inexclusion', it can readily be interpreted retrospectively as 'evidence' that foreign bodies do indeed belong elsewhere, if not necessarily by race or citizenship, then by personal sentiment, national allegiance or cultural affiliation.

'The community to which we belong' – what is it? All too often, it appears as a choice between native and foreign (or West and East, white and black, coloniser and colonised):

Either identity A or Not A. But the immigrations had left one feeling one was both, split by a dividing line which might also be seen, paradoxically, as the line along which the pieces join together. A borderline identity, belonging to both sides or neither? (Maharaj, 1991, p. 80)

As long as this stark choice of separate, mutually exclusive categories remains – A or Not A – the question of 'the community to which we belong', even if posed as 'both sides or neither?', will remain unanswerable. ('Both sides *and* neither' would get closer, but remains predicated on an idea of 'sides'.)

Rather than confining oneself within the homeland of Western 'inexclusion' or opposing it with one that derives from an imaginary East, there is another possibility: to challenge the distinction which produces this division. Instead of tolerating an ascribed place as 'dirt' or opposing it with reference to another part of the map, this reconstructs that map in order to undermine the boundary upon which those responses are based. This third sense of imaginary homeland is suggested by Rushdie towards the end of his article, and forms the basis of choreographer Shobana Jeyasingh's own 'Imaginary Homelands' essay (1995). Jeyasingh illustrates this with reference to her own dancework entitled, appropriately enough, *Making of Maps* (1991):

I suppose the first thing I thought about when I made *Making of Maps* was the question of heritage . . . . For me, my heritage is a mix of David Bowie, Purcell, Shelley and Anna Pavlova, and it has been mixed as subtly as a samosa has mixed itself into the English cuisine. (Jeyasingh, 1995, p. 193)

Apart from these Westerners, her heritage also includes the Indian dance style Bharata Natyam, which she learnt as a child. 'The reason *why*,' she writes, 'is rooted in certain historical events.' It's a teasing statement, for instead of the expected answer 'because I happen to be from India', she goes on to explain that it was 'a direct result of the British presence in India' (*ibid.*). Already the division between a Western and an Eastern heritage is complicated and blurred: they are intimately implicated with each other.

The starting-point for *Making of Maps* was suggested by a medieval European map made in 1300. On this map, Jerusalem is placed at the centre of the world, with other locations, both historical and mythical, defined in relation to it. It suggests a symbolic map of the world in which the map-maker lived, expressing his concerns and viewpoint. Jeyasingh took this idea and applied it to herself, as 'an Indian dancer living in Britain' (programme note, 1995).

The piece, for five women, opens with one dancer sitting on the floor, her eyes closed, as if travelling within her imagination. That imagination is represented by the other dancers: two of them mark out the stage with the formal spatial designs and directions of Bharata Natyam, while the other pair examine the floor space, pushing themselves across it as if to get the lie of this land. These contrasting styles of movement – the traditional and the exploratory, the defined and the undefined – form the two poles of the imaginary world which the dance invents.

The score too moves between these poles. Its basis is a classical Indian composition by composer and singer R. A. Ramamani. This is incorporated into a score by Alistair MacDonald, which mixes in the everyday sounds of the city street, adding in snippets of radio music, fragments of conversation, the sonorous timbre of the violin, the chiming of church bells.

Against this vivid collage of sound, the dancers first demarcate the stage space in a series of circular formations, and then personalise it, inhabiting it with both classical and idiosyncratic nuances. Sometimes the vocabulary is strictly classical, at other times it is individual. Often both are on stage at the same time, and connections are made between them: a dancer in a classical pose shifts sideways, or is pulled off centre by another, until she overbalances, falls, and rolls. Although the basis of the dance movement is rooted in the objective clarity of a tradition (Bharata Natyam), it is re-routed towards the complexity of urban life, where traditions evolve, merge, disperse.

The piece finishes with the same dancer sitting in a meditative posture as at the beginning, as if still imagining her journey. Around her, the other four dancers face in different directions, hinting at paths that are yet to be mapped, journeys still to be made. The score ends with a soundscape of the city, an open-ended evocation of the flux of everyday life which was, Jeyasingh says, 'the only way to end the dance' (*Making of Maps* education pack, 1993).

By placing herself at the centre of the work, Jeyasingh maps out a configuration in which she is not, by virtue of her Indian background, a foreign body adrift in the modern urban world, but an active participant in its construction. Although *Making of Maps* is 'a personal map of an Indian dancer living in Britain', it is not limited to these beguilingly simple but manifestly inadequate linguistic terms ('Indian', 'Britain'): instead, its starting-point is their interdependent complexity, and in the process of transgressing the border between them it transfigures their relation from fixed and separate categories into one that is more fluid, mobile and contingent.

CONFIGURATIONS OR COLLABORATIONS?

If *Making of Maps* is explicitly concerned with interrogating, obscuring, restructuring or dissolving the boundary between İndia and Britain, other works by Jeyasingh presume this remapping in order to focus on a more specific subject: a narrative sequence, for example (*Correspondences*), or the relations between different styles of moving (*Raid*). The understanding of a dancework does not, however, derive solely from the choreography (or the choreographer, for that matter), but also from the prior knowledge and concerns that we bring to it, for example the received ideas of race and culture referred to at the beginning of this chapter. From within these terms, Jeyasingh's work appears as problematic, difficult to place: dirt of the unsettling kind that cannot be located on the current map. One way of replacing it on this map is to interpret the interferences, the 'noise' that her choreography produces, from within the language of multiculturalism. Perhaps the clearest illustration of this is Jeyasingh's early work *Configurations*.

During the 1991 tour of Jeyasingh's company, two local newspapers misprinted 'Configurations' as 'Collaborations' (*Harrow Observer*, 22 October 1991; *Ealing and Acton Gazette*, 23 October 1991).[4] The slippage between these two words is revealing: it is symptomatic of the different ways that the work is understood, and highlights a contest over definitions.

Originally choreographed in 1988 as a solo, *Configurations* was reworked for a duet, a trio, and finally as a quartet; it is this last version to which I refer. *Configurations* is for the most part an exploration of the formal qualities (*nritta*) of Bharata Natyam: how the steps, gestures and positions of the traditionally solo style can be composed into group designs and spatial patterns. Phrases are dissected, repeated and varied in different directions, and the dancers move in and out of unison through the devices of canon, symmetry and opposition – formal procedures which create a highly articulated texture of time and space; a sparkling, crystalline geometry. Its aesthetic impulse is modernist (the structure of the dance is its own subject), and, with its classical basis, it could be likened to the impulse behind, say, Ashton's *Scènes de ballet*, or Balanchine's formalist work.

Balanchine liked to work closely with music, and in *Configurations* Jeyasingh does the same. Traditionally, the precise, complex rhythms of Bharata Natyam footwork are matched by the musical accompaniment; here, instead of traditional music, Jeyasingh used a commissioned score from Michael Nyman, whose systematic methods of composition corresponded well with the mathematical permutations of Bharata Natyam footwork. The score was in fact composed *to* the dance, and Jeyasingh was 'very disciplined' with Nyman in setting its metres. The result is a dance in which the rhythms of the music and the movement correspond almost note-for-step.

Yet while Balanchine and, say, Stravinsky were granted the status of individual artists working together from within their separate fields of choreography and music, *Configurations* was understood not as an artistic collaboration but as a cultural one. On one level, nothing could be more self-evident: Jeyasingh's choreography remains largely within a recognisable classical Indian style, while Nyman's music is very much part of the Western contemporary music scene. Yet this division into parts is nowhere to be found within the aesthetic qualities of the dancework *itself*, for there could scarcely be a more intimate unity of music and dance. Rather, it is based upon a prior knowledge of what constitutes the East and the West.

If *Configurations* allowed a relatively easy separation of East with dance and West with music, Jeyasingh's later work has complicated this division. She has extended her exploration of Bharata Natyam both in terms of structure (a project initiated by *Configurations*) and in terms of vocabulary, for example by using the floor, by distorting its iconic poses, by adding everyday movement, or movement from sport, martial arts and yoga. She has commissioned a piece from modernist (white) British choreographer Richard Alston, with whom she shares many aesthetic concerns (*Delicious Arbour*, to music by Purcell); and in *Making of Maps, Romance** *... with footnotes, Raid* and *Duets With Automobiles* (a short television film directed by Terry Braun) she has used scores which cut and mix a Western and an Eastern composition. Although this intermingling of cultural references has confounded the easy separation of Eastern and Western *heritages*, there has nevertheless remained in reviews of her work a concern to discern and classify Eastern and Western *influences*.

The conception of Jeyasingh's work as a cross-cultural hybrid has become something of a commonplace, though it is one that she has vigorously contested (and if it is less common now than five years ago, this in no small part due to Jeyasingh herself, who has been – of necessity, I suspect – rather more vocal than many other choreographers). But it would be too easy, I think, to dismiss this conception as simply 'wrong', for it seems to be almost a self-evident truism: yes, there is both East and West in her work. A more useful approach would be to see it as a disagreement over the how the word 'hybrid' is understood.

Hybridity, as Robert Young observes (1995, p. 21), is itself a hybrid term. At its simplest, it implies the merging of two separate entities into a single compound, the resultant hybrid being made up of its component parts. This view corresponds to the idea of multiculturalism described above, in which separate cultures are seen as coexisting together:

Today the notion is often proposed of a new cultural hybridity in Britain, a transmutation of British culture into a compounded, composite mode. The condition of that transformation is held out to be the preservation of a degree of cultural and ethnic difference. (Young, 1995, p. 23)

The critical concern to separate and demarcate the East and the West within Jeyasingh's choreography is an example of this 'multiculturalist' approach. What she objects to is not, I think, that the idea that there is East and West in her work, but the simplistic way those 'elements' are defined.

Underpinning this definition is an association of the West with modernity: the experimental, individual, progressive and new is seen as implicitly Western, while the traditional, religious, ethnic and exotic is assigned to the East.[5] Take, for example, this statement: 'Shobana Jeyasingh is our leading experimentalist in blending classical Indian dance with contemporary Western music and ideas' (*Time Out*, 9.10.91). The contemporary is Western (not just its music, but its *ideas*), while the classical is Indian. Or this: 'Jeyasingh reappears as a choreographer on a voyage of discovery in the world of European contemporary dance . . . at the temple of experimental dance, the Place Theatre' (*Morning Star*, 12.3.93). Contemporary dance is a European phenomenon which this non-European 'discovers', in appropriately orientalist fashion, in a temple. The same review goes on to reinforce the company's status as visitors to this European temple: 'The company, still swinging their amazing pigtails, flexing their delicate fingers and stamping their flawless feet, remain indisputably Indian.' Or this: in order to make Indian dancing 'easily accessible to Western eyes', 'the traditions of ancient lands had been sacrificed to the new cities' (*Guardian*, 18.10.91).

These reviews express in more sophisticated language a common audience response: either that the dance looks more 'Indian' than 'contemporary' (as if they were mutually exclusive categories), or that its modernism is a Westernisation and hence a corruption (a 'sacrifice') of Indian tradition. The celebration of cultural diversity in Jeyasingh's work thus becomes a containment of the 'other' culture within the narrow confines of tradition: 'AfroAsian artists are removed from the authentic space or experiences of the modern age. As a result, all signs of modernity in their work become *in*-authentic representations' (Araeen, 1991, p. 19).

The possibility that an Indian classical tradition can in itself form a basis for experiment is overlooked: that the use of the floor in *Making of Maps* may derive from the Bharata Natyam style – with its low centre of gravity and strong downward pull – rather than from the influence of Western contemporary dance; that the multi-directionality which Jeyasingh investigates may arise from its articulate spatial structure, clear directions, and strong visual design rather than from the influence of Merce Cunningham.

The 'contemporisation' of Bharata Natyam is not necessarily therefore a Westernisation. This is not to deny that Jeyasingh may cite influences from Western contemporary or indeed classical dance (which are as much a part of her environment as of any other British choreographer); it is to object to the commonplace notion that modernism, experimentation and invention can only be borrowed from the West, so that modernity is seen not as a confluence of different heritages, but as the influence of one upon another.

This multiculturalist understanding of hybridity is rather literally 'commonplace': two separate entities, the East and the West, share the same space. It is a straightforward idea which presupposes the existence of the East and the West as separate categories, each with its own essential qualities, and reinforces them as such. Robert Young (1995) argues that the idea of hybridity was central to nineteenth-century racial theory, for it was through hybridity that separate races were defined. Here, hybridity is used to separate and define cultures. That these cultural divisions are also racial ones suggests that this strategy is not so far removed from the racial ideologies of the last century as many would like to think. The celebration of Jeyasingh's work as a cross-cultural hybrid may thus do no more than affirm the divisions – cultural and racial (the two are often conflated) – which she implicitly or (in *Making of Maps*) explicitly contests.

There is, however, another sense of hybridity, in which the hybrid is not seen as a compound of separate parts, but a new form that is incompatible with the division which defines them *as* separate parts. This is a more unsettling sense, for the hybrid cannot be placed on the map of prior knowledge. From within that map it is registered as a disturbance, an anomaly, 'noise'; fusion is seen as confusion.

In order to move beyond this static, self-perpetuating position it is necessary to attend to the internal workings of the dance itself; for dance is not simply a reflection of its context, but also the source of its own emergent meanings. The aesthetic structures of Jeyasingh's choreography suggest that it cannot be simply described as a cultural compound. To date, Jeyasingh's aesthetic interests have formed a relatively consistent framework – a regard for the form and texture of movement, an attention to structural rigour, more abstract than representational: modernist. (Even *Correspondences,* with its narrative of exile and return, is interpreted in a sequence of abstract episodes, and in the final section – thrillingly titled 'The Mock Theta Functions' – dissolves into a spectacle of pure mathematics.) It is through formal experimentation that old maps can be overwritten and restructured into new configurations. Instead of referring to prior knowledge, this exploration activates the potential for connoting new meanings; it presents more than it represents. So, as described above, the separation of *Configurations* into two distinct cultural modes ignores the internal coherence of music and movement. From within its own terms, *Configurations* is not a cultural hybrid, but a hybrid of two media: music and dance. And in *Making of Maps*, by placing herself at the centre ('an Indian dancer in Britain') rather than between the poles of India and Britain, Jeyasingh reorders that polarity into a more open, complex configuration. Through her abstract, modernist procedures, she navigates a pathway along the precarious edge between the known and the unknown, dancing on the very cusp of possibility.

HERE BE DRAGONS

A number of writers have proposed that new formations in art (or, more generally, in cultural representations) can prefigure social identities. Raymond Williams, for example, in his concept of 'structures of feeling', argues that emergent social groups that have yet to be positioned within the dominant regime of representation (the hegemonic map) may find points of identification in the emergent meanings articulated in art. Art, by creating new configurations, pushes at the 'edge of semantic availability' (Williams, 1977, p. 134), enabling new meanings to be imagined, and hence new possibilities for identification.

The dominant regime described at the beginning of this chapter relies upon a particular formation of race, nation and culture. As I suggested, this leaves British Asians in a contradictory position. They are given a choice of either assimilating into a culture which defines them as out of place, leading to the experience of 'inexclusion', or attempting to identify with a country of origin to which they can no longer belong. In his witty and poignant story 'The Courter', Salman Rushdie expresses this dilemma:

> But I too, have ropes around my neck, I have them to this day, pulling me this way and that, East and West, the nooses tightening, commanding *choose, choose.*
>
> I buck, I snort, I whinny, I rear, I kick. Ropes, I do not choose between you. Lassoes, lariats, I choose neither of you and both. Do you hear? I refuse to choose. (Rushdie, 1994, p. 211)

The choice between a motherland of origin and a fatherland of adoption is frankly Oedipal: either identify with the mother (from whom you are irrevocably separated) or with the father (which necessarily involves an act of repression). The traumas of these impossible demands are expressed by Roger Sinha, first in *Burning Skin* (choose the West), and then in *Pehla Safar* (choose the East). Neither are satisfactory.

Jeyasingh (like Rushdie, in fact) does more than refuse to choose: she refuses the validity of the choice. Instead of struggling within these Oedipal terms (like Sinha), she opts for a less nuclear, more extended family. *Making of Maps* stands at a critical distance from Sinha's dilemma, invoking his predicament without itself being an example of it. In the process of redefining herself on the map, Jeyasingh reconfigures it. In doing so, she charts a new terrain in which those anomalous creatures, the British Asians, may find a point of identification that is not impossibly self-contradictory or confined to an imaginary ghetto. By getting 'under the skin' of cultural boundaries, by loosening the links between race, place and culture, her work can speak to the experience of diaspora. As she said in a television interview, 'I am inventing my own ethnicity' (*The Colour of Britain*, BBC, 1994).

Is this ethnicity a hybrid? It depends on the viewpoint: a hybrid is not so much a thing as a way of understanding. We all, in fact, have plural identities that shift with context, place and time, often in contradictory ways; in short, we are all hybrids. But this ordinary, everyday hybridity is not generally conceived as such: hybridity seems to be recognised only when its elements are seen as somehow *essentially* incompatible; that is when a cultural border has been crossed, such as the imaginary one between East and West. So it is the existence of the border which defines the elements, not the other way round: 'A boundary is not that at which something stops, but, as the Greeks recognized, the boundary is that from which *something begins its presencing*' (Martin Heidegger, quoted in Bhabha, 1994, p. 1).

Jeyasingh is, then, not necessarily creating a cultural hybrid; rather, by assuming that hybridity is already there, though it may be unrecognised, she attempts to transform the way that it is understood: 'I don't want to divide between East and West, nor do I see myself as bringing them together. History has already done that' (*India Mail*, 2.3.95). We might say that she attempts to change an exceptional hybrid into an ordinary one, to transfigure the simple binary of East and West into a more complex configuration, which, paradoxical though it may seem, makes it more everyday. This is not to dissolve into that commonplace of multiculturalism, the cultural melting-pot, but to complicate the simplistic terms in which ethnicity is thought, the way that knowledge is structured, and the way that borders are mapped.

On medieval maps, the areas of uncharted terrain beyond the edges of the known world were imagined to be populated by strange creatures that could only be conceived as monstrous hybrids composed of elements that were already known – mermaids (half-woman, half-fish), griffons (half-lion, half-eagle), dragons (half-bat, half-lizard). In the modern age, that uncharted terrain is cultural, and those hybrids now appear not at the edges of the map, but at its very centre: the city. Here – in the modern urban metropolis – be dragons. These noisome products of colonial and post-colonial traffic have come home to roost; must they – we, I – too be imagined as monstrous creatures, impossible compounds that can only speak with forked tongues?

NOTES

1. For a lucid discussion of the reduction of 'relative' to 'equivalent', see Wilden, 1980, pp. xxxvi–xxxvii.
2. I should add that within the UK England remains precedent: the Irish, Scots and Welsh have a different relation to the notion of Britain from the English. These internal differences within British national identity are not, however, the subject for consideration here.
3. For an investigation into the relations between multiculturalism, popular imperialism and the connoisseurship of the urbane white city-dweller – the *flâneur* – see Shields, 1994.
4. Wherever this mistake came from, it seems very unlikely to have arisen from the dance company.
5. Modernity is not, of course, the only dimension which affects how Jeyasingh's choreography is seen, though it is the one I consider here. Gender, for example, is another, and one which has its own relations to modernity and ethnicity.

REFERENCES

R. Araeen, 'The Other Immigrant: The Experiences and Achievements of AfroAsian Artists in the Metropolis', *Third Text*, Vol. 15 (Summer 1991), pp. 17–28.
H. Bhabha, 'The Third Space' in J. Rutherford (ed.), *Identity: Community, Culture, Difference* (London: Lawrence & Wishart, 1990), pp. 207–21.
H. Bhabha, *The Location of Culture* (London: Routledge, 1994).
I. Chambers, *Migrancy, Culture, Identity* (London: Routledge, 1994).

M. Douglas, *Purity and Danger: An Analysis of the Concepts of Pollution and Taboo* (London: Routledge & Kegan Paul, 1966).

F. Fanon, *Black Skin, White Masks* (London: Pluto Press, 1986).

P. Fryer, *Staying Power: The History of Black People in Britain* (London: Pluto Press, 1984).

P. Gilroy, *There Ain't No Black in the Union Jack* (London: Routledge, 1987).

P. Gilroy, *Small Acts* (London: Verso, 1993).

S. Hall, 'Cultural Identity and Diaspora' in J. Rutherford (ed.), *Identity: Community, Culture, Difference* (London: Lawrence & Wishart, 1990), pp. 222–37.

S. Jeyasingh, 'Getting Off the Orient Express', *Dance Theatre Journal*, 8, 2 (1990), pp. 34–7.

S. Jeyasingh, 'Imaginary Homelands: Creating a New Dance Language' in *Border Tensions: Proceedings of the Fifth Study of Dance Conference* (Guildford: University of Surrey, 1995), pp. 191–7.

S. Maharaj, 'The Congo is Flooding the Acropolis: Art in Britain of the Immigrations', *Third Text*, No. 15 (Summer 1991), pp. 77–90.

G. Moorhouse, *India Britannica* (London: Paladin, 1984).

S. Rubidge, *Romance* ... *with footnotes* (London: Shobana Jeyasingh Dance Company, 1996).

S. Rushdie, *Imaginary Homelands: Essays and Criticism 1981–1991* (London: Granta, 1991).

S. Rushdie, *East, West* (London: Jonathan Cape, 1994).

R. Shields, 'Fancy Footwork: Walter Benjamin's Notes on Flâneurie' in K. Tester (ed.), *The Flâneur* (London: Routledge, 1994), pp. 61–80.

M. Stokes, 'Place, Exchange and Meaning' in M. Stokes (ed.), *Ethnicity, Identity and Music: the Musical Construction of Place* (Oxford: Berg, 1994), pp. 97–115.

R. Visram, *Ayahs, Lascars and Princes: The Story of Indians in Britain, 1700–1947* (London: Pluto Press, 1986).

A. Wilden, *System and Structure: Essays in Communication and Exchange*, 2nd edn (London: Tavistock, 1980).

R. Williams, 'Structures of Feeling' in *Marxism and Literature* (Oxford: Oxford University Press, 1977), pp. 128–35.

R. Young, *Colonial Desire: Hybridity in Theory, Culture and Race* (London: Routledge, 1995).

OTHER SOURCES

The Colour of Britain, BBC, 1994.

Making of Maps education pack (book and video), London: Shobana Jeyasingh Dance Company, 1993.

Another useful source is the special issue of *Choreography and Dance, South Asian Dance: The British Experience*, ed. A. Ayer, 4, 2 (1997).

Part II
Stepping Out

6 Ballroom Blitz
Helen Thomas and Nicola Miller

'Every once in a while I suddenly find myself dancing.'
'I suppose it must be some kind of affliction.'

Fred Astaire and Ginger Rogers in Top Hat

Every week, so we are led to believe, some five million people in Britain find themselves dancing (Johnson, 1993), or, at least, go to an event that includes dancing. The focus of this chapter is oriented towards one dance genre, ballroom dancing, through a discussion of certain issues that emerged from a qualitative study of particular dance events and activities that take place regularly in an established dedicated ballroom dance-hall (the *Rivoli Ballroom*) in south-east London.[1] The concern here, in part, is to raise these issues through what may be termed as 'snapshots' of aspects of two of the dance activities, the competitions and the tea dances, and the voices of the people who were interviewed, as opposed to providing a systematic account of this research setting. The inquiry also generated certain questions concerning research methods and strategies, which will contribute to recent discussions on the use of ethnographic methods for the analysis of dance contexts and practices (see, for example, Martin, 1995; Ness, 1996a, b; Novack, 1995; Thomas, 1996). However, it should be noted that this study represents the first stage of a larger project which will compare and contrast the events, and dance preferences of participants, in relation to age and gender differences, in an older-style venue such as the one under discussion here, with other more recently established 'dance' venues that have sprung up in pubs in south-east London. Thus, any conclusions that we might wish to draw from this initial study can only be tentative.

RESEARCH SETTING

The initial research interest was fuelled by what appeared to be a resurgence in the popularity of more formal 'couple' or 'touch' dancing in the 1990s, after many years of decline, which was given voice through a number of press reports, magazine articles and listings (see for example, Fidler, 1994; Smith, 1995). It was envisaged that the research setting of the Rivoli Ballroom would provide an interesting starting-point for exploring this apparent resurgence because it had a history, and thus could offer the possibility of considering the relative weight of the claims concerning the renewed popularity of formal social dancing over time, at least in this venue. Moreover, this particular setting was intriguing because it is a well-known landmark in the area. Although most local people could tell you where the dance-hall is, the majority seem blissfully unaware of the variety of dance activity that takes place there, or, indeed, what it looks like from the inside.

Standing opposite a train station and a library, the Rivoli Ballroom is sandwiched between a hairdressers and a paint shop, on a parade of local shops, in what is now a working-class, multi-racial residential area of Crofton Park in the inner-city borough of Lewisham in south-east London. At first glance, from the outside, it looks more like an old-fashioned 1950s, pre-Odeon-style picture-hall, than anything else. This is hardly surprising, as it was just that before it was transformed into its current splendour as a ballroom in the early 1970s. There is a rumour that its history dates back before the days of cinema, and that from around the middle of the nineteenth century, a music-hall of somewhat dubious repute had stood on the site. The local cinema historian, however, disputes this (George, 1987). Rather, he maintains, it was a purpose-built, 600-seater cinema, which opened in 1913 as the Crofton Park Picture Palace. This cinema, and others nearby which opened around the same time, were situated in residential areas which had expanded rapidly between 1880 and 1900 and which were increasingly coming to house a lower middle-class and working-class population of 'clerks and artisans' (Coulter, 1994). The local paper stated that the Crofton Picture Palace, which was clearly attempting to be seen as a respectable concern in those early days when the cinema had a rather questionable reputation, sought to cater for the 'select residential population roundabout', and to that end, was intent on avoiding the 'vulgar' or 'sensational' in its selection of programmes (George, 1987). The cinema had a rocky passage in its early years, with the licence changing hands many times over a short period. It was also renamed several times and finally became the Rivoli in 1929. The Rivoli finally closed its doors as a cinema in 1957. It became a dance-hall in 1960 and subsequently for several years, like a large number of old cinemas, it became a bingo-hall, with dancing on Tuesdays and Saturday evenings. In 1970 it closed for refurbishment, and two and a half years later it was reopened as a dedicated ballroom. The rather scruffy, nondescript exterior of the dance-hall, with flush pay-booth on the left-hand side of the entrance, however, gives no indication of the lavish, glittering artifice that lies within. The contrast between the almost DIY appearance of the exterior of the ballroom, which is painted in yellow and blue emulsion, and the crafted design of the interior is quite striking. The decor of the ballroom is fashioned on the lines of the grand Viennese ballrooms of the late eighteenth and nineteenth centuries. In the 1920s, the newly-created *palais de danse*, such as the Hammersmith Palais, which opened its doors in 1919, aimed to cater for the urban working classes who wanted dance in the new styles, but could not afford to frequent the exclusive West-End hotels and restaurants where their more wealthy peers danced. With their large halls and spacious, sprung floors to dance on, to the sounds of the latest music played by full live bands, the *palais* were designed to give the appearance of luxury and grandeur for the pleasure of the working classes that had formally been reserved for those higher up the social scale. The Rivoli Ballroom evokes the earlier past of the great balls and the more recent 'retro' style of the *palais de danse*. It is hardly surprising that it is used regularly for films, pop videos and fashion photo shoots. The walls of the hall are lined with red velour, with patterned panels encrusted with diamanté and gold-painted wood panelling. There are 200 wall-lights which highlight the opulent appearance of the red and gold. The tables and the red velvet seating are set around the edge of the sprung maple dance-floor, with two revolving glitter balls, three large chandeliers and numerous smaller ones hanging down from the ceiling. There is a raised stage across the breadth of the far end of the hall, large enough to take a small dance band, complete with sound system and a large selection of dance records. There are two bars, a rather sumptuous 1960s one with gold flock wallpaper and matching upholstered seating, and a more everyday bar/buffet reminiscent of a 1950s ice-cream parlour, with booth seats. The regular dance programme includes the traditional afternoon 'tea dances', evening dances to bands or records, beginner and intermediate ballroom classes, 'singles' night, practice sessions, monthly competitions, exhibition evenings, and private lessons by professional ballroom dance teachers. Although the focus is on ballroom dancing, there are sessions to cater for the latest dance craze, such as salsa, or line dancing.

METHOD

The approach taken here builds on previous work (see Thomas, 1993, 1996), and is broadly ethnographic in character. Ethnography has a long-established tradition in social and cultural anthropology and over the past thirty or so years has gained considerable ground in sociology and related areas such as social psychology. The critiques of ethnography in the social sciences have emerged not only from survey or quantitative researchers (see Hammersley, 1992) who see ethnography as lacking in scientificity, but also, although on somewhat different grounds, from within postmodern cultural anthropology (see Clifford, 1986), where it is viewed as a colonising ethnographic gaze. Recent ethnographic studies by dance anthropologists, such as Cowan (1990); Drewal (1992); Ness (1992) and Novack (1990), have drawn on contemporary reflexive ethnographic approaches in anthropology, along with the insights of structuralist and postmodern/poststructuralist thought, for their studies of dance as a 'complex cultural practice' (Novack, 1995). For the purposes of the discussion, at this particular juncture, however, ethnography is taken to refer 'primarily to a particular set of methods'.

> In its most characteristic form it involves the ethnographer participating, overtly, or covertly, in peoples' daily lives for an extended period of time, watching what happens, listening to what is said, asking questions – in fact, collecting whatever data are available to throw light on the issues that are the focus of the research. (Hammersley and Atkinson, 1995, p. 5)

There were two researchers (Nicola Miller and Helen Thomas), who, over a period of six months, observed the various levels of ballroom activity that took place at the Rivoli, conducted interviews with women and men participants at tea dances, practice sessions and competitions, and on occasions, took part in classes. Before gaining access to the research setting, we interviewed two women in their forties who had taken ballroom classes at the Rivoli the year before, a group of three women and one man in their twenties who had been going to a newer venue in a pub in southeast London, and a couple (man and woman) who frequented a venue in the centre of town. Eleven people were 'formally' interviewed and taped using a semi-structured questionnaire which was altered to take account of the dance context, for example, whether the individuals were involved in competitive dancing, tea dancing, or in some aspect of teaching or demonstrating. On a number of other occasions, however, the loosely-based questionnaire proved to be a stumbling block in the research. On a certain level, we found that ballroom dancing, like a number of sports,[2] is a highly competitive 'closed' world in which everyone seems to know everyone else, or, at least, everyone else who matters. There were occasions when some individuals, particularly professionals (teachers), were wary of being taped, despite guarantees of anonymity, in case their 'voices' would be recognised, and perhaps they would be seen to be treading on someone else's toes (the invisible [at least to us], yet ever-present, hierarchy). At the same time, dedicated ballroomers are only too well aware that their public image is less than 'chic' and may wish to be prudent in what they say, so as not to be misconstrued. They proved to be very skilled at thwarting any attempts to engage them in a semi-structured interview setting, preferring just to chat 'off the record'. After such occasions, the researchers would compare notes and discuss the issues that emerged through these more open-ended discussions. These informal 'chats' helped us to see both the strength and the fragility in what increasingly came to seem like a microcosm of the ballroom-dancing world.

For the most part, the research was conducted overtly, although in the instance of the classes, Thomas did not reveal to the other learners during the breaks, or the male partners, that there was another 'hidden' element to this participation, although the teacher was informed by the owner of the Rivoli, who acted as our 'gatekeeper' into this field of ballroom dancing. After taking into account the ethical questions that have been raised in relation to covert research (see Hammersley and Atkinson, 1995, pp. 263–87), it was decided that, in this context, it was legitimate not to reveal to the co-learners that there was a researcher in their midst. Although both researchers are familiar with contemporary dance, neither had any real foundation in ballroom. The main aim of participating in the classes, in the first instance, was to experience learning ballroom dancing in order to be able to gain an understanding of what it entailed in terms of bodily skills, how it compared with our own knowledge base, and so on, as opposed to offering a detailed account of the interaction in the classes. This, in turn, would feed into the interviews, the informal discussions, and the other overt participant observation aspects of the study. The other participants in the classes, unlike the interviewees, were not going to be referred to directly in the study. In a manner of speaking, in this instance, the subject/object of the research was the researcher herself. Moreover, from about ten minutes into the first class, the dancing became a real pleasure in and of itself, rendering the idea of separating extrinsic from intrinsic considerations, even for analytic purposes, as redundant. This, in turn, contributed to a questioning of traditionally received notions regarding the distinctions between outside/inside (objectivist/subjectivist, far/near) research strategies, which have been the subject of much debate and criticism by advocates of reflexive approaches in sociology (for example, see the discussions on feminist ethnography in Stanley, 1990).

STRICTLY BALLROOM

And by day, Alf is a bus driver and by night he is a sequin sewer.
Andrew, an amateur ballroom dancer

Competition dancing takes place at the Rivoli about once a month on a Sunday during the day. As with all such events in Great Britain, the competitions are governed by the rules set down in the official *Rule Book* of The British Council of Ballroom Dancing (BCBD) which was formed as a result of a conference of various teachers' associations in 1929 as the Official Board of Ballroom Dancing (OBBD), with the aim of establishing 'a co-ordinating organisation to enable teachers to work together on uniform lines' (BCBD *Rule Book*). The OBBD played a major role in the consolidation and the establishment of the 'English Style' (waltz, foxtrot, quickstep and tango) of ballroom dancing, the basis of which had been set out in 1924 by five leading dancers, including Josephine Bradley and Victor Sylvester, who had been brought together by the Imperial Society to form its Ballroom Branch in that same year. The 'English Style' forms the basis of what is now referred to as the 'International Style'. Competition dancing first came into vogue in Britain just after the First World War and to begin with there was no delineation between the amateur and the professional dancer (Richardson, 1948). But, with the increase in competitions, it became clear that rules had to be set down regarding amateur and professional status and so tentative attempts were made at formulating guidelines, under the auspices of the editor of *The Dancing Times*, and these were subsequently used in three World Championships. As a result of a conference of amateurs, professionals, dance teachers and dance-hall managers in 1926, *The Dancing Times Rules* were revised to define amateur status, and with the establishment of the OBBD, new rules were brought in which subsequently displaced *The Dancing Times Rules*. Although the primary function of the Board was and is concerned with the control of all matters pertaining to competition dancing in England, Scotland and Wales, it has also become interested in promoting social dancing (Franks, 1963).

Stepping into the ballroom at the Rivoli on a Sunday afternoon when the competition is in full swing proved to be a fascinating and bewildering experience. To begin with, the sight of the lavish, yet mannered, styling of the contestants as they swished effortlessly across the floor doing their set pieces, bathed in the light of the chandeliers, and set against the backdrop of the red and gold décor, with onlookers dressed in ordinary clothes, and other contestants in their ballroom best, standing or sitting around the edge of the floor, was so other-worldly that it seemed as if we had been dropped into a period film-set designed to exude the kitsch and the glamorous in the same instant. The setting also seemed to bring to life certain typifications of ballroom dancing that were all too familiar, at least at a common-sense, taken-for-granted level. These, however, almost like the setting itself, were real and illusory at the same time.

Despite the popularity of films like *Strictly Ballroom* and *Scent of a Woman* or, perhaps, because of them, ballroom dancing, more often than not, remains the butt of jokes in the popular press and the media. Mention to colleagues or friends that you are researching in this area and almost without exception, the first thing they will want to know is, 'have you started sewing on the sequins yet?' The stereotypical images of the female ballroom dancer bear more than a passing resemblance to the seemingly unchanging images that have been paraded before our eyes on our television screens over the years in *Come Dancing*, the longest-running television series in the UK. On the one hand, there is the stereotype of the 'modern' ballroom dancer (waltz, foxtrot, quickstep and tango), who could be anything from sixteen to fifty, complete with the piled-up, coiffed hairdo glued to her head, face coated in pan-stick make-up, heavily made-up eyes, and glossy lips with a fixed, wide smile. She is adorned in a bright yellow, peacock blue, lime green or pink chiffon dress, with sequined bodice and full calf-length skirt (the hemline goes up or down according to the fashion of the day), which, edged at the bottom with ostrich feathers (or the like), stands away from and moves with the body, with the aid of layers of nylon net underskirts. Attached to the dress is a long, matching chiffon scarf which flows behind her (Isadora Duncan-style) as she is turned and shown by her partner, and to complete the look she wears matching satin high-heeled shoes. The conspicuous consumption of her dress and the raised, slightly backward tilt of the upper body, long neck line and high head orientation, and the formalised lifted positioning of the arms, which combine to give off an air of elegance and 'class', hark back to a former time and a higher class from which, in part, the 'English style' of ballroom dancing was derived. Her partner's dress and comportment, coded to complete the artifice, as Fiske and Hartley (1993) point out, are derived from the evening dress of the Edwardian upper class with white tie, winged collar and black tails. The gender distinctions which are emphasised through the dress codes and the dances themselves, with the man leading and the woman following, also seem to belong to a different era. Although some of the younger dancers we spoke with stressed that the idea of the man leading and the woman following is somewhat old-fashioned and that the aim is to work as one (see also Peters, 1991 on this issue).

The dress code and the demeanour of the other female stereotype, the Latin American ballroom dancer, evokes a more overt sexuality to fit in with the body movement required by the samba, rumba, cha-cha-cha, and *paso doble*. Her hair is slicked back close to her head (rather like a Flamenco dancer), revealing the full contours of her heavily made-up face and neck. Rather than being engulfed by layers of chiffon, she appears to be practically naked; wearing a close-fitting skirt, slit to the waist, revealing an expanse of leg and thigh, a skimpy top with almost no back which shows off her tanned body, and very high-heeled, open-toed shoes which give added length to the legs, and help shift the body weight forward over the front of the foot. The male Latin dancer look, designed to show off the streamlined body shape, is reminiscent of John Travolta in *Saturday Night Fever*, with slimline fitted trousers, open-necked shirt and raised heel shoes.

In their discussion of competitive ballroom dancing on television, Fiske and Hartley (1993) argue that the dress codes and bodily attitudes of the modern ballroom dancers express, on a cultural level, the competitive principle embedded in the hierarchical but relatively stable class structure of British society. Whilst the dancers' dress and demeanour are borrowed codes from a higher social stratum in a different era, nevertheless, they are used to 'assert their contemporaneity and ordinariness'(Fiske and Hartley, 1993, p. 41). Viewed in this light, the ability to move up the class system becomes a matter of performativity. This, in turn, according to Fiske and Hartley (*ibid.*), 'makes it possible to reconcile one of our culture's central paradoxes: the maintenance of a relatively stable class system with competitive ideology'. As we shall demonstrate later in this chapter, the 'English Style' is both a product of the class system and of the vernacular.

Historically, dress has been a symbolic battleground on which the old has been confronted by the new or on which the dominant hegemonic groups have sought to retain their position in the social hierarchy. The war between the aristocracy and the ascendant bourgeoisie was fought out symbolically on the dress and adornment front, as witnessed by the sixteenth-century sumptuary laws. Moreover, as Bourdieu (1993) has pointed out, in the contemporary arena of cultural capital there is a certain correspondence between the fields of 'haute couture and haute culture'. On a more everyday level, Willis *et al.* (1990) have demonstrated the important 'symbolic work' that is carried out by the ways in which young people routinely use clothes to 'express and explore' their own specific individual identities.

Thus, dress codes are not quite as trivial as they might at first appear. They perform an important symbolic function in relation to the embodied self and its relation to the outside world. We relate to them on several levels: the social, the psychological and the aesthetic (Wilson, 1985). The body's boundaries do not simply stop at the skin. Dress and adornment occupy an interesting position in relation to the body's boundaries. Clothes can be seen to mark the boundary of the body of the self and the social world. Our clothes stand at the interface between the physical body and the social body. All societies, to a greater or lesser extent, dress the body. And if we agree with Douglas (1973) that the body is a symbol of society and that dress and adornment occupy the space between the body and the outside world, then it is likely that they will also perform symbolic functions. Dress links the body to the social world, but it also separates the body from the outside world. Dress, as Wilson (1985) has argued, 'is always unspeakably meaningful'. In some respects clothes seem to have a life of their own, through the material, colour and styling, they speak of class, gender and culture. Clothes can reveal, cover over or transform the appearance of the body of the wearer. They can make individuals feel differently about themselves in different social situations and can affect the way they walk, talk and express themselves.

Nevertheless, in reality, as Fiske and Hartley (1993) point out, we do not believe that the complexity of the class structure is reducible to a matter of dress and bodily codes. If we return to the dancers in the competitions, we can see that there is a certain irony at work in their behaviour because they know, and also they know that we know, that they are giving off the illusion of belonging to another class while, in reality, being situated in another. The semiotics of the dress, the dancers' demeanour, and the dances themselves, declare 'that they are not what they appear to be pretending to be' (Fiske and Hartley, 1993, p. 42). The ballroom dancers' clothes are doubly coded to appear, on the one hand, as if they are something they are not, while on the other, the 'over the top' glitter and gaudiness of the attire denote that the 'classiness' is a pretence. At the same time, however, the ritual enactment of this pretence is only achievable at some financial cost, which seems to call into question Fiske and Hartley's (1993, p. 41) description of the spectacle of competitive ballroom dancing on television as a mythic enactment of the Cinderella fairy-tale. Currently, the price of a new ballroom dress begins at around £1800 (the price of a handmade designer collection garment) for quite a simple one and the best ones, we were informed, are made in Italy (ironically, the home of classic styling in the world of *haute couture*) and therefore have to be imported, which, in turn, gives these dresses an aura of a touch of class. The men's tail suits are also expensive; one competitor stated in an interview that his suit cost £2000. The women's shoes cost around £60 a pair. One mother we spoke with who surveyed her daughter's performance (for commitment as well as skill) in the practice sessions and the competitions, indicated that her daughter wears out a pair of shoes in about six to eight weeks. But the attire is only the beginning. In addition, and more routinely, there are the private lessons, at around £36 for three-quarters of an hour (these can be more or less expensive, depending on the reputation of the teacher), the practice sessions, the competition fees and the travelling expenses. The serious ballroom competitors we spoke with train five or six nights a week and go to competitions on a Sunday. Thus, the pursuit of ballroom at competition level involves some considerable financial investment on behalf of the competitors, or their parents if they happen to be juniors, that would put pressure on the purse strings of the middle classes, let alone Cinderella. In terms of lifestyle, however, the C1s or C2s, who appear to be the mainstays of competitive dancing, tend to have more disposable income in proportional terms than those immediately next to them (up or down) on the Registrar General's social class index.

The competition dances themselves are highly formalised versions of, for example, the waltz, the foxtrot, the quickstep and the tango, which often seem to bear little relation to the social dances that are taught in classes up and down the country. Some social dancers we spoke with considered that competition dancing, as portrayed in *Come Dancing* in particular, was partly responsible for the decline in popularity of ballroom dancing over the past twenty-five years or so, precisely because of the highly ritualised character of the dancing and the dress. But, in reality, the social dances have also been formalised in terms of tempi and steps, so there is a kind of double transformation at work in the competition version of the dances and it could be argued that the latter allows more scope for 'creativity'. A number of social dancers we talked with were keen to point out that competition dancing is not ordinary or 'real' dancing, and that with a little practice it is possible for novices to acquire enough skills to enable them to move confidently around the dance-floor for their own pleasure. Ironically, the skills of social dancers who frequent the tea dances, as we will discuss later, are sufficiently high enough in themselves to deter a mere beginner from taking to the floor during one of these sessions.

Just as social dancers are concerned to distinguish their activity from competition dancing, so a number of competition dancers are intent on getting away from the image of dancing as a pastime or hobby. They point to the idea of competitive dancing as a sport which can match other major sports in terms of the commitment, training and stamina that it necessitates. Ruth Gledhill (1996), for example, in her defence of ballroom dancing as a sport, points to yet another stereotype when she says that 'the image of the ballroom dancing remains one of a faintly humorous tearoom activity indulged in by those in their middle years'. Gledhill is a journalist who competes with her husband on the amateur circuit and has written on both the 'romance' and the 'rigour' of ballroom dancing in the national daily broadsheet she works for (see also Gledhill, 1995). Leaving aside the ageist comment in the above quotation because it will be addressed in the section on the tea dances, Gledhill's general tenor in the article echoes the concerns of several of the amateur competition dancers and the professionals (teachers) we spoke with at the Rivoli (see the BCBD rules on amateur and professional status). Although the British still have some of the best dancers in the world, such as the professional world champions, Karen and Marcus Hilton, and the best teachers, the lack of support and patronage for ballroom dancing in this country varies inversely with the growth of support and patronage in other countries like Holland, Germany and Japan. While the Hiltons are fêted and 'mobbed in the streets in Japan' (Margolis, 1993), they are unlikely to merit a more than passing glance in the streets of their home town of Rochdale, or the Streatham area in suburban south London, which happens to be the world mecca of ballroom, where they teach and have a second home. The following extract from our interview with Andrew, a top amateur championship dancer, which took place after one of the evening practice sessions, sums this up:

> Ballroom, Latin American dancing, competitively, is an amazing thing . . . . We've got these tremendously fit people who are tremendously artistic, who are world champions, and yet they have not an ounce of recognition. And they dedicate more of their time and life to it than anybody else . . . . You got rugby players who can't win a rugby match, you got footballers who can't win a football match . . . and you got tennis players who are horrendous . . . . And they get millions of pounds ploughed into their personal sports – for what! To see the *foreigners* [our emphasis] win it. Now we got world champions [in ballroom dancing] in this country and we get no recognition at all!

At the same time, on another level, the growth of interest in ballroom in other countries is welcomed by the amateur competition dancers and professionals we spoke with, because, one suspects, they genuinely love the pursuit and want to see it expand and be celebrated on a global plane. This attitude also finds a voice in the *Ballroom Dancing Times'* coverage of major competition events in other countries. Through our discussions with the dancers, it became clear that a great deal of their sense of themselves is tied up in their commitment to ballroom dancing. This is not so surprising when one considers the time, effort and money they put into what is viewed from the outside as a faintly ridiculous, but quaint, suburban hobby. At an individual level, the elevation in the status of ballroom, albeit in other countries, may be seen by them as a confirmation of their self-investment in this pursuit. However, the fact that the 'foreigners' not only value ballroom, but also throw more money in its direction, means that they can, and do, tempt some of the best British teachers away to train their dancers. The implications that follow from this for the training of 'home-grown' dancers, coupled with the low status of ballroom dancing in Britain, have led to growing fears that Britain is in imminent danger of losing its world dominance in the field that it invented and subsequently colonised under the guise of the 'English style'.

Although the competition dancers are only too well aware that, like theatre dancers, they are 'performing' when they dance in the competitions, they nevertheless have a version that their dance movement is 'natural' as opposed to artificial. It soon became clear to us that, for most of the people we talked with, 'proper' dancing *means* ballroom. Except for Andrew, who has begun to take ballet lessons, and a female competition dancer who had been a ballet teacher, theatre dance did not appear to feature in their minds as 'real' dancing, just as the social dancers did not think that competition dancing constitutes 'real' dancing'. To begin with, this narrow and rather divisive view of what counts as dancing was surprising to us. On reflection, however, there is a similar kind of closure and division at work in regard to the various genres of theatre dance, as well as to other kinds of dancing outside the theatre, which we were party to, at least implicitly, in the early stage of the research. What is interesting here, is that through the research process, the researchers can come to question their taken-for-granted assumptions, which in turn can lead to looking at the problem with new eyes. The harnessing of this process, in part, leads to what Glaser and Strauss (Glaser and Strauss, 1967) term 'the discovery of grounded theory'. That is, it is through the processes of, in this case, ethnographic research, that ideas and concepts may be generated,[3] as opposed to being superimposed on the research from the outset in a rigid fashion, by means of some over-arching *grand* theory. This does not mean that the ethnographer enters the field as a blank slate. Nor does it necessitate a view that ethnographic writing is an entirely separate enterprise from reading. Ethnographers, whether they are anthropologists or sociologists, bring their intellectual tradition with them to their writing, even when they stand against it, and thus the discipline 'writes itself through their work' (Hammersley and Atkinson, 1995). However, as Glaser and Strauss (1967) advise, researchers should use their written sources in a spirit of creativity as opposed to dogmatism, to assist in the generation of concepts. The basic premise of 'grounded theory' implies that the initial assumptions that researchers begin with may be found lacking, as a result of the engagement in the field, and thus may require thinking through in a new way.

The idea that ballroom dancing – and here we are focusing on the 'modern' dance section – is somehow 'natural' was perplexing, given the codification of the steps, posture, holds, dress codes and strict tempi involved. In our discussions with dancers, the distinction between the 'natural' movement that is the starting-point of ballroom was contrasted with the artificiality of ballet, which seemed to be the only form of theatre dance that people were familiar with. Andrew, for example, pointed out that ballroom dancing (in contrast to ballet) 'was derived from a social element' and that it is 'based on a normal walk . . . there's is nothing that's exaggerated', unlike the 'exaggerated turn-out' in ballet. Moreover, ballroom dancers, unlike ballet dancers, are constantly told to go through the floor: 'you go from the back of the heel, through the foot and out through the toe, so you can move the body along the foot and along the floor in a smooth way'. Andrew also considered that the body stance and the arm positions of ballet were more artificial than ballroom:

> Ballet dancing is a slightly different way of holding your arms . . . [and] a very *exaggerated* way of holding yourself . . . you have a very open back and you have a very open hip area. The thighs [and] . . . the feet are turned out because you are looking for the most stable position . . . . Because ballroom dancers are moving across the floor, they don't need that wide base . . . they're not in a static position.

But not only are ballroom dancers continuously shifting the weight, but as two people are meant to move together in perfect balance and poise (with the man leading and woman going backwards), they also have to be sensitive to their partner with whom they are in bodily contact from the hip to the diaphragm, if they are to achieve the appearance of 'free and flowing and effortless' movement in the upper body that is required for 'the first-class competition dancer' (Moore, 1986), while in reality, underneath, as Andrew indicated, the legs 'are galloping across the floor'.

The aesthetic of ballet, according Andrew and Jack, who had been a competition dancer in his youth, does not transfer easily on to the dance-floor. Jack's wife was a ballet teacher but, he said, 'she was hopeless at ballroom . . . it's a completely different discipline. Whereas ballroom dancing's a very *natural* movement, ballet is certainly not.'

The contrast between the lower body doing all the work and smooth upper body in contemporary ballroom dancing which Andrew's comments allude to, bears a certain resemblance to the canons of deportment in dancing in *A Treatise on the Theory and Practice of Dancing* by James P. Cassidy, which was published in Dublin in 1810 (before the acceptance of the waltz in British society):

> In order to dance well, the body should be firm and steady; it should be particularly motionless, and free from wavering, while the legs are in exertion, for while the body follows the action of the feet, it displays as many ungraceful motions as the legs execute steps, the harmony, the

exactness, firmness and perpendicularity, equilibrium in a word, of all those beauties and graces that are so essential to make dancing give pleasure and delight. (cited in Aldrich, 1991, p. 93)

The idea that ballroom dancing is based on 'natural movement', in fact, forms the core of the 'English Style'. As indicated above, this was first codified by the five dancers/teachers who formed the first Ballroom Committee of the Imperial Society in 1924. This, in effect, made formal the break between 'modern' dancing and what we now call 'old-time dancing' (rotary waltz, polka, quadrilles, lancers, and sequence dances), that had begun in earnest in 1910, with the influence of a dance called the Boston, and had continued with a spate of other new dances that emerged in response to the revolution in syncopated dance music, ragtime, that stemmed from across the other side of the Atlantic. The new forms of social dancing which emerged over the next several years, such as the tango, the one-step, maxixe, foxtrot and the Castle walk, were profoundly influenced by the great American dancers, Irene and Vernon Castle. The Boston was first introduced to Britain around 1903, but did not make an impact until around 1910 (Richardson, 1948, pp. 18–20), when it rapidly displaced the waltz, which had been the undisputed champion of the ballroom for many years. Although the Boston was danced to waltz music, it had little else in common with it apart from the music. The Boston was a smooth-flowing dance, with a right hip to right hip hold, so that the man's feet were outside the woman's. Unlike the waltz, which was essentially a turning dance, the Boston was primarily a linear dance, with intermittent turns. It was based on a natural walking style using the flat of the foot, with the weight being transferred on each step. This 'natural' walking step was in direct contrast to the 'artificial turned-out position of the feet', founded on the five positions in ballet, which had formed the basic posture for all dancing up to that point (Franks, 1963, p. 162).

Although the popularity of the Boston declined rapidly after 1914, nevertheless, according to Richardson (1948), its style of movement, and particularly its 'natural' walking style, was in large part responsible for the initial growth of the 'English Style'. The desire for new movement styles and new dances from around 1911 seemed to be fulfilled by the introduction of the Argentine tango into England via Paris. For several years prior to the First World War, London went 'tango mad', and 'tango teas' became all the rage in hotels and restaurants where the public could dance.

The 'democratisation' of ballroom dancing, which reached its zenith with the spread of the *palais de danse* in the 1920s, had begun in the middle of the nineteenth century with the establishment of the popular assembly rooms. Prior to the First World War, the popular assemblies had expanded to include 'shilling assemblies'. These were usually run under the auspices of a local dancing academy and took place on Saturday evenings at a local town hall in urban areas or the village hall in the rural areas. Although the gap between the kinds of dances that were danced by different classes in society, and between urban and rural areas, had all but disappeared by the first decade of the twentieth century, the class distinctions remained visible in relation to where they danced and also how they danced (Rust, 1969). In the popular assemblies, for example, the waltzes were played at a much slower tempi than in the places frequented by those higher up the social scale. An indication of the importance of the relation between class and style of dancing around that time may be seen in three pictures (see Plate 2) reproduced in Edward Scott's book *Dancing as an Art and a Pastime* which was published in 1892. However, what eventually came to comprise the equivalent of 'high-class' dancing in the modern style did not emerge from the traditional breeding ground of dance etiquette, the upper stratum of society. But, rather, as Rust (1969) points out, the measurement of skill and grace on the dance floor came to be measured in inverse proportion to social status. As Richardson (1948, p. 90) comments, the 'development of the "English Style" was in the hands of the frequenter of the Palais and the public dance halls, and not those in the smart West Enders'. Thus, it was forged through the rhythms of the vernacular. The vernacular, however, is idiosyncratic and, in some people's eyes, potentially unruly (somewhat like the masses) and in order to prevent it erupting into chaos, it needs to be homogenised (see Back, Chapter 10 in this volume). The state of ballroom just after the end of the First World War was viewed by some, who were most certainly not of the vernacular, in this light. The freedom in the dance steps and the divergent styles of dancing to be found in the ballroom were viewed as 'artistic bolshevism' (Richardson, 1948, pp. 42–3) and the concern arose to set out some basic rules of 'good form'. In 1920, the year after the opening of the Hammersmith Palais, Richardson, who was editor of *The Dancing Times*, and a key figure in the development of ballroom and English ballet (see Sayers, Chapter 8 in this volume), chaired the first of three conferences of teachers of ballroom to attempt to 'call a halt to freakish dancing before it became something worse' (Richardson, 1948). This was to be the beginning of the standardisation process that paved the way for the evolution of competition dancing and the 'English Style'. Viewed in this light, the proposition that the 'development of the "English Style" was in the hands of the frequenter of the Palais and the public dance halls' needs to be treated with some caution.

THE TEA DANCES

I've only got to set my toe in a dance hall and the adrenaline starts flowing. I can feel that music even before it starts. My big toe tells me as soon as I step through the door, that I want to get on that floor and dance. And I think here [at the Rivoli] more so. I just come down those stairs and I can't wait to get my shoes on.

Annie, 75 years – tea dancer

Gledhill's (1996) identification of ballroom dancing's problems as lying in its image as a 'faintly humorous tea-room activity indulged in by those in their middle years' may serve to betray her own stake in the competitive arena and thus blind her to the dominant stereotype. Although Donnie Burns MBE (numerous times World Professional Latin Champion) also recognises that 'ballroom dancing has a credibility problem' (see *The Times*, 17.10.93, p. 12) in Britain, he lays the blame more squarely on the shoulders of the stereotype advanced by *Come Dancing* along with 'the fake tans, the sequins' (*ibid.*). Burns suggests that the *real* dancing is there to be observed on practice nights, away from the glitter, the glamour and the artifice. However, the tea dances at the Rivoli suggest themselves as another, rather different alternative. Here there is an opportunity to watch competent, and often much more than competent, ballroom and Latin dancing in its least alienated form.

According to Rust (1969), the consolidation of the popularity of tea dancing in the 1920s was a result of the emergence of simplified dances with more straightforward steps, and there was a turn away from the exhibitionism which had previously prevailed. For Franks (1963), the important factor was the emergence of the *new* 'French' tango craze which was easier than the earlier version of 1911 and more suited to the smaller dance-floors of drawing-rooms and restaurants (Richardson, 1948), as was the syncopated, jazzy foxtrot. Today these claims are echoed in the explanations of the popularity of ceroc, the French dance form said to have emerged as a popular simplification of the jitterbug and the lindy hop (*Strictly Dancing*, Channel 4, 1996). However, it is the centrality of the dancing which seemed and continues to appear to characterise the tea-dance phenomenon. Although tea dances do take place in the evenings, they are held more often in the afternoon, dispelling a contemporary image of social dancing as a by-product, 'a little something for the ladies', in an otherwise male, alcohol-centred evening's entertainment.

The continuing popularity of tea dancing, although not on the scale of the post-war years, is attested to by their being advertised in many of

London's local papers. There is also *The Tea Dancer*, an insert magazine in *Dance Diary*, the south-east London dance magazine, which details events and classes across Greater London and further afield. As the dances are weekday afternoon events which are held in various venues such as church halls and community centres, there appears to be an assumption that the main interest group is retired people, although there is evidence of a growing interest in tea dancing amongst the gay community.

During our visits, the afternoon tea dances at the Rivoli, held on Tuesdays, Thursdays and Fridays (there are also social dance events on most evenings) were attended exclusively by the over-55s. When asked about her choice of the Rivoli as her preferred venue for dancing, Annie, who doesn't live locally, described it as being 'special'. She pointed to the quality of the dance-floor, 'the luxurious décor', the 'beautiful chandeliers' and the 'comfortable furniture' as contributing to its distinctiveness. Whilst it is tempting to suggest that the Rivoli attracts the more discerning amongst the tea-dancing fraternity, in reality there are more pragmatic issues at stake. Although the Rivoli is very reasonable in terms of its admission charges (£2.50 for an afternoon's dancing in comparison to the £7–£8 which can be charged in the centre of town, according to Annie) and it is located on the main road in Brockley opposite a train station, it is still not very accessible to those who rely on public transport. Annie suggests that the weather is an important factor in how busy the afternoon sessions are, and reports that fear of travelling in the dark keeps many away from the evening sessions in the winter.

The age range of the dancers may suggest initially that the tea dancers at the Rivoli are a particularly homogenous group about which many generalisations may be made. On closer analysis this proved not to be the case, although there were uniting aspects of these dancers as a group. The emphasis was certainly on the dancing rather than the tea, with most people pausing through single dances before returning to the floor with a renewed and surprising energy. Although there were obvious differences in the abilities of the dancers, the general level of skill was daunting and thus prohibiting to the complete novice, and despite reassurances that it was both acceptable and easy to join the dancers dancing the 'social waltz' (the simplest of dances), in the face of the quick-footed, whirling confidence before us we remained unconvinced and gracefully declined the invitation to participate.

With closer attention it became apparent that the difference between the dancers lay not only in their abilities but also in their dress, their preferences for particular dances, and their tendency to either remain with the same partner all afternoon or to dance with many different partners.

According to Annie, many of the dancers (both men and women) had learnt their dancing as a matter of course in their 'courting days', and certainly some of the women wore dresses that looked like they might be well-kept 1950s originals.

Annie began learning ballroom dancing, like many others, validating her accomplishments through 'taking medals' awarded by the different examining bodies of the dance teachers' organisations, who are all corporate members of the BCBD. These require the dancers to demonstrate their competence in a range of prescribed steps and sequences under examination from officials from the awarding body. Here there is a consonance between the teaching of ballroom and Latin dancing and ballet, tap and modern dancing, which refers back to the time when the different dance styles were united by the same over-arching council. Though the latter three may be more usually taught to children and young people, they share as their main objective the progression up a prefigured scale of externally assessed achievement. At the tea dances there may have been people who were 'practising' in order to progress in terms of this scale, but for the majority it seemed that the dancing was an end in itself. Within this majority there seemed to be a further differentiation between those who had a certain level of competence with which they were satisfied and others, like Annie who, although disenchanted by the medals system which she felt took away some of the enjoyment of dancing, remain keen to learn and improve their dancing continually. The tea dances offer the opportunity for such dancers to dance with many different partners, a skill in itself. For Annie a good partner is someone who shares her desire and enjoyment of learning and who wants to talk about dancing. She advises dancing with someone much better than yourself as the best way of learning.

Though untrained in the assessment of ballroom dancing, our knowledge of other dance forms led us to pick out, as the better dancers, those men who seemed to be gliding effortlessly across the floor, leading their partners in fluid, yet rapidly-changing sequences in which they both looked confident. These qualities Annie equates with a 'natural ability' for dancing which she contrasts with the unfortunate 'dancing by numbers' style of many otherwise accomplished male dancers. In the technical language of ballroom this is referred to as 'floor craft' – the ability to change sequences to fit the dancing space, thus avoiding collisions with other dancers whilst retaining the fluidity of the movement. Those who 'dance by numbers' lack this ability to anticipate and adjust – unwilling to depart from their prepared sequences of steps and directions, they stop when faced with obstacles and thus break the rhythm of the movement.

Annie is unequivocal in her differentiation between the roles of men and women as part of the dancing couple. Without any self-consciousness she places herself as part of a pre-feminist generation by stating that the woman is reliant on the man to lead her. It is clear, however, that it is *we* rather than she who are concerned about the relative importance of the man and woman who form the couple. Annie attends both tea dances and classes across south-east London. Having learnt the women's steps of particular sequences, she then turns her attention to the men's steps, so that she can teach them to partners at other classes. Occasionally, she can also be seen partnering other women at the tea dances, thus helping to make up for the shortfall of men. When asked about the qualities that make a good female ballroom dancer Annie was more direct and technical, after having pointed out the woman's role in avoiding collisions: 'what I do is, if I see that there's a dangerous situation coming up, I dig my partner in the back, which gives him a clue that he's got to be wary, you see'. She pointed to the importance of footwork and posture, detailing the correct use of both. However, she finished by indicating the importance of being 'dressed for dancing'. Although her overriding concern seemed typical of her generation of dancers, that of neat self-presentation, her suggestion that you could have too many sequins and feathers was tempered somewhat by her admission of being 'a bit of a glittery person myself', and so not adverse to 'quite a bit of fancy'.

The initial conclusions to be drawn from observing the afternoon tea dancing at the Rivoli would seem to confirm some of the stereotypical images which it conjures up in the uninitiated. These preconceived images derive their power from their being held by the dominant groups in society (Featherstone, 1995). Despite the misrepresentation with which they are imbued, they serve to confirm the older generation as outsiders, as they dare to experience their bodies in alternative ways to those prescribed by late capitalism's consumer culture. Here were a smartly-dressed group of people, in the later stages of life, observing, almost without exception, the etiquette of the ballroom, sipping tea and enjoying particularly the sequence dancing, the pre-set dances which afford the safety of everyone moving in the same direction and doing the same steps at the same time. However, anything more than a cursory glance reveals an energised, skilled, heterogeneous activity practised not by 'old people' but by *dancers*. As a counter-balance to the popularity of the sequence dancing, another favourite is the rumba. In the ISTD (The Imperial Society of Teachers of Dancing) handbook of *Ballroom Dancing*, the rumba is described as having

completely fascinating rhythms and bodily expressions which enable the woman dancer to express her grace and femininity and the men to show her off in this way while himself feeling the spell of the music and the sheer joy of being alive. (ISTD, 1992, p. 80)

For Annie, who finds the sequence dancing a bit predictable and boring, the rumba is appealing because you can 'put everything into it'. Indeed, the rumba brought forth a display of dancing which was both subtle yet sensuous, defying the arrogance of younger generations who would claim a monopoly in terms of physical sensuality.

If the scene does awaken a sense of nostalgia, making reference to the largely mythical 'good old days', it does so through the voices and memories of Annie and her co-participants who remember having to get to the Rivoli as the doors opened to secure a seat. Now, with the odd exceptions in the evenings, it seems that the phenomenon of tea dancing may be growing old with its dancers, which in part calls into question the assumption of resurgence with which we began. The younger generations seem to be interested in ballroom and Latin only in so far as they might provide a means of self-validation in terms of medals or in the competitive arena. This is not to dismiss the hours of practice and the high level of skill demanded by these contexts; however, they do differentiate themselves as practices from the social enjoyment of dancing as an end in itself. In terms of social dancing, the younger people seem attracted by the latest crazes of, for example, line dancing or ceroc. This is probably as it should be, since it is how social dancing has been developing during the past 150 years, through the 'polka craze', the different versions of the tango and the foxtrot to the more direct antecedents of today's crazes, the jitterbug, the jive and the Lindy hop. However, sitting in the Rivoli Ballroom it is tempting to hope that there is something perennial about this form of dancing, that the owner of the ballroom is right when he suggests it will be back in five years time, rescued from its marginality as an enjoyable, unalienated social pastime. This hope is further fostered by Annie's enthusiasm and experience in social dancing. 'I've done the Salsa, I've tried them all, but I still go back to the ballroom dancing.'

NOTES

1.   This research was funded by Goldsmiths' College. We would like to thank the owner of the Rivoli Ballroom for being our 'gatekeeper' (Hammersley and Atkinson, 1995) and facilitating our almost always smooth entry into the world of ballroom. We are also grateful to those people who gave up

their time to be interviewed, and those who spent time talking with us in classes, competitions and practice sessions.

2. The notion that ballroom dancing is a sport and not simply a hobby or a leisure activity is subject to much debate at the present time (see Gledhill, 1996). The International Dance Sport Federation has been provisionally recognised by the International Olympic Committee and there is a possibility that competitive dancing may appear in the Olympic Games in 2004.

3. Although we do not agree with Glaser and Strauss's desire to make ethnography scientific, nevertheless, we find some of their ideas extremely useful.

REFERENCES

E. Aldrich, *From the Ballroom to Hell: Grace and Folly in Nineteenth-Century Dance* (Evanston, IL: Northwestern University Press, 1991).

BCBD *Rule Book* (London: British Council of Ballroom Dancing Ltd).

P. Bourdieu, *Sociology in Question*, trans. and ed. Richard Nice (London: Sage, 1993).

J. Clifford, 'Introduction: Partial Truths' in J. Clifford and G. E. Marcus (eds), *Writing Culture: The Poetics and Politics of Ethnography* (Berkeley, CA: University of California Press, 1986), pp. 1–26.

J. Coulter, *Lewisham: History and Guide* (Stroud: Alan Sutton Publishing, 1994).

J. Cowan, *Dance and the Body Politic in Northern Greece* (Princeton, NJ: Princeton University Press, 1990).

M. Douglas, *Natural Symbols* (Harmondsworth: Penguin, 1973).

M. T. Drewal, *Yuuba Ritual: Performers, Play, Agency* (Bloomington, IN: Indiana University Press, 1992).

M. Featherstone, 'Introduction' in M. Featherstone and A. Wermick (eds), *Images of Aging: Cultural Representations of Later Life* (London: Routledge, 1995).

C. A. Fidler, 'All the Right Moves', *Vogue*, 160 (May 1994), pp. 172, 210.

J. Fiske and J. Hartley, 'Dance As Light Entertainment' in S. Jordan and D. Allen (eds), *Parallel Lines: Media Representations of Dance* (London: John Libbey, 1993), pp. 37–50.

A. H. Franks, *Social Dance: A Short History* (London: Routledge & Kegan Paul, 1963).

K. George, *Two Sixpennies Please: Lewisham's Early Cinemas* (London: Lewisham Local History Society, 1987).

G. L. Glaser and A. L. Strauss, *The Discovery of Grounded Theory: Strategies for Qualitative Research* (London: Weidenfeld & Nicolson, 1967).

R. Gledhill, 'Love At First Waltz', *The Times: Weekend*, 19.8.95, pp. 1, 3.

– 'Dancing around the Question of Sport', *The Times*, 23.5.96.

M. Hammersley, *What's Wrong with Ethnography?* (London: Routledge, 1992).

M. Hammersley and P. Atkinson, *Ethnography: Principles in Practice*, 2nd edn (London: Routledge, 1995).

'Hot Blooded in Hamilton; Scene; Scotland', *Sunday Times*, 17.10.93, p. 12.

ISTD, *Teach yourself Ballroom Dancing*, 2nd edn (London: Hodder & Stoughton, 1992).

A. Johnson, 'Rhythm and Hues Attract New Wave to Ballroom Dance Floor', *Guardian*, 14.8.93, p. 6.

J. Margolis, 'Waltz and All; Cover Story', *Sunday Times*, 25.4.93, p. 9.

R. Martin, 'Agency and History: The Demands of Dance Ethnography' in S. L. Foster (ed.), *Choreographing History* (Bloomington, IN: Indiana University Press, 1995), pp. 105–15.

A. Moore, *Ballroom Dancing*, 9th edn (London: A. & C. Black, 1986).

S. A. Ness, *Body Movement and Culture: Kinesthetic and Visual Symbolism in a Philippine Community* (Philadelphia, PA: University of Pennsylvania Press, 1992).

– 'Dancing in the Field: Some Notes from Memory' in S. L. Foster (ed.), *Corporealities* (London: Routledge, 1996a), pp. 129–54.

– 'Observing the Evidence Fail: Difference Arising from Objectifications in Cross-Cultural Studies of Dance' in G. Morris (ed.), *Moving Words: Rewriting Dance* (London: Routledge, 1996b), pp. 245–69.

C. J. Novack, *Sharing the Dance: Contact Improvisation and American Culture* (Madison, WI: University of Wisconsin Press, 1990).

– 'The Body's Endeavours As Cultural Practices' in S. L. Foster (ed.), *Choreographing History* (Bloomington, IN: Indiana University Press, 1995), pp. 177–84.

S. Peters, 'From Eroticism to Transcendence: Ballroom Dance and the Female Body' in L. Goldstein (ed.), *The Female Body: Figures, Styles, Speculations* (Ann Arbor, MI: University of Michigan Press, 1991), pp. 145–58.

P. J. S. Richardson, *A History of English Ballroom Dancing 1910–1945; The Story of the Development of the English Style* (London: Herbert Jenkins, 1948).

F. Rust, *Dance in Society* (London: Routledge & Kegan Paul, 1969).

R. Smith, 'Ballroom Dancing: A Way to Get Back "in Touch"', *Dance Magazine*, 69 (1995), pp. 54–7.

L. Stanley (ed.), *Feminist Practice* (London: Routledge, 1990).

H. Thomas, 'An-other Voice: Young Women Dancing and Talking' in H. Thomas (ed.), *Dance, Gender and Culture* (Macmillan: Basingstoke, 1993).

H. Thomas, 'Dancing the Difference', *Women's Studies International Forum*, 19, 5 (1996), pp. 505–11.

P. Willis, with S. Jones, J. Canaan and G. Hurd, *Common Culture* (Milton Keynes: Open University Press, 1990).

E. Wilson, *Adorned in Dreams: Fashion and Modernity* (London: Virago Press, 1985).

OTHER SOURCES

Strictly Dancing: Jive and Swing (A Wild and Fresh Production for Channel 4, 1996).

7 Cyborgs, Nomads and the Raving Feminine
Maria Pini

The aims of this chapter are broadly twofold. First, I want to examine certain aspects of contemporary rave culture, with particular reference to the subject positions opened up within this to women. To this end, I will be drawing upon personal accounts collected in a series of interviews conducted over the past two years with women involved in rave and post-rave clubbing in and around the London area. Second, I want to explore the resonances that these accounts have with certain poststructuralist feminist attempts at developing new narratives and configurations through which to think mind, body, technology, physicality, self, other and the relations between these classifications. The concern therefore is to consider the extent to which rave, as a lived social practice, resembles the kinds of theoretical formations being imagined by certain feminists in their strategic construction of particular Utopias and political fictions. Hence, the conclusion of this chapter considers the relationship between rave, which can be read as opening up modes of being which are not structured around traditional dualisms of mind/body, self/other, physicality/machine, and the kinds of configurations being mapped out by Donna Haraway in her chapter 'Cyborg Manifesto' (Haraway, 1991) and subsequent commentary on this piece (Penley and Ross, 1991), and Rosi Braidotti in *Nomadic Subjects* (1994).

One aspect of this analysis involves considering whether these new 'feminist figurations', to quote Braidotti (1994), allow dance to be freed up from the kind of rationalistic reasoning which, as Andrew Ward (1993) clearly argues, has traditionally guaranteed its neglect by academics. I am not however, solely concerned with shifts in academic thinking, and the ways in which these shifts enable us to speak differently about dance. I am equally interested in how rave has transformed the meanings of social dance. Hence, although I agree with Ward (Ward, 1993, p. 29) that 'recent developments in cultural analysis map out a conceptual and theoretical terrain that make more likely a rigorous appreciation of dance', I also believe that recent developments within social dance culture itself are equally significant in making this appreciation likely, and in bridging the gap between the popular and the academic imagination. This chapter, then, should be

111

read as an attempt at bringing into communication a particular contemporary popular practice such as rave with a particular body of contemporary philosophical enquiry. It is at the point of their intersection that I have personally been located for the past three years of researching femininity and social dance practices. For some length of time I found this location a tense and contradictory one, attempting as I was to 'read' dance through 'theory'. More recently however, my interest has shifted towards a consideration of how rave can be read *in parallel* to these heady philosophical debates, as itself constituting a popular cultural refiguring of the world: a refiguring which problematises the same dualisms and conceptual frameworks currently under attack from this body of feminist philosophy. Hence, the material and discursive assemblage which makes up rave can be seen to articulate a particular, historically specific version of subjectivity and its relation to the space around it. Rave, then, is seen as comprising a collection of thinking, articulating bodies in motion; bodies which, to adapt Susan Foster's (1996, p. xi) phrase, 'develop choreographies of signs through which they discourse'. Rather than seeing rave as 'meaningless' (Rietveld 1994), or falling into the trap of viewing the dancing body generally as a form of physical and hence pre-linguistic expression (Thomas 1986), this analysis starts from the premise that rave 'speaks'. It 'speaks' from a specific historical and cultural position. Bringing the raver into communication with the figures of the Cyborg and the Nomad then, highlights the extent to which a drive to reinterpret the world and to provide the space for alternative articulations of subjectivity do not belong exclusively within the realm of high philosophy, or much more generally, within the realm of verbal or written language. My project therefore involves a strategic obscuring of conventional distinctions between 'high philosophy' and popular culture. This move to affect an encounter between the raver, the Cyborg and the Nomad, however, is not an attempt to appropriate rave into the arms of high theory. That is, it is not a bid to suggest that the raver must be read through these philosophical works, or that the raver is simply, or *really*, an *example* of these figurations. Rather, one can, in the words of Braidotti, draw a 'flow of connections' between seemingly unconnected forms or signifying practices. In elaborating upon her notion of a nomadic shifting she writes:

> It is *as if* some experiences were reminiscent or evocative of others: this ability to flow from one set of experiences to another is a quality of interconnectedness that I value highly. Drawing a flow of connections need not be an act of appropriation. On the contrary; it marks transitions between communicating states or experiences. Deleuze's work on lines

of escape and becoming is of great inspiration here; nomadic becoming is neither reproduction nor just imitation, but rather emphatic proximity, intensive interconnectedness. Some states or experiences can merge simply because they share certain attributes. Nomadic shifts designate therefore a creative sort of becoming; a performative metaphor that allows for otherwise unlikely encounters and unsuspected sources of interaction of experience and of knowledge. (Braidotti, 1994, p. 5)

Finally, bringing together *actual* ravers with theoretical figurations like the Cyborg and the Nomad, whose statuses hover somewhere between reality and Utopia, clearly entails going beyond conventional divisions between fact and fiction; between lived practice and the theoretical formulation of fictional figurations. As I will indicate, the lived practice of rave cannot be separated from the 'texts' or 'fictions' which make up its meanings. The personal accounts drawn upon here are thought of as 'textualised' inasmuch as they are clearly threaded through with particular themes or fantasies. In this sense, the raver is as much about a confusion of accepted splits between corporeality and fiction as is the Cyborg or the Nomad. The women's accounts drawn upon here speak of the complexities of a present state and at the same time reveal a particular set of fantasies about a future; a future wherein the woman can move beyond the conventional confines of female physicality, or at least redefine these confines. Hence the female raver, like the Cyborg and the Nomad, can be seen to be involved in a wider staking-out of the physical and linguistic possibilities currently open to women.

DANCE AND THE LIMITS OF THE HUMANIST SUBJECT

I will return to the figures of the Cyborg, the Nomad and the raver shortly. I want to begin, however, by indicating some of the ways in which dance has come to signify within academic thought. Helen Thomas has pointed out that it has become almost standard to begin a piece on dance by pointing to the relative absence of work on the subject (Thomas, 1993). Indeed, the neglect of social dance by academics has been well documented by cultural analysts keen to establish it as a serious area of academic inquiry. Some have argued that this neglect simply reflects a wider, more general marginalisation and trivialisation of cultural practices associated with femininity (McRobbie, 1984). Others, like Richard Dyer (1990) and Susan McClary (1994), writing specifically on social dance, have pointed to the historical tensions between left-wing scholarship and popular pleasures

which are centred on the physical and the sensual, and which therefore fail
to conform to accepted notions of the 'political'. And, as Ward's (1993)
work shows, the rationalist and functionalist tendencies which can be seen
to characterise the sociological gaze serve to ensure social dance's neglect,
or its easy interpretation as a means to some other (more 'meaningful')
end. For Helen Thomas, this neglect is also partly related to the fact that
dance is often read as 'unlanguageable'; as a means of *bodily*, and hence
pre-linguistic expression (1986). All of these arguments indicate the limited ability of existing interpretative frameworks to accommodate social
dance. They signal a discontent with what traditional theoretical formations allow dance to mean. Thomas's (1993) ethnographic work also illustrates the difficulties which dancers *themselves* experience in languaging
their practice, and hence highlights the difficulties in 'speaking' dance
through available linguistic categories. Something about dance, then, can
be seen to resist easy incorporation into existing linguistic classifications
and for this reason it has often been seen as representing an 'other' language; one which, in Ward's terms, lies beyond the phallocentric limits of
rationalism (Ward, 1993).

Indeed, the concept of 'The Dance' has been appropriated by some feminist and other critical philosophers as a metaphor to signal alternative, non-
phallocentric representations of human subjectivity. Luce Irigaray (1989),
for example, poses dance as a female alternative to Freud's concept of the
'fort da' game, and as a means by which the little girl stakes out her own
subjective space in relation to the mother. The metaphor of the dance,
then, is used by Irigaray to indicate the ways in which the female child
discovers and appropriates her own subjective territory. Dance here serves
to get at a form of subjectivity which is not structured around a clear
distinction between attachment and separation. As opposed to the 'fort da'
game which involves the casting-away and recapturing of a ball of string,
and hence the symbolic playing-out of the development of subjectivity in
terms of a linear, backwards and forwards motion – which signifies an
attempt to control loss – dance is used to signal the formation of feminine
subjectivity in terms of a set of gestures based on gyrations and circularity.
The dance, in Irigaray's terms, puts the female child in touch with the
cosmic, maternal world whilst at the same time securing her separation
from the mother. This separation, unlike masculine separation, is not one
based on mastery, nor is it one which ever achieves full autonomy. The
girl is never fully separate from the mother. Instead, 'the girl has the
mother in some sense in her skin' (Irigaray, 1989, p. 133). Hence, dance
serves in Irigaray's work as a means by which to imagine a form of
subjectivity different from phallocentric representations. It enables her to

1. *Duets with Automobiles* (1994) a dance work for the screen choreographed by Shobana Jeyasingh and directed by Terry Braun. Photo by Terry Braun, reproduced by kind permission of Illuminations.

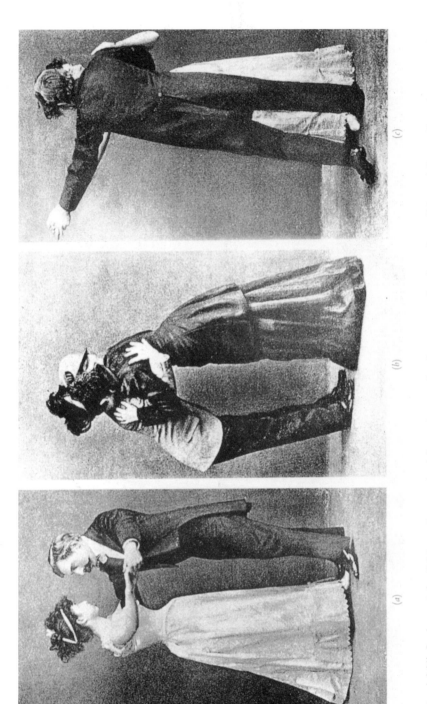

2. (a) High-class style, (b) low-class style, (c) no class style; three reproductions from Edward Scott, *Dancing as an Art and Pastime* (London, Bell & Sons, 1892)

3. The ballet class taking tea. Reproduced by courtesy of the Royal Academy of Dancing

4. (*above*) *Censored steps*; interracial dancing in Ipswich, England, c. 1942

5. (*right*) The Jitterbugging Marauder; Nazi propaganda, Holland, 1944

describe a set of relations not based on a clear split between subject and object, or between interiority and exteriority. Irigaray has been repeatedly criticised for the essentialism of her position. However, this work is perhaps most usefully considered, as it is by Braidotti (1994, p. 3), as a political fiction 'committed to the radical task of subverting conventional views and representations of human and especially female subjectivity'. Seen in this way, dance provides Irigaray with a means by which to formulate an alternative account of female subjectivity, one which aims at disturbing a phallocentric model constructed around a framework of dualisms.

Jacques Derrida (1991) also turns to the concept of dancing as a means by which to indicate a mode of non-phallogocentric being. In an interview with Christie V. McDonald, he responds to a question about the meaning of Emma Goldman's statement, 'if I can't dance, I don't want to be part of your revolution', and suggests that perhaps this 'maverick feminist' was:

> thinking of a complete other history: a history of paradoxical laws and nondialectical discontinuities, a history of absolutely heterogenous pockets, irreducible particularities, of unheard of and incalculable sexual differences; a history of women who have – centuries ago – 'gone further' by stepping back with their lone dance, or who are today inventing sexual idioms at a distance from the main forum of feminist activity with a kind of reserve that does not necessarily prevent them from subscribing to the movement and even, occasionally, from becoming militant for it. (Derrida, 1991, p. 442)

Unlike Irigaray (1989), Derrida (1991) is keen to avoid any notion of what he calls the 'eternal Feminine'. Instead, he uses the metaphor of dance as a means by which to get at a certain unfixing of a 'truth' of femininity, and claims that dancing 'is the displacement of women'. He therefore relates dancing to the destabilisation of sexual categories, including the category of 'woman' as an unproblematic basis for a revolutionary feminist politics. What he reads into the dance, are the possibilities for disrupting established 'spaces' and escaping 'those residences under surveillance'. Dancing therefore becomes a metaphor through which to imagine a certain disorganisation of subjectivity; a history not based upon continuities, dualisms and consensus. Derrida also utilises the term choreographies in the construction of his 'dream of the innumerable'. Unlike the term 'organisation', this enables him to suggest a set of interconnections and movements based upon dissymmetry and multiplicity, rather than upon order and homogeneity.

Both Irigaray and Derrida, in their different ways, turn to the concept of 'Dancing' in their attempts at constructing alternative representations of human subjectivity and inter-subjectivity; representations which highlight the limitations of humanist models. Their different works can therefore be situated as part of the growing philosophical move to produce alternative languages, or figurations. Included within these figurations are, as I have mentioned, Haraway's (1991) 'Cyborg' and Braidotti's (1994) 'Nomadic Subject'. Elizabeth Grosz's (1994) 'Mobius Strip' and Deleuze and Guattari's (1982) 'Bodies Without Organs' are also included here. All of these works constitute attempts at intervening in, and disrupting established linguistic categories and conceptual schema. For Irigaray (1989) and Derrida (1991), the dance provides one way of imagining a formation not organised around linearity, coherence and dualism. It provides a means of representing a mode of being wherein mind and body are not separable; wherein the body does not move towards a final, singular rationality and wherein the subject is no longer the individual, boundaried, Liberal Humanist 'self'.

'The Dance', as it is utilised as a concept by Irigaray and Derrida, is precisely that: a concept, an abstraction. Because their works function at the levels of language and imagination, 'Dance' is appropriated as an idea. This is problematic inasmuch as an idealised version of 'Dance' functions as an umbrella term for all that is not rational or phallogocentric. Whilst it is important to recognise that the experiential and corporeal states associated with dance often cannot be translated into functionalist or rationalist terms, it is equally important not to essentialise dance – as the above works clearly run the risk of doing. I therefore want to leave these philosophical abstractions and turn towards contemporary popular dance culture, and the embodied experiences of this. What is the relationship between the actual rave dancer and the philosophical conception of 'The Dance' as it appears in the works cited above? If 'The Dance' as a concept can serve to indicate non-phallocentric formations; formations which destabilise existing linguistic categories (in Derrida's terms), or which pose subjectivity in terms of circularity rather than linearity (in Irigaray's work), then to what extent can these formations be grounded in the lived experiences of contemporary social dance? To what extent does the rave dancer approximate 'The Dancer' as an alternative non-phallocentric representation of subjectivity? To what extent can s/he be seen to embody an alternative vision of the world? And to what extent can the personal narratives of the women quoted below be seen to signal a popular reframing of the world; a reframing which parallels the academic refiguring being developed within new feminist configurations?

Before embarking on this discussion, however, it is important to indicate the significance of centring this work around femininity, and show why and how I am using women's accounts in this analysis. Situated, as we are, in an intellectual climate within which the categories of male and female are subjected to increasing problematisation, the use of the term 'woman' to refer to a universal, fixed subject is no longer tenable. However, within this climate, there is equal concern to avoid either a slippage into a form of relativism as though this were the only alternative to universalism, or an abandonment of issues of sexual difference simply because these are shown to be intersected by a complex range of other factors. Hence feminist thinkers like Judith Butler (1993), Elizabeth Grosz (1994) Rosi Braidotti (1994) and Donna Haraway (1991) demonstrate a concern in their works to return to the sexual specificity of corporeality; to reintroduce the body into discussions on subjectivity. Rosi Braidotti, for example, argues that her work stems from:

> the political will to assert the specificity of the lived, female bodily experience; the refusal to disembody sexual difference into a new allegedly 'postmodern' and 'antiessentialist' subject, and the will to reconnect the whole debate on difference to the bodily existence and experience of women. (Braidotti, 1994, p. 160)

Following Braidotti and other contemporary 'corporeal feminists' (Grosz, 1994), I consider the category 'women' as a term which enables us to hang on to the sexual specificity of bodies whilst at the same time acknowledging that this sexual specificity is not enough to assume a sameness between all women. Hence, I would locate my work within the contemporary move to recognise the incompleteness of the category of 'woman', whilst at the same time refusing any resort back to the liberal humanist, sexually non-specific notion of the 'individual'. Where I speak of 'women', then, I do so with a recognition that subjectivity is grounded within the sexually-specific body, but that a multitude of differences exist between these sexually-specific embodiments.

My concern to look particularly at the situation of women within contemporary social dance cultures also arises from a desire to make sense of the many claims made by women for rave's liberatory potential. Elsewhere, I have illustrated how women involved in early British rave experienced this scene as sexually progressive inasmuch as it enabled an escape from the traditional associations between dancing, drugged-up woman and sexual invitation (Pini, 1997). Hence, the experiences of rave cannot not be detached from the sexually-specific body. I illustrated how even Utopian claims about rave's apparent ability to erode sexual differences (as well as other social differences) had to be grounded within the sexually-specific, because this perceived erosion obviously has particular implications for femininity. For example, a woman's perception that rave affords her an 'ungendered' sense of self clearly implies an escape from a body which is always already specifically coded, and such a claim would carry different implications and speak of different issues were it uttered by a man.

Drawing upon women's personal accounts, is not an attempt to 'uncover' the 'true' significance of rave. Rather, these accounts are seen as embodied, and hence located, representations of the wider material and discursive assemblage which makes up the multi-layered significance of Rave. Primarily, my concern is with how, within this wider assemblage, the female raver is produced – and is also a producer.

RAVING WOMEN

In an earlier work (Pini, 1997) I highlighted the obvious inability of academic feminism to make sense of the kind of Utopian claims made by women ravers regarding the apparent ability of rave to dissolve social divisions based upon sex, sexuality, age, race and class. Rave failed to conform to the kinds of 'political' movements favoured by left-wing academics, and for this reason was either ignored, or read as retrogressive in terms of its sexual politics (McRobbie, 1994). What is striking about early commentaries on rave is the clear failure of academic feminism to recognise what was (either explicitly or implicitly) feminist about these claims. All of the women quoted in this paper saw rave as a movement away from sexual pick-up, or at least away from what one interviewee, Ann, referred to as the 'cattle-market element' of previous forms of clubbing. Nearly all interviewees emphasised how important they felt it was that rave was primarily about dancing, and the fact that men seemed to dance, and enjoy dancing as much as women. Significant here was the fact that rave events seemed to provide few, if any, non-dance spaces where one could sit/ stand and simply watch others dance. In many of these accounts, associations were made between traditional dance-clubs and large groups of non-dancing men standing around bars, 'surveying the talent', as one of the women put it.

What seemed to be rave's main appeal to these women, however, was its ability to both offer them new ways of experiencing themselves, and to transform their understandings of inter-subjectivity. I therefore suggested that rave could be seen as the representation of a different kind of politics. This politics is not one concerned with 'changing the world', but rather with the constitution of a particular mind/body/spirit/technology assemblage which makes for alternative experiences of the self. Indeed, having since read Susan McClary's work, I find a renewed sense of commitment to my earlier reading. McClary suggests that:

> The musical power of the disenfranchised – whether youth, the underclass ethnic minorities, women or gay people – more often resides in their ability to articulate different ways of construing the body, ways that bring along in their wake the potential for different experiential worlds. (McClary, 1994, p. 34)

In drawing upon this suggestion, one can see a radical reframing of the body within rave and, as a consequence, the emergence of experiences which many claim are entirely new to them. Indeed, participants often refer to rave as constituting a different 'world'. Within this 'world' the 'self' is no longer an individual, boundaried one. Rather, subjectivity is restated in terms which do not reproduce traditional distinctions between mind and body, self and other, physicality and machine. One can also see that the 'ecstatic dancing body' produced within this configuration represents a form of sexuality which is difficult to define in terms of any clearcut desire. I now want to develop some of these issues and look more closely at the nature of this seemingly different experiential world.

The interviews drawn upon in what follows have been conducted over the past two years. In particular, I will be drawing specifically upon seven of the more in-depth of these (although others will be referenced). These seven are most useful to the present because they deal more directly with issues of sexuality and physicality (as opposed to those interviews within which participants spoke more about the 'formal' aspects of rave, such as the differences between musical styles and the historical developments of rave). All of these interviewees are between 25 and 30, which makes them relatively old for 'ravers'. However, this sample proved to be interesting in that these women – because of their age – seemed to have reflected more closely upon their experiences of raving. This is primarily because these older women feel they will soon have to 'give up' or 'let go' of 'raving', so that they don't become what one woman has described as 'saddies'. All interviewees are white, and although they were not asked to define their sexualities, all are referring primarily to their involvement within heterosexual rave scenes (as opposed to the growing number of specifically gay events). Six of these women classified themselves as either working class or 'educated working class'. These interviews attempt to draw out what many women described as the 'loss' of their individual sense of self, and examine the kind of 'self' that was reconstituted in place of this. Three particular aspects of the rave experience were concentrated upon and these have been broken down as follows: (1) the seeming 'loss' of the individual self to a wider 'body', (2) perceptions of technology and (3) the place of sexuality within this wider 'body'.

The apparent 'loss' of self mentioned above has been commented upon by Tim Jordan, who claims that: 'In these vast celebrations, usually called raves, participants gradually lose subjective belief in their self and merge into a collective body, whose nature is best captured by Deleuze and Guattari's concept of the Body without Organs' (1995, p. 125).

A very typical illustration of this theme is given in Amy's account, where she states: 'Yes, it's really like you have spread out of your own individual boundaries and lose your limits. You feel like you really are bigger, or part of something bigger.' Amy's statement clearly echoes one made by Jane, who says: 'Although you're aware of yourself, you're in something bigger than yourself. And so you can just spread out and – especially when you're on "E" – your boundaries are just so stretched out, it isn't you any more. It's a whole thing.'

This idea of losing oneself is also accompanied in these accounts by a notion of involvement within an interconnected totality, and hence participants speak of being part of something bigger, or as Jane puts it, 'the whole thing'. Kate gives a very clear illustration of this: 'It's like being part of one big, coordinated animal that just moves, and you're part of it. And it doesn't really matter if you personally stop dancing because even if you just stand there, it carries on and you still feel like you are part of it.'

A notion of a general interconnectedness, then, is central to all of these women's accounts. The individual body is seen as just one component within a wider, interconnected circuit. Subjectivity is therefore restated in terms which do not reproduce traditional divisions between self and other and which arguably challenge liberal humanist notions of the bounded, unique individual as the centre of awareness (Geertz, 1979, p. 229). Hence, although it is possible to speak of 'subjectivity' within rave, the *individual* subject is de-centred, and consciousness is given over to the 'wider' body constructed in the process. The 'self' of rave also indicates a departure from liberal humanist models inasmuch as there is a strong drive within this to move beyond rationality, and even, as Elaine puts it, beyond sanity. She says: 'Rave is about going to the edge, which represents the edge between sanity and insanity. It's about "losing it".' Amy says: 'It's best for me when I feel like I can go completely mad usually when I dance until I feel like I've expressed every single anxiety or pressure and it all comes out. It's like a safe space for going mad.'

The sense of connectedness mentioned above does not simply apply to the loss of the individual self to a wider, communal body, but also applies to understandings of mind/body relations. Later on in our interview, Kate states that:

No, it's not just a body thing. It's not that your mind isn't there or that you're brain-dead. Absolutely not, because I always feel hyper-aware. Even a trance-like state isn't the same as being totally brain-dead because you can get so stimulated by things you see. And you can also get very emotional. So, it's not like you're like a stone-cold zombie. You *feel*, so it's very emotional. You don't actively 'think'. Like it's not like you have to force yourself to concentrate. You kind of relax into this feeling of wholeness.

This stress on 'wholeness' clearly echoes certain 'New Age' ideas about mind and body 'balance'. Indeed several of the interviewees described their experiences as 'spiritual'. Related to, and furthering this sense of connectedness between mind, body and spirit, between individual and crowd, is a theme of a wider 'synchronicity' of individual components within what comes to look increasingly like a complex, mechanic network. Music, for instance, is seen as working 'through' the body; as connecting the inner with the outer. Miriam says: 'You're not separate from the music. The music *is* you. You are part of the music and there's no relationship even, 'cause you're one.'

This theme of synchronicity is clearly illustrated by Chris, who describes her first experience of a rave as follows:

I could really feel the thumping of the music going right through me, and everything seemed to be in real harmony. Like the beat of the music and the strobes and the visuals. The crowd also looked really in tune with it all. I was amazed at how everyone seemed to dance at the exact same pace. Like, everything was going as one. It all moved together.

In these accounts, therefore, no easy split is made between physicality and technology. Significantly, Chris uses the terms 'every*thing*' and '*it*' to refer not only to technical elements but also to the dancers, which are dehumanised, and given the same status as machinery. I will return to this aspect shortly, when the relations between technology and physicality are discussed in more depth.

Clearly, the use of the drug Ecstasy or 'E' is an important feature of the rave assemblage, and plays a central role in the production of the state described by the women quoted above. Helen says of her experiences of Ecstasy: 'I feel very happy and sometimes this feels very strong. I feel very affectionate, as though I'm in the bosom of my family and I feel very friendly and like smiling at everyone. It makes me feel confident and sexy and relaxed.'

Miriam describes her 'E' experiences as follows:

Well, when you're 'coming up', you know it 'cause your heart feels like it's exploding. And your heart feels like, like you're in love almost. No, it's much more intense than that. You *feel* love. Like you *are* love. Do you know what I mean? It's not a question of *feeling* love, it's just there all the time. It's everywhere, like you're surrounded by love . . . . It feels like I'm in another state of being, but that everyone else is there too. You see everyone as part of you and you are just thinking of harmony. Yes, harmony.

Although, as these statements indicate, 'E'-use plays a central role in the experiences of the rave event as another 'world', this cannot be seen as 'causing' this experience. Many women stressed that they often 'raved' without using the drug. The significance of Ecstasy, then, is best understood by recognising its inseparability from the wider mind/body/spirit/technology assemblage mentioned above. 'E' can be seen as an important chemical component of this assemblage, as a component which, along with other material and discursive aspects such as music, visuals, the organisation of time, space and bodies, produces particular embodied experiences. These embodiments, therefore, have to be understood as part of a wider machinery which produces them as such.

Descriptions of inter-bodily relations within these women's accounts also indicate the emergence within rave of modes of sexuality or eroticism which are 'blurred' or difficult to define. Many women clearly experienced difficulty in pinning down the nature of their feelings, in response to my question 'would you describe the "ecstatic state" as sexual?' Often responses were couched in confused or contradictory statements such as 'yes it is, but no it isn't'. Miriam describes her experiences as 'orgasmic, but not sexual' and three of the interviewees use the term 'auto-erotic'. What is also clear from these accounts is a strong pleasure which participants experience in looking, and seeing other participants in a state of 'ecstasy'. Often this 'look' seems to be sexual, and one woman describes 'getting off' on watching her female friends dancing. Another, Jill, says: 'I think my feelings – if they're sexual – apply to everyone, women and men alike. I do like looking at other women dance, and sometimes this gets very strong, almost like an attraction.'

Kate tells me: 'I never really focus on men when I'm dancing. In fact, I like looking at women much more. My mates seem to say that too. We often come out and someone says "did you see that woman? She was really gorgeous."'

One could argue then, that within the 'ecstatic moment', and along with the blurring of individual boundaries, sexual boundaries are also blurred. The kind of attractions mentioned by these women, however, seldom 'go anywhere' and both Kate and Jill make this point. Kate stresses that 'it doesn't *have* to go anywhere'.

Kate's statement could be seen to reinforce claims being made that rave (or that rave dance-floor activity) constitutes a form of 'post-sex' (*Passengers*, Channel 4, 16.9.95). What these women's accounts clearly point to, however, is the difficulty experienced in giving shape to these experiences in language. This is obviously related to the difficulty experienced by dancers more broadly, in describing their feelings (Thomas, 1993). Similarly, it can be argued that an appreciation of dance generally requires what Ward (1993, p. 29) calls 'the recognition of erotic possibilities beyond phallocentric limits'. I am therefore not denying that something within dance *generally* presents a resistance to easy interpretation. Many of the aspects highlighted here can be seen as important features of *all* social dance. What I am suggesting is that rave accentuates this 'something', making the 'ecstatic' dance-moment its central *raison d'être*. Hence the production of this ambiguous and arguably chaotic moment becomes its major drive. No previous social dance culture has placed so much emphasis on dance in itself. Similarly, no previous social dance culture has witnessed such enormous and intense involvement by such a diverse range of people. Russell Newcombe claims that: 'It would be no exaggeration to say that raving is now one of the main reasons for living for a huge group of socially diverse people aged between 15 to 35 years' (Newcombe, 1991, p. 1).

As mentioned earlier, there are clear crossovers between rave and the 'New Age'. This link becomes apparent in many interview accounts which stress notions of 'wholeness', 'harmony' and 'spirituality'. However, it is important to highlight a basic contradiction which runs through these personal accounts and which clearly undermines this 'harmonious', love filled 'world'. This contradiction revolves around the tensions between paying large amounts of money for 'pills' (which are very possibly 'duds', especially if bought from a stranger) and entry into events, and the 'world of love' which is sought after. In my earlier work I referred to a 'text of positivity' which, I argued, worked largely to conceal the negative aspects of rave (Pini, 1996). However, in the light of subsequent research, and developments within rave itself, it appears that there is now a greater cynicism threaded throughout personal experiences of rave. This is primarily because people have become more used to rave, and witnessed its commercialisation and incorporation into the mainstream. As a consequence, there is a noticeable detachment from an investment in the promise that rave might lead to profound changes within the world at large, an investment which was clearly evident at the beginnings of the movement. Therefore, although many of these women speak of the creation of an alternative world, there is a clear recognition of the temporary and contradictory nature of this world. Catherine's statement demonstrates these tensions

and illustrates the way that participants can live within these contradictions, and still give in to a temporary, and 'total', as she puts it, absorption
within events:

> It *is* all very expensive and I can't tell you how often I've been ripped
> off with buying pills which turn out to be nothing, or aspirin or some-
> thing. And I also have a problem with the way that many of these things
> are guarded by big, aggressive-looking men who basically treat you like
> shit even though you're paying money to get in. It's the same in clubs
> too. Everyone's paying a fortune for drinks, and you see how much
> some of the kids must have payed for their clothes, and it's all a bit sad
> that it costs so much to be amidst it all – to be in that kind of 'loving'
> state. But, it doesn't ruin things for me. I mean, it's just a passing
> thought, and if it's good, I still get totally into it.

Although Catherine's account offers a particularly clear demonstration
of the contradictions involved in the rave experience, her account is not
uncommon. Thus, there is a clear recognition in these personal accounts
of the partiality of the 'harmonious' world created within the rave event.
In short, many of these women's accounts indicate how rave exists, within
their wider day-to-day lives, as something which they move in and out of,
recognising the context-specificity of the experiences it produces.

CYBORGS, NOMADS AND RAVERS

To return to my title, I have attempted to illustrate some of the themes
which emerged out of women's personal accounts of rave, with the aim of
laying the ground for a consideration of the interconnections between
Haraway's 'Cyborg', Braidotti's 'Nomad' and the Raving Feminine. To
draw together the above, it is possible to see how within rave, subjectivity is restated in relational and ecological terms of an 'ecstatic', dancing
body; terms which undermine traditional dualisms between mind and body,
between interiority and exteriority, and between physicality and machine.
The 'ecstatic moment' can thus be seen as a release from monadic interiority
– an outburst which represents less the escape of mind from body than the
absorption of the individual into a wider body.

This wider 'body', however, is no longer simply the physical human
body, or a combination of these. Rather, this 'body' includes technology
(in the forms of music, lighting and drugs) and, therefore, is perhaps best
understood in terms of a mind/body/technology assemblage. I have, in this

chapter, concentrated mainly on one aspect of this assemblage – the embodied experiences of this. However, in highlighting the centrality of technology within this 'body' I have also attempted to show how technology
is an important 'actor' within this constitution. Hence, although I have
been working with personal accounts, these are located as part of a wider
machinery. It is then, possible to see within the constitution of the rave,
an erosion of the limits between the corporeal and the technological, and
in this sense it comes close to illustrating Haraway's claim that 'not all
actors have language' (Penley and Ross, 1991, p. 3). What Haraway is
attempting to imagine are possibilities for human/technology relations which
do not reproduce the active/passive split of the world which prioritises
language-bearing agents over other non-human actors. What we can see
within the particular mind/body/technology assemblage produced within
rave is a positive female engagement with technology – an engagement
which recognises the fluidity of borders between the human and the non-
human, and which signals a move away from perceptions of 'technology'
as 'out there somewhere'. Within the personal accounts discussed here,
one aspect of this engagement manifests itself as an experience of having
somehow been released from the rigid limitations of their sexually-marked
selves, through having become 'something bigger'. In comparing rave
with other forms of clubbing, many interviewees claimed that within the
rave they do not feel restricted to their bodies; bodies which, when 'drugged-
up' and dancing, have conventionally been marked as sexual invitation.
This in turn opens up the possibilities for these arguably 'Cyborgian' women
to be what Haraway calls 'bad girls' (Penley and Ross, 1991, p. 19). They
can safely share in the kinds of night-time and often illegal adventures
traditionally the preserve of men, and engage themselves in an ecstatic
unfixing of identity boundaries in the process. Taken in this light, the raver
can be seen as an embodied representation of the kind of non-phallocentric
subjectivity which Derrida sees within the concept of the 'Dance'.

Barbara Bradby (1993) makes a similar point, but with reference specifically to the particular relations between female voices, techno-music and
sexuality. She sees, within the particular female body/technology assemblage which emerges from the use of women's vocals within dance music,
'resultant Cyborgs' which 'transgress the boundaries of Enlightenment
equation of women with nature' and which therefore challenge stereotypes
about women (Bradby, 1993, p. 157). Although Bradby's focus is primarily
upon musical production, the 'Cyborgs' she finds here are equally evident
at the level of musical consumption on the dance-floor where bodies are
seen as being 'taken over' or 'controlled' by technology. An illustration of
this comes from Catherine, who says:

You just *can't* stop sometimes. It's like you're being pushed to dance. I guess it's the drug as much as anything but it's the lights and the crowd too. That first time was really strange for me. Everyone around me looked like they were chopped-up by the strobes. I mean, I could see heads here, arms there, all flashing up at different moments and it was actually a bit freaky. Then, when I got into it, it was amazing . . . . You feel like you are a robot.

Rosi Braidotti (1994, p. 3) claims that with the 'Cyborg', Haraway is proposing 'a high-tech imaginary, where electronic circuits evoke new patterns of interconnectedness and affinity'. As I have suggested, this imaginary offers one very clear way of understanding the relations of the different components which make up rave, including inter-subjective relations. A centrally significant theme which emerged from the interview material was a sense of interconnectedness with others which was temporary and not based upon clear identity classifications. Many interviewees stressed the importance of rave being primarily a non-verbal space. What we can see within this space are the emergence of affinities not based around language, but around ecstatic bodily relations. This also becomes clear if, for example, rave is compared with more explicitly 'political' youth movements, based around the development of 'statements' and hence around the consolidation of an 'identity'. If rave has attempted to 'politicise' itself, this has been in defence of its right to hold on to its space, a space within which, arguably, what is produced is a sense of chaos and ambiguity. Within this space, attention is not directed towards an individual performer, speaker or band. Instead, within the dark, loud and crowded space of events participants themselves become both audience and performer simultaneously, and give themselves over to an engagement with usually anonymous others. Ann tells me:

At parties for instance, you have to talk to people, and nowadays I find that tiresome. Also, sometimes you can't join in conversations because maybe you know nothing about what they're discussing. In a rave, you can get on with people without knowing them. You can actually get closer.

Similarly, Miriam says of raving: 'You didn't have to say anything – it was that simple.'

Hence rave can be seen as providing a space for alternative kinds of connections to be made, connections based upon a certain unfixing of identity categories. To an extent, it can be read as being organised around a kind of 'non-identity'. However, it still offers a sense of belonging within a whole. What we see within rave, then, is an unlikely combination between holism and partiality, and as I illustrated above, women can temporarily engage within a kind of New-Age notion of a 'whole', whilst recognising the context-specificity of this and the contradictions inherent within it. This clearly resonates with Rosi Braidotti's image of the Nomadic Subject:

> Being a nomad, living in transition, does not mean that one cannot or is unwilling to create those necessarily stable and reassuring bases for identity that allow one to function in a community. Rather, nomadic consciousness consists in not taking any kind of identity as permanent. The nomad is only passing through: s/he makes the necessary connections that can help her/him to survive, but she never takes on fully the limits of one national, fixed identity. (Braidotti, 1994, p. 33)

Braidotti's statement clearly echoes that process whereby the raver moves into the space of an event, makes connections with other bodies (which, as Ann says, enables a closeness with others which is stronger than one based upon speech) and leaves, never likely to meet any of these bodies again. Braidotti's work finds a particularly clear illustration within big, outdoor rave events, held in unfamiliar surroundings which have often taken hours to get to.

Although I indicated earlier that the 'politics' of rave could not be seen as an attempt to 'change the world', this is not the same as saying that it is apolitical. A very clear politics exists within rave. This politics involves the construction of new forms of connectedness between differences. However, it is difficult to see how this base might become anything more like a recognisably political 'movement', given that what seems to be heavily resisted within rave, are homogenising claims over its identity. Perhaps for this reason we need to move away from the traditional expectations we have of youth cultures. These expectations revolve around a reliance on 'youth' (itself a very selective category) to ignite some kind of wider revolutionary spark. Perhaps rave's 'politics' are best understood by looking to how, within events, we can find new articulations of the world. In this sense, rave can be located as a popular, and embodied parallel to the heady philosophical debates of certain poststructuralist feminists trying to construct alternative political fictions. If the new articulations which emerge within rave are to lead to anything 'bigger'; if its loosening-up of identity, and its provision of new modes of femininity are to be carried any further afield, then only time will tell. Indeed, as Haraway (Penley and Ross, 1991, p. 20) says of the role of these new feminist political fictions, and what they can lead to, 'it's undone work'. This is not to invoke an evolutionary paradigm. Rather, it is to suggest that only in time will we know whether the articulations of subjectivity which are being developed within both contemporary feminist philosophy and contemporary social dance practices will impact upon a wider, more general consideration of sexed subjectivity.

This chapter has sought to bring rave, as a lived social practice, into communication with the figures of the Cyborg and the Nomadic Subject. Indeed, Haraway suggests that we need, within these new attempts at refiguring the world, 'ecstatic speakers' (Penley and Ross, 1991, p. 86). It can be argued that the female raver, with her drive towards the maximisation of pleasure, her ability to move beyond the limitations of a conventionally-coded femininity, her merging with machine, and her ecstatic moments of 'madness', provides an interesting angle to these debates.

To close, it is important to point out that the reading of the new 'feminist figurations' presented in this chapter may not be wholly 'faithful' to the authors' works. But, as both Haraway (1991) and Braidotti (1994) seek to challenge notions of authenticity and originality, and offer their fictions up for strategic interpretation, their creative use in the present hardly seems problematic. The concern has been to bridge a gap between new feminist figurations which stand ambiguously between fictional Utopias and descriptions of a postmodern world, and the lived, social practice of rave. As suggested earlier, the lived practice of rave cannot be neatly separated from these fictional Utopias, as one thing which is obviously threaded through these women's accounts is an equally Utopian dream of moving beyond the confines of conventional femininity. As Haraway indicates, her own image of the Cyborg is something which both seeks to invent new languages, and at the same time describe a present social condition. As Constance Penley writes: 'Most Utopian schemes hover somewhere in between the present and the future, attempting to figure the future as the present and the present as the future' (Penley and Ross, 1991, p. 8).

REFERENCES

B. Bradby, 'Sampling Sexuality: Gender, Technology and the Body in Dance Music in Popular Music', *Popular Music*, 12, 2 (May 1993), pp. 5–176.

R. Braidotti, *Nomadic Subjects: Embodiment and Sexual Difference in Contemporary Feminist Theory* (New York: Columbia University Press, 1994).

J. Butler, *Bodies that Matter: On the Discursive Limits of Sex* (London: Routledge, 1993).

G. Deleuze and F. Guattari, *A Thousand Plateaus: Capitalism and Schizophrenia* (London: Athlone Press, 1982).

J. Derrida, from '"Choreographies"' in P. Kamuf (ed.), *A Derrida Reader: Between the Blinds* (New York: Harvester Wheatsheaf, 1991).

R. Dyer, 'In Defence of Disco' in S. Frith and A. Goodwin (eds), *On Record* (London: Methuen, 1990).

S. Foster (ed.), *Corporeal Realities* (London: Routledge, 1996).

C. Geertz, 'From the Native's Point of View: On the Nature of Anthropological Understanding' in P. Rabinow and W. M. Sullivan (eds), *Interpretive Social Science* (Berkeley, CA: University of California Press, 1979).

E. Grosz, *Volatile Bodies: Towards a Corporeal Feminism* (Bloomington and Indianapolis, IN: Indiana University Press, 1994).

D. J. Haraway, *Simians, Cyborgs and Women: The Reinvention of Nature* (London: Free Association Books, 1991).

L. Irigaray, *The Gesture in Psychoanalysis* in T. Brennan (ed.), *Between Feminism and Psychoanalysis* (London and New York: Routledge, 1989).

T. Jordan, 'Collective Bodies: Raving and the Politics of Gilles Deleuze and Felix Guattari', *Body and Society*, 1, 1 (March 1995).

S. McClary, 'Same as it Ever Was: Youth Culture and Music' in A. Ross and T. Rose, *Microphone Fiends: Youth Music and Youth Culture* (New York and London: Routledge, 1994).

A. McRobbie, 'Dance and Social Fantasy' in A. McRobbie and M. Nava (eds), *Gender and Generation* (Basingstoke: Macmillan, 1984).

A. McRobbie, *Postmodernism and Popular Culture* (London: Routledge, 1994).

R. Newcombe, *Raving and Dance Drugs* (Liverpool: Rave Research Bureau, July 1991).

C. Penley and A. Ross, 'Cyborgs at Large: Interview with Donna Haraway' in C. Penley and A. Ross (eds), *Technoculture* (Minneapolis, MN and Oxford: University of Minnesota Press, 1991).

M. Pini, 'Women and the Early British Rave Scene' in A. McRobbie (ed.), *Back to Reality: New Readings in Cultural Studies* (Manchester: Manchester University Press, 1997).

H. Rietveld, 'Living the Dream' in S. Redhead (ed.), *Rave Off* (Manchester: Manchester University Press, 1994).

H. Thomas, 'Movement, Modernism and Contemporary Culture: Issues for a Critical Sociology of Dance' (unpublished Ph.D. thesis: London University, 1986).

H. Thomas, 'An-Other Voice: Young Women Dancing and Talking' in H. Thomas (ed.), *Dance, Gender and Culture* (Basingstoke: Macmillan, 1993).

A. Ward, 'Dancing in the Dark: Rationalism and the Neglect of Social Dance' in H. Thomas (ed.), *Dance, Gender and Culture* (Basingstoke: Macmillan, 1993).

OTHER SOURCES

Passengers (Channel 4, 16.9.95).

8 Madame Smudge, Some Fossils, and Other Missing Links: Unearthing the Ballet Class

Lesley-Anne Sayers

> I wonder how many balletomanes realise the extent of the profession at all, or even the fact that there is this flourishing industry, something almost apart from the art they love?
>
> (Haskell, 1934, p. 194)

With its French terminology, peculiar rituals, traditions and paraphernalia, the ballet class has become a feature of both provincial town and city life. Surrounding the practice itself is a plethora of manuals, guidebooks, syllabi, educational videos and school prospectuses. There are specialist magazines, regulating bodies, shoe and clothing shops. The ballet class appears in fiction, photography and educational debate; there are medically- and anatomically-based considerations, even feminist evaluations. The subject of the ballet class currently has 30,000 entries on the World Wide Web, to say nothing of the art itself, which has been associated with diverse subjects ranging from fairies to physics. An 'industry' certainly, and one that can be looked at in many different ways. But something 'almost apart from the art'?

My particular interest in the ballet class lies with its history in Britain, and above all with finding its social history and cultural significance. The history of the ballet class in twentieth-century Britain is inseparable in many respects from the history of the two major providers of ballet classes, the Imperial Society of Teachers of Dancing (ISTD) and the Royal Academy of Dancing (RAD). As such the development of the ballet class in Britain, and its rapid export to the Commonwealth, former colonies, other outposts of Empire and beyond, has not gone unchronicled. But in comparison with the history of ballet as an art form, the social history and significance of the amateur ballet class, its role in provincial town and city life, its relationship to class and to culture, its images and ideals, its place in the British imagination, are all relatively unexplored territory. This brief chapter offers a collage of selected material relating to various aspects of the ballet class in fact, fiction, and personal memory. It searches for the role of the ballet class in amateur British practice, for its qualities, aspirations, and dominant imagery.

'HAPPY PRINCESSES, PLEASE'

The practice of classical ballet extends back to the court of Louis XIV where it developed as part of the glorification of monarchy. If we could deconstruct the steps themselves, we would no doubt unravel centuries of socially as well as artistically significant pillaging and transformation. In addition to courtly and peasant folk-dance origins and evidence of their place in the hierarchy of forms, and the stylized mannerisms of seventeenth-century social etiquette, we would undoubtedly find also an evolving aesthetic of ideal male and female bodies and their qualities and roles in social and aesthetic space. In the steps and rituals we might expect to find encoded memory, evidence of mutations, mergers, influences absorbed and transformed, changing ideals; an evolution of form. But how many children lining up at their weekly ballet class know the significance of a *ronde de jambe* beyond what it is as a step and perhaps what it can do for your legwork? Rather than a perception of ballet as an evolving art form, the idea that it represents certain 'absolutes' is perhaps more dominant. For example, ballet has long held a reputation as the finest training for virtuoso theatre dancing. It has been celebrated throughout its literature in Britain as at least the Western dance form that carries the highest aesthetic value, i.e. its capacity for 'beauty', for formal sublimity, and the grand style. Above all these 'absolutes' perhaps, shines the sense of ballet as a refined, profound and established tradition.

> Thus, the ballet, which has been quite unaffected by social eruptions – political, religious, or technological – and has survived the French Revolution of 1789, European revolts of 1848, and the Russian Revolutions of 1905 and 1917 as a court style, is, in essence, untouched. (Kirstein, 1971, p. 17)

Ballet teachers, struggling to keep abreast of changes in the growing syllabi and changes to regulation practice dress, might be less impressed by ballet's consistencies. So too might anyone paying attention to the impassioned, even furious, debates between supporters of the Cecchetti method and the Vaganova style in professional training. Some things do change, if not the essentials. Look after all at a ballet of Petipa and then at one by William Forsythe. Look at the very bodies of ballerinas and compare for example those ethereal sylphs hovering above the earth in romantic lithographs with photographs of buxom Victorian ballet dancers peering flirtatiously over their fans; or compare the demure, downcast gaze of later British heroines – the queenly Markova and Fonteyn, with the splayed body of Sylvie Guillem setting out the extended compass points of today's increasingly svelte balletic body in space.

Of course the amateur ballet class has very little to do with ballerinas. For every child who becomes a professional ballet dancer thousands will have been called to the barre.

> The pupil grasps the bar. Before moving, one must stand well. Pelvis is centered, neither tipped back nor forward. Abdomen is drawn in, diaphragm raised. Shoulders drop naturally; head is straight, eyes front. Arms are carried downward, rounded from shoulders to finger tips. The desired 'turn-out', in which, with heels together, the feet are spread to form an angle of 180 degrees, supporting the erect upper body, is only slowly gained. (Kirstein, 1971, p. 5)

Watching a primary-level class however, in a suitably elegant Edwardian house, I was reminded that the amateur ballet class can also have everything to do with ballerinas. The class consisted of a group of five-and six-year-old girls in various shades of pale pink. Their hair swept back into buns, their white socks held in place with ballet-style crossed-over shoe ribbons, they hovered in uncertain rows like a stray tribe of pantomime fairies. One had come in a home-made tutu, the others sported the regulation accessories. The three at the front were soon to take their examination and one had already assumed an unmistakably balletic form of affectation along with a respectable turnout. The two rows behind, new recruits from pre-primary, were particularly lovable with their turned-in knees, bewildered faces, coyly held-out skirts, and their fervent attempts to move in the same direction. Even walking around the room was a serious business and began by placing imaginary crowns on their heads. They remained intent and solemnly involved in circumventing the room despite the teacher's repeated cries over the music of 'happy princesses, please'. After the curtsies at the end of class I asked them what they liked about ballet. 'Skipping' they all said enthusiastically. Did they dislike anything? 'Stretches' said one or two. Had anyone seen a ballet? One thought she had seen *Cinderella* on television, the others were unsure. 'Did anyone want to be a ballerina when they grew up'? Every hand shot up immediately. 'Why?' I asked. They thought very hard. A five-year-old said she liked dancing in front of people. Then one said 'because it's beautiful' and that word spread in agreement around the group. 'What is beautiful'? I asked. 'The ballerinas', they chorused.

'FRIVOLOUS AS THEIR FROCKS'?

The sense of perfection, beauty and sublimity that spectators of all kinds have found in the practice as well as the performance of ballet has motivated many a pen more than ballet's social and cultural significance. The sense of nature idealized and of beauty has been prevalent in describing the art form. Ballet is an evocative subject, and that is almost as true of the ballet class as of ballet in performance. The rows of obedient children with disciplined bodies performing ritual exercises at the barre in professional training has been the subject of numerous photographic studies. The legions of little girls flocking into back-street amateur ballet studios can be just as enigmatic. The buns, pink tights and trappings are a uniform for a ritualized and altogether extraordinary act. The piano (sadly today often replaced with a tape recorder), the mirrored walls and the French words, the discipline, the ritual and regimentation transforms the shabbiest surroundings and can readily captivate the spectator. Here is a fascinated layman, E.I., describing a ballet examination class in the *Manchester Guardian* in 1927.

> One would not as a rule consider it a privilege to be allowed to attend an examination of candidates in any subject . . . . But the hour is full of interest when the candidates are dancers more or less highly skilled in the art of the ballet . . . . There is a certain severity about the scene, pretty though the dancers are and frivolous as their frocks might appear to the uninitiated. The committee were told that it would be impossible to persuade all the candidates to wear the regulation white satin bodice, frilled white ballet skirt, and pink silk tights, but they said it must be done, and it was. So now when the examination begins three sides of the huge room are lined with fairies, who differ in age and still more in height, but are all dressed exactly alike. They stand there, with one hand on the rail, their feet in a straight line, ready for the word of command. (E.I., 1927, p. 8)

Fairy imagery in describing ballet and ballerinas is not unusual. In December 1921, for example, *The Times* reported that visiting the Russian dancers at the Alhambra Theatre was to spend time in a region of fairyland (Packer *et al.*, 1980, p. 106). The combination of perceiving in ballet both a serious art form and the appeal of its surface charms often forms a fascinating and even amusing tension, particularly in the writings of the predominantly male writers drawn to describe the subject earlier in the century. Despite the fact that in reintroducing ballet as a serious art form to Britain in the early twentieth century, Diaghilev's *Ballets Russes* celebrated male at least as much as female dancing, ballet has been seen and described largely through attention to female bodies and feminine associations. (Sayers, 1993, pp. 164–80). Here is E.I again following up a tribute to ballet as a serious mental as well as physical discipline, with a sudden indulgence of what has most captivated his attention:

> But the prettiest things are the pirouettes, when all around the room the girls, standing with one hand on the barre, suddenly rise on tiptoe with a birdlike movement and twirl themselves round. Well, even the ignoramus can see the defects . . . the uncertainties and lack of balance, but it is as pretty to watch as if these were fluffy white birds. (E.I., 1927, p. 8)

The ballerina has often been evoked with rather trivializing imagery that colludes with her artistry to disguise, or perhaps even deny, the skill and strength required to produce the image. The ballerina has been a focus point in the 'seeing' of ballet and both through her and as something separable from her, ballet has been seen as representing extremes of aesthetic value.

> 'Ballet' came to mean a troupe of girls in fluffy white skirts doing a pretty-pretty toe-dance, to music of saccharine triviality. In fifty years this tradition became so firmly entrenched that it is still powerful; it can be seen, in all its purity, in dance competitions and provincial pantomimes. (Hall, 1947, pp. 10–11)

> Ballet in its very purest sense, is to the Dance as a whole what European Poetry is to Literature. (Heppenstall, 1936, p. 25)

> Men of good taste and good sense in all ages have inveighed against the insipid mummeries and lavish pantomimes of the Ballet. It was in Thomas Rymer's language, the conspiracy of Circe and Calypso against poetry and good sense. Its dumbness implied a decadence of the word; its triviality, a decadence of emotion. (Sayers, 1937)

> The geometry of the classical ballet, the outwardness of the classical ballet and the harmonious gradualness of its forms, are an emblem of the European spirit. (Stokes, 1942, p. 88)

The terms of ballet appreciation reflect ballet's shifting standing from music-hall entertainment to expressive art form, and also, perhaps, something of both its courtly origins and the salacious associations of nineteenth-century 'ballet girls'. This duality in appreciation, in our ways of seeing ballet, perhaps also surfaces in the contrasting qualities of the amateur ballet world. The aristocratic values associated with ballet can make a poignant contrast with the social context of its amateur situation and practice. The predominant image of the ballerina is something of both the pantomime fairy and the sublime swan; as such she is a useful vanguard for the ballet industry with her ability to appeal on a variety of levels. In turn the academic qualities of the classical technique can form a fascinating contrast with much of ballet's superstructural imagery. But does the 'meaning', imagery and associations of ballet in amateur practice relate simply and straightforwardly to ballet as an art form in the theatre, or does it have something of its own, peculiar history relating perhaps as much to other factors as to the art form itself?

MADAME SMUDGE AND THE TAGLIONI CHANGES

E.I.'s account of an examination class in 1927 was written at a time when the Association of Operatic Dancing (now the RAD) was, along with the ISTD, beginning to make inroads into the establishment of the discipline and tradition in Britain. Ballet had conquered London 200 years earlier with the French Romantic Ballet, but it was not until the Russian conquest prior to the First World War that a British tradition began to take root. Traditionally ballet was taught in England by a very few foreign teachers. Amongst them was Madame Katti Lanner, whose 'National School of Dancing' provided dancers for the Empire ballets in the late nineteenth century. In 1872 Leon Espinosa, who had studied at the Paris Opera and became a dancer with the Bolshoi, also settled in London, where he opened a school. His wife and daughter specialized in tap as well as ballet and his son, Edouard, became one of the founders of the RAD in 1920. With the Russian dancers, in the early twentieth century, came teachers who were to do a great deal to encourage and enable the development of ballet teaching in Britain, amongst them the Italian dancing-master Enrico Cecchetti and Madame Seraphine Astafieva.

When Anna Pavlova first inspired new audiences for ballet from 1910 onwards, London was not short of dancing. The Duncanesque dancer Maud Allan was a household name following the success of her infamous *Salome*. Danish ballerina Adeline Genee was immensely popular with the British public. The names of British dancers also appear: Phyllis Bedells at the Empire Theatre, Margaret Morris and her Child Dancers, Ruby Ginner and Ninette de Valois (Richardson, 1947). Ballet and ballroom had not yet separated in amateur dancing classes, and would not do so for some time to come (see Thomas and Miller, chapter 6 in this volume). The ISTD had been in existence since 1904 but had not split into its ballroom and the-atrical branches (Dickie, 1992). Manuals on ballroom dancing reveal the use of ballet's turnout and five positions of the feet. There was a great enthusiasm for all forms of dancing, from new social dances to Duncanesque ideas of 'classical' dance. The term 'Operatic' had to be used to distin-guish the distinct discipline of traditional ballet training.

> Five positions of feet and arms support the subsequent academic vocabu-lary. All traditional schooled action starts and stops with these positions, which have their subliminal logic in the carrying of torso by legs and feet, and in initiating movement for every key hinge of the body. Start-ing with the five positions in succession, practice at the bar commences with half-bends (demi-pliés), slow continuous lowering and straighten-ing of the knees, followed by the deeper full bends (grands pliés), in which the heels leave the ground. Arms coordinate in large sweeps with the deeply sinking and fully rising body. Port de bras, or carriage of the arms, frames the body, as, next, it dips forward and back. A large family of elementary 'beats' (battements tendus dimples, battements jetés, petits battements, frappés, soutenus) forms the substructure for smaller move-ments of the feet that, when mastered, permit the further fractioning into sharp and rapid movements later required for acrobatic brilliance in turns and jumps. (Kirstein, 1971, p. 5)

Those working in Britain in the 1920s with a firm knowledge of the classical ballet technique were very few; the majority were unschooled and taught without regulation and without the need for even a basic know-ledge of anatomy. In the struggle to establish the distinct form of classical ballet, and perhaps also its hegemony over other forms of dancing, the *Dancing Times*, under its editor, P. J. S. Richardson, was to play a crucial role. In 1916, pressed by Edouard Espinosa, it called for the establishment of an 'Examining Body' and the publication of a 'Syllabus of what every Teacher ought to Know'. In 1920 the RAD's official examinations specif-ically for ballet teachers began.

The demand for what was at least popularly understood as ballet ap-pears to have been considerable. In 1922 Espinosa apparently reported that the number of novitiates was 'too great for comfort' and found the stand-ard 'decidedly poor' (Parker, 1995, p. 11). Perhaps also in evidence is the struggle between a tradition attempting to establish itself in a nation's culture, and that culture attempting to invest in 'ballet' its own ideals. In a lecture demonstration of 1922 Espinosa is said to have referred to an unknown girl who:

had received two years training in London, and was considered excellent by her teacher. The child danced for me, fine toes, well shaped girl,
naturally graceful in arms, legs and body, but was using positions and
steps absolutely against all rules, technique or laws of art. I requested
. . . an assemble – she executed a series of kicks. I asked her for the five
positions – they were wrong. I handed her a syllabus of the elementary
examination – she knew practically nothing of it. But she said she did
know the 'Taglioni changes'. Needless to say, there is no such step.
(Espinosa, 1922, in Parker, 1995, p. 10)

There may be no such step in the canon of classical ballet, but steps
such as the 'Taglioni Changes', no doubt 'illegitimate' offspring of various dance forms, could arguably represent a lost and undocumented part
of our dance heritage. The Taglioni Changes looked nostalgically back,
perhaps, to the sylphs and sylvan glades of the Romantic ballet, freshly
inspired by the ethereal beauty of Pavlova's dying swan, and perhaps drew
also on a mixture of ballroom steps and music-hall ballet style. A history
of the ballet class in twentieth-century Britain might start with the suppression of uprisings of ballet-inspired, but 'illegitimate' and anatomically
unwise, dancing practice. The place of ballet however, in the evolving
amateur response to the ideals of 'artistic' dancing, which came to be
dominated by classical ballet, is perhaps equally significant.

The social history of ballet dancing integrating with the aspirations,
ideals and fashions of the dancing public in Britain is recorded in the
photographs, advertisements and articles in the *Dancing Times*. Arnold
Haskell has provided an amusing caricature of one early manifestation of
the British 'artistic' dancing teacher:

Madame Smudge – ten letters after her name- and her successful pupils.
Madame Smudge, a fat woman with a smirk, was shown dressed in
pseudo-Greek draperies with a bandeau around her forehead and the
pupils were draped around her bulky form in winsome elfin poses. On
a table were exhibited the cups, shields, medals and other trophies
annexed by Madame's winsome elves. The whole thing was a source of
the greatest amusement to me. I used to cut them out and gloat. What
an anthology they would make, what gems for the découpages of a more
than usually morbid surrealist. I never dreamed of any possibility of
contact with this strange world. (Haskell, 1951, p. 236)

Of those that flocked to learn 'fancy dancing', toe dancing, operatic
dancing, or any of the forms that drew some inspiration from ballet in the
1920s, few could have seen ballet as a developed collaborative art form as

brought to London by Diaghilev's *Ballets Russes*. The ideal of Pavlova however, as the epitome of ballet, was widespread and, unlike Diaghilev, Pavlova toured to provincial stages all over Britain. Pavlova inspired numerous child imitators as well as legions of admirers. Ninette de Valois recounts her experiences as a child performing on pier-heads all over England prior to 1914: 'I was Pavlova and danced "The Dying Swan" – dying twice nightly on all the coastal piers, for my "death" was always ferociously encored' (de Valois, 1977, p. 3).

In the realm of fiction, amateur balletic aspiration and its social pretensions in back-street dance classes from between the wars has been evoked and satirized in Angela Carter's *Wise Children*. Twins, the 'Chance' sisters are stage dancers and also the unacknowledged illegitimate children of Sir Melchior Hazard, a great Shakespearian actor and representative of the legitimate theatre.

> We used to run a little school, in those days, the Brixton Academy of Dance . . . . We'd done it up in a Thames green Regency-stripe wall paper. We put in a big mirror. The little girls laboured with sweat mustaches on their upper lips. One, two, three. (Carter, 1992, p. 35)

> One, two, three, hop! See me dance the polka. Once upon a time, there was an old woman in splitting black satin pounding away at an upright piano in a room over a haberdasher's shop in Clapham High Street and her daughter in a pink tutu and wrinkled tights slapped at your ankles with a cane if you didn't pick up your feet high enough. Once a week, every Saturday morning, Grandma Chance would wash us, brush us and do up our hair in sausage curls . . . . One, two, three, hop. Big mirrors blooming like plums with dust along the walls. I can see us now, in our vests and knickers and our little pink dancing slippers, dipping a curtsy to our reflections . . . . Everything smelled of sweat and gas fire. The old woman thumped the piano and Miss Worthington in her droopy tutu showed us how to fouette, poor thing sixty if she was a day . . . . We did our exercises at the barre. Nora's bum in her navy-blue bloomers jiggled away in front of me like two hard-boiled eggs in a handkerchief. We'd turn around, then she could feast her eyes on mine . . . . To tell the truth we lived for that dancing class. We thought that was what the week was for, for Saturday mornings. (Carter, 1992, pp. 53–4)

What Carter has drawn upon so richly is the pretensions of the ballet class; the absurdity of its 'sausage curls' and curtsies, and of a set of values upheld, regardless of context, within Britain's entrenched class system. My own experience of ballet class as a child in the late 1960s and early

1970s was not so very different from the picture drawn by Carter of the Brixton Academy of Dance. Certainly my image of ballet came not from having ever seen it, but from a miraculously transmuted, and certainly incredibly potent idea of a pale, sparkling and winged feminine ideal somewhere between a dying swan and a sugar-plum fairy. Had my mother not decided that an RAD-trained teacher was important, I could easily have attended a weekly class, that Espinosa would undoubtedly not have approved of, in the small Welsh village where I lived. As it was I took the bus to the nearest town where an official ballet school resided on the top floor of an old tenement block in a grimy side-street. After climbing seemingly endless flights of brown lino-covered stairs you could see, through the murky sash windows, the rooftops of a provincial seaside town. Behind a curtain in a draughty side-room mothers helped their shivering daughters to don their finery and sweep their hair up into buns. Pink tights, satin slippers, leotards and hairnets transformed very ordinary children into special beings. Inside the ballet studio mirrors and barre circumvented three walls. In one corner Mrs Davies would sit at the piano in a fur coat with a small one-bar electric fire at her feet and wink at us in the mirror while the RAD teacher put us carefully through our syllabus. In the other corner sat a row of ballet-committed mothers. Aspiration ran high and examination results were excellent. But standing at the barre we looked down on the disused Plaza Cinema across the street, a one-time music-hall that was a lot closer in space and possibility than Covent Garden.

What happens, once asked a worried Arnold Haskell, to the thousands who enter the children's ballet examinations?

> With few exceptions ... the chorus, musical comedy, marriage, with, let us hope, a happy ending, and several daughters to continue 'mummy's tradition' and go one better. They may become a shade more graceful than they would have been, help a worthy profession and a few charities, while their number accounts for the really fine audiences we enjoy. (Haskell, 1934, p. 196)

The star of our school was a gorgeous creature seemingly destined for greatness. She had black hair parted down the middle, a slender, sylph-like body, large, downcast dark eyes and a lyrical sweep to her easily extended *developpé* that was both inspirational and humbling. She got honours for all her examinations, went on to full-time ballet school and was next heard of dancing topless on ocean liners.

Each exercise is planned to prepare one part of the body for ultimate virtuoso requirements. The deep bend (plié) stretches the Achilles tendon;

pointing with leg extended, knee straight (battement tendu) frees the entire leg from the hips. These exercises are repeated often, usually in four directions in units of eight – front, side, back, and side. Dancers are trained to be completely ambidextrous. Lessons liberate the body from instinctive muscular habit. In its stoic simplicity, daily schooling, as spectacle, possesses the lean elegance of a well laid-out palette, colours freshly squeezed, or a perfectly controlled chromatic scale fingered on the piano. (Kirstein, 1971, p. 5)

At 14 some girls from my dancing school would dance in the seaside summer shows. Snobbishly devoted to a more elevated image of classical ballet, and predicting parental response, I never considered joining in but would voyeuristically hang out with them at their constant rehearsals. With pink feathers glued to sequined leotards that just managed to cover carefully-padded bras, they would high-kick to the director's emphatic calls of 'come on, sell it, sell it', which made them smile all the harder and thrust out their limbs, their chests and their 'personalities' with everything they had. It was both a rich and lurid contrast and yet also a live-wire connection to the disciplined ballet class in the back streets. At the local comprehensive school, if you had your 'head in the clouds' and were not inspired by the prospects of motherhood, or a career in catering, nursing or hairdressing, ballet offered an almost spiritual alternative, a hope, a way out: 'To tell the truth we lived for that dancing class. We thought that was what the week was for, for Saturday mornings' (Carter, 1992, p. 54).

In an age when most women were trapped in the home as wives and mothers, the 'liberated' figure of the ballerina reflects both her unusual physical freedom and also the fact of her dubious social position. It was a commonplace that dances were not 'respectable', yet nevertheless their popularity was intense. Their image was to be found in prints, in porcelain; the name of the Sylphide advertised parasols; stage coaches were called after dancers; the ballerinas were fêted wherever they went. Even Queen Victoria doted upon the ballet. (Clarke and Crisp, 1978, p. 46)

'... THE FINEST FORM OF PHYSICAL CULTURE?'

Many parents no doubt still send their daughters to ballet to promote traditional female virtues of grace, charm and elegance, as well as good co-ordination and deportment. (There are still very few boys to be found in amateur ballet classes.) The realities of pursuing ballet dancing as a profession however, are for many not all that different today as they were for the Chance sisters or teenage aspirant swans in provincial seaside towns during the 1970s: one-night stands on lengthy tours with unsubsidized companies, poor pay and conditions and a limited career expectancy.

When the class shifts onto the open floor, exercises from the bar – but now without its help – are repeated and developed. Movement progresses off the floor into the air, as the separate male or female specialties are accentuated. (Men do not dance on toe; girls do not jump very high). Girls, on toe-point, move almost imperceptibly in feathery runs (pas de bourrée). Boys start to execute multiple turns (pirouettes) and broad leaps (grands jetés). Petite batterie, or small jumps with beats (changements de pieds, royales, brises), in which feet, held close together, change neatly and briskly, inches off the ground, lead to entre-chats, the familiar interlacing beats that, when multiplied, are the spectacular trademarks of male dancers. (Kirstein, 1971, p. 5)

Given such a very small chance of real mastery, the limited possibilities of practising ballet in adulthood, the disciplined and difficult nature of the technique, its rather 'old-fashioned' attitudes towards masculine and feminine roles and qualities, and its exclusivity in terms of ideal body shape, it is perhaps surprising that so many pursue ballet so ardently. The question of what the ballet class has to offer the amateur once-a-week child, and the physically unsuited, has often been raised. Certainly the children's examination systems have been specifically designed to meet amateur needs, as well as provide an early training for, and means of talent-spotting those few who can take it further. Although the line has been drawn at accepting the disabled child, good results in the children's examinations can be attained by those whose physical shape means they have no hope or intention of becoming professional ballet dancers. The fact that there are adult classes in ballet, often taken by a range of women some of whom are well into retirement, also testifies to the fact that the appeal of the technique and the pleasure of practising it goes beyond professional aspiration. The principle of ballet as more than a training for the professional is long-standing. Here is E.I. again from 1927:

It becomes clear as the exercises go on that to practise classic dancing aiming at perfection is to receive a very fine mental as well as a physical training. The necessity for unflagging attention to secure precision in every movement, the rhythm of the movements, and the fact that there is only one right way, make the mind as flexible and as disciplined as the muscles. One feels enthusiastically that every child in a civilised community should go through such a course of training, though what

Lord Eustace would say to the suggestion one knows only too well.
(E.I., 1927, p. 8)

Certainly, by the 1960s, it was not unusual for doctors to prescribe ballet
as a postural corrective where there was no structural defect requiring
medical intervention, and this practice may have started much earlier.

The Association from the first never hesitated to press the view that
ballet classes should not be viewed simply as preparing girls (or boys,
for that matter – though there were always few of those) for a professional career. As Philip Richardson put it, 'when properly given, classes
form the finest form of physical culture, the best corrective of the minor
bodily ailments and one of the pleasantest steps in the direction of
mental culture which a child can have'. (Parker, 1995, p. 13)

Yet the ballet class is undoubtedly ideal-centred rather than child-centred.
'Oh I shall be so glad not to have to think of placing my body correctly,
and all those awful positions of the arms and legs!. I can just be sturdy and
unimaginative and my self!' (Estoril, 1957, p. 68). As the training progresses
the presence of the mirror and the central idea of correcting one's body
and movement in relation to the ideal can undermine just as easily as
mastery of the technique can inspire confidence.

Jenny, for all her practical common sense, stifled a faint sigh that she
was plump and ungraceful . . . . Most of the students looked charming,
the music was attractive, and there were many skilful dancers in the
Selswick School, even though Madame knew that so few of them could
ever hope to reach the status of ballerina. (Estoril, 1957, p. 67).

The darker aspects of the serious pursuit of ballet as a career have been
documented by Dr L. M. Vincent in his book *Competing with the Sylph.*
Dr Vincent presents typical case-studies of those who fall victim to punit-
ive dietary regimes, to bulimia, anorexia nervosa and what he describes
as 'a vicious, self-destructive obsession'; a concern 'with weight and diet,
with looking like a ballerina' (Vincent, 1979, p. xii). But ballet's discipline, its exclusivity, its difficulty, its association with 'calling' and self-
sacrifice, that it is in the main a career peaked and finished in youth, may
only add to its mystique.

THE CHARMED, LUMINOUS, ENCHANTED SPACE

There is undoubtedly a great sense of pleasure to be experienced in practising classical ballet technique without the need for any aspiration to

professional performance. It involves perhaps the technique's particular clarity of linear definition and geometry, the sense of centring the self within a body attuned to seemingly universal principles of harmony and order. For girls the unearthed, sublime and airy plane of existence, and magical associations, opened up as a possibility by the pointe shoe, with its potent symbolism, undoubtedly adds to its attraction.

> Ballet ... is human bodies behaving in an unusually lovely manner, seeming to tend towards an ideal pattern, the Platonic Idea of movement. The condition of all such lovely behaviour is perfect obedience to certain rhythmic and harmonic laws .... Dancing, generally, is a great heightening of the natural tensions of human movement. Ballet ... is such a superlative heightening, such a complete epitome and pure essence, that it will often have to be regarded, in the contrary sense, as an absolute and closed art, which must not be adulterated with lower forms of dancing. (Heppenstall, 1936, p. 18)

No doubt the success of the ballet class has much to do with the nature of its technique and its relationship to virtuosity, as well as to its cultural ideals and ability to appeal on a variety of levels. But it may also have something to do with ballet's occupation of the space for 'serious' dance. That is to say ballet may have been invested with, and may still carry the value of the dance form most artistically, spiritually, aesthetically, and perhaps even 'ethically', meaningful. 'The primary concern of dance is with the expressive exploration and creation of moral meaning and spiritual value through the medium of the body' (Abbs, 1991, p. xii).

Contemporary Dance, stemming from American and European Modern Dance forms, has challenged classical ballet's hegemony in this respect, providing alternatives to its technique, its ideals and its sexual politics. Yet outside major cities it is still comparatively difficult to find high-quality Contemporary Dance classes. Through schools and youth dance groups Contemporary Dance probably attracts a wider social mix than does ballet, but it has not made significant inroads into the private studios, nor has it developed the kind of establishment bodies so effective in creating and maintaining the high standards of classical ballet teaching. Like ballet in its early days, Contemporary Dance classes are often taught by those with an inadequate training in and understanding of the techniques and art form. It is often confused with jazz and disco, seen as an opportunity to explore any form of dance or as a vehicle for free expression in movement. In comparison with the understanding of defined technique, clear criteria for excellence and disciplined examination structure offered to amateurs studying ballet, it is a poor relation. In addition, for adults many dance studios offer a ballet class, but the alternatives on offer outside major cities are likely to be ballroom, yoga, jazz or aerobics.

In addition to its 'seriousness', ballet is also a particularly glamorized profession and, like other gateways to 'stardom', it is surrounded by a 'mythology', by superstition and belief in fate, destiny, innate genius and calling, that serve to unearth and romanticize the art form and its training. The history of ballet literature in Britain reveals the active romanticization of the art form. Here, for example, is Kathleen Crofton recounting the beginning of her 'history' as a member of Anna Pavlova's *corps de ballet*:

> Before World War 1, into a remote hill station of the North-West Frontier Province, British India, came the words 'Anna Pavlova'. They were heard, repeated rather haltingly at first, turning themselves with strange inflexions round the unfamiliar Sahib's and Memsahib's tongues .... one day a small girl caught them – or did their magic catch her? She asked her mother 'What is Anna Pavlova?' 'A dancer', came the answer, 'a Russian dancer. They say she is the greatest dancer in the world'. Touched by the spell, from that moment the child found herself being drawn, slowly but irresistibly from the everyday world into the charmed circle of the dance, the centre of which was luminous with the enchantment of Pavlova. (Crofton, 1956, p. 73)

ORPHANS, FAIRIES AND PRINCESSES IN CHILDREN'S BALLET FICTION

Children's ballet fiction reflects aspects of both ballet's history in Britain and its mystique; it is a rich source for understanding the idea of ballet training in contemporary aspiration and imagination. For example, when Noel Streatfeild wrote *Ballet Shoes* in 1936 it was still necessary for Posy, the ballet dancer of the three orphaned Fossil sisters, to be taught by a Russian émigré called 'Madame'. Ballet was, in 1936, still considered a Russian art form. By the 1950s however, children's ballet fiction begins to reflect an English tradition. Veronica Weston, the orphaned heroine of Lorna Hill's books, studies at first with one of the many Madames of children's ballet fiction, a Madame Violetta Wakulski, whose lineage is 'part Italian, part French, and part goodness knows what! Added to that she married a Russian' (Hill, 1950, p. 16). She quickly moves however, to study with a very English Miss Martin and is destined for Sadler's Wells. In Jean Estoril's children's ballet fiction, written from the late 1950s, the heroine, Drina, attends an altogether English establishment, the Janetta

Selswick School of Dancing. The Russian heritage of the ballet teacher in earlier children's fiction is even mocked: 'Miss Selswick is Madame, though she's not foreign like most of the teachers in all those idiotic stories about the ballet', says one of the characters. 'She doesn't say, "Ah, ze leetle one ees going to be ze dancer most pair-fect"' (Estoril, 1957, p. 23).

Veronica Weston, the 1950s heroine, is quite different from 1930s heroine Posy Fossil; she fails examinations, has to work hard and is only transformed into a beauty when she dons her ballet costume. Children's ballet fiction reflects the development of understanding ballet from something entirely foreign and exotic to becoming accepted as both 'English' and a serious and respected art form. It reflects also many of the ideals invested in ballet and its place in a hierarchy of dance forms. When one of the children is sought to entertain the guests at a garden fête it is suggested that Veronica dance the Sugar-Plum Fairy. Aunt June is not immediately impressed:

> 'Dance?' she repeated, as if she'd never heard of the word. 'You don't mean that atrocious tap dancing, I hope?' 'Oh no, Aunt June!' I exclaimed. 'Caroline means ballet' .... 'Ballet is one of the arts', said Sebastian's voice from the window. 'You couldn't get anything higher class than ballet'. (Hill, 1950, p. 142)

The romanticization of ballet dancing in children's ballet fiction relates directly to the star-centred nature of the art form and its fairy-tale associations. As in fairy tales there are an abundance of orphans, little rich girls do not tend to do very well, and if the shoe fits the heroine is assured a happy-ever-after ending. Ballet dancing itself continued to be heavily romanticized in children's ballet fiction throughout the 1950s. For example, the idea that the right place for the waltz in *Les Sylphides* is a forest glade rather than a theatre stage is expressed in Lorna Hills's *A Dream of Sadler's Wells*:

> Then, before I had recovered from my daydream, another melody came floating out of the window – a dreamy melody ... a melody that made you think of green woods, and graceful larch boughs of glimmering water and the pale evening sky ... the Waltz from 'Les Sylphides' .... Before I knew what I was doing, I had kicked off my heavy shoes, thrown aside my cardigan, and was dancing. There, in my faded cotton frock, my feet bare, on the strip of velvet lawn which was my first stage, I danced the Waltz as I had never danced it before. The lacy, arching trees, the emerald turf, the pale host of a new moon between the larch boughs – I put them all into my dancing. It wasn't till afterwards, when

I thought it over, that I realised I had danced the Waltz in its rightful setting – a woodland glade. (Hill, 1950, p. 148)

With Posy Fossil the romanticization of ballet is achieved largely through the idea of predestination. Posy is the abandoned child of a great dancer who arrives at her adopted family with a pair of ballet shoes tied around her. Similarly, Estoril's orphaned Drina has a mysterious desire to dance from the time she takes her first steps and she and the reader gradually discover that, like Posy Fossil, her mother was a great dancer who died tragically young. However, by 1979, the romanticism that is so much a part of ballet fiction is noticeably beginning to give way. The heroine of Jean Richardson's ballet books, Moth, has both her parents. The series begins with Moth failing her audition to White Lodge. She is not described in terms of a 'born dancer', as much as a girl determined to make herself into a dancer. But the author's surface attempt at down-to-earth character-ization is perhaps betrayed by her heroine's name, and even a disparaged Moth pauses to wonder if 'perhaps ballet was a superior world to which you either belonged – or you didn't' (Richardson, 1979, p. 34). By 1994 however, Mal Lewis Jones's series begins by reversing entirely the the-matic use of predestination as an association with balletic success. Nasty, spoilt Amanda Renwick, the principal's favourite, who is cast in all the leading parts, suffers under a huge psychological burden, a secret that leads her first to theft and then to mental collapse; she is the only daughter of a once great ballerina who died in childbirth at the height of her career. All her genes, wealth and privilege do not make her as good as otherwise ordinary but talented heroine, Cassie. Lewis Jones's book is concerned with the psychological burden of parental expectations as well as with the certainty that only true talent and hard work, quite separate from anything associated with predestination or birthright, wins through in the end.

The steps may be the same for all these fictional ballet heroines but a great deal of changing cultural context separates the romanticism of Noel Streatfeild's little Fossils in *Ballet Shoes*, destined for stardom, and the 'bun heads' of the most recent *Scrambled Legs* series destined for a life on diet coke. Perhaps though the ballet 'industry' should be wary of any fall from grace of its fairies, swans and sylphs in children's ballet fiction; like monarchy itself, the ballet business may well need its mystique to secure its place in the British social fabric. For younger readers of ballet fiction, however, star-centred spotlit fantasies and fairy-tale associations appear to reign unchallenged. A glance at the images of ballerinas in very young children's fiction reveals the common association of ballerinas with fairies and vice versa. Next to fairies must come princesses and butterflies in terms of popular imagery associated with ballet. Patrick Yee's book *Helen the Little Ballerina* (1994), for example, attempts to introduce the very young reader, perhaps starting their pre-primary or primary class, to the basic positions of the feet and to the idea that practice makes perfect. To keep the attention of his young readers however, Yee draws on typical imagery and association, perpetuating the all-too familiar stereotypes. Helen is obsessed with ballet. Ballerinas appear on everything from her school bag to her best dress. Above her bed hangs a picture of the most famous ballerina in the world, Maxima Maximova. She goes every Saturday to class where she learns the positions of the feet and how to skip and curtsy. Then there is the announcement of the end of term performance of *Dance of the Butterflies*. 'Would she ever be good enough to be the Flower Princess?' ponders Helen after class. 'I think you could be the Princess if you practise', says her mother. When her big night arrives she dons her pink satin shoes and her pretty pink tutu. Her mother puts up her hair and puts on her flowery head-dress. After a bravura performance she is given a posy of flowers. 'Everyone clapped and cheered. Now Helen knew what it felt like to be a proper ballerina.'

If the profundity of ballet's aesthetic significance resides in the main with its nature as an evolving tradition, its trivialization, romanticization, elevation and vulgarization form a lively alternative history. There are perhaps many histories of ballet that remain to be written, histories that have nothing to do with Sadler's Wells, the Ballet Rambert or the influence of Diaghilev. Histories that is of an industry, almost apart from the art form – but intimately related to its development.

NOTE

With thanks to Wendy Gill, AISTD; the Patricia Newman School of Dancing, Cheltenham; Susan Hughes-Parry; Sheila Davis and Barbara Oats.

REFERENCES

P. Abbs, 'Preface' to P. Brinson, *Dance as Education* (London: Falmer Press, 1991).
A. Carter, *Wise Children*, Vintage edn 1992 (London: Chatto & Windus, 1991).

M. Clarke and C. Crisp, *Ballet in Art* (London: Ash & Grant, 1978).

K. Crofton, 'Chorus' in A. H. Franks (ed.), *Pavlova* (London: Burke Publishing Co. Ltd, 1956).

N. de Valois, *Step by Step* (London: W. H. Allen, 1977).

S. Dickie, 'The Origins of the ISTD', *Dance Now*, 1, 1 (Spring 1992) and 1, 4 (Winter 1992/93).

E. I., 'Our Operatic Dancers', *Manchester Guardian* (5.7.27).

J. Estoril, *Ballet for Drina* (London and Sydney: Macdonald & Co., 1957).

F. Hall, *Ballet* (London: The Bodley Head, 1947).

A. Haskell, *Balletomania* (London: Victor Gollancz, 1934).

A. Haskell, *In His True Centre* (London: Adam & Charles Black, 1951).

R. Heppenstall, *Apology for Dancing* (London: Faber & Faber, 1936).

L. Hill, *A Dream of Sadler's Wells* (London: Evans Brothers Ltd, 1950).

L. Kirstein, *Movement and Metaphor* (London: Pitman Publishing, 1971).

M. Lewis-Jones, *Ghost at the Ballet School* (London: Hodder Children's Books, 1994).

J. Malcolm, *Scrambled Legs* (series) (UK: Lyons, 1991–).

A. Packer *et al.*, *Fairies in Legend and the Arts* (London: Cameron & Tayleur Ltd, 1980).

D. Parker, *The First Seventy-Five Years* (London: Royal Academy of Dancing, 1995).

J. Richardson, *The First Steps* (London: Knight Books, Hodder & Stoughton, 1979).

P. J. S. Richardson, 'A Chronology of the Ballet in England 1910–1945' in A. Haskell (ed.), *Ballet Annual*, first issue (London: Adam & Charles Black, 1947).

P. J. S. Richardson, 'Classical Technique in England' in A. Haskell (ed.), *Ballet Annual*, second issue (London: Adam & Charles Black, 1948).

L. A. Sayers, 'She might pirouette on a daisy and it would not bend' in H. Thomas (ed.), *Dance, Gender and Culture* (London: Macmillan, 1993).

M. Sayers, Review of 'Apology for Dancing', *The Criterion* (London: January 1937).

A. Stokes, *Tonight the Ballet* (London: Faber & Faber, 1942).

N. Streatfeild, *Ballet Shoes* (London: J. M Dent & Sons Ltd, 1936).

L. M. Vincent, *Competing with the Sylph: Dancers and the Pursuit of the Ideal Body Form* (Kansas City, MO: Andrews and McMeel, Inc., 1979).

P. Yee, *Helen the Little Ballerina* (London: Orchard Books, 1994).

9 Safe Sets: Women, Dance and 'Communitas'

Barbara O'Connor

INTRODUCTION

The recent success of *Riverdance: The Show* in Britain and the US has given Irish dance a certain cultural cachet beyond its traditional milieu. At home in Ireland it is likely to have the effect, at least temporarily, of an increase in the number of young girls, and perhaps, even some boys, attending step-dancing classes and diligently practising their steps in the hope of becoming future Jean Butlers or Michael Flatleys.[1] The subject of this chapter, however, is the increase in activity in another form of Irish dance – set dance. The revival of set dancing has been ongoing for around fifteen years now and one of its most striking facets is the transference of what was historically a form of rural dance to the city, where it now occupies a place as one of the most popular forms of recreational dance.

At one level the re-emergence of set dancing in the city can be viewed as part of a wider interest in dance as a leisure activity. Other popular forms of recreational dance currently include ballroom, jive and Latin American. At a more specific level, it is only possible to suggest some general reasons for the revival, since there is a dearth of sociological analysis on the topic. This is hardly surprising, since the sociological analysis of dance in Ireland is only just beginning and can be placed in the general context of the marginalisation of dance in Western sociology generally (see Thomas, 1995). However, there has been some welcome and useful comment on the set-dance revival from other sources. For instance, Tubridy (1994) places it as following on, a decade later, the revival of traditional music in the 1960s which, in turn, he places in the context of the folk-music revival generally. In my opinion, the international success and acclaim of traditional Irish music at this time marked the beginning of a reawakening of interest and pride in indigenous cultural forms, and was instrumental in turning round a sense of inferiority which had its origins in a colonised past, and a project of modernity in which national and rural cultural practices respectively were denigrated. It could also be suggested that more recently, membership of the European Union has generated some desire to maintain a distinctive ethnic culture. The last twenty years have also witnessed a

149

substantial growth in internal cultural tourism, so that people from the city come into more contact with set dancing in the country. In some cases this kind of cultural contact may be underpinned by an ideology of rural romanticism where traditional cultural practices such as set dancing are sought as a way of accessing an 'authentic' folk culture. I would suggest, too, that changes in migration patterns have led to an increase in internal rural–urban migration resulting in larger numbers of rural people living in the city with a knowledge of, and interest in, set dancing.

In an attempt to address some of the above issues I chose to explore the current popularity of set dancing in terms of the pleasures and meanings associated with the practice itself. The perspective adopted here could be loosely called a critical one in the sense that the experiences of dancing as described by the participants are explored and then interpreted in the light of the social and cultural environment of the dancers. I set out to explore the pleasures and meanings of set dancing by talking to a number of women who do set dancing as a leisure activity in Dublin city.

Set dancing is a form of social dancing which has been popular in rural Ireland for at least the last two centuries. It is a group dance, perhaps most akin to American country dancing, for those not familiar with the genre. It has its origins in the cotillons and quadrilles introduced into Ireland in the eighteenth century and has been gradually adapted to local conditions and music to emerge as a much faster and more exciting genre than the eighteenth-century counterpart. The set requires eight people (four couples) and the basic steps used are jigs, reels and hornpipes. The set very often begins with the four couples in a square with two top and two side couples (standard position) and frequently ends in the same position, though there are a number of variations on this. Each set consists of a number of figures or individual dances which vary both within the set and between sets. The number of figures in a set varies between four and six. The dancing involves various movements around the set, so that while one is dancing as a couple it is not the 'closed couple' of ballroom dancing but an open couple dancing very often in relation to, or with, other members of the set (I have included the fifth figure of 'The Lancers' and 'The Caledonian', both frequently danced sets, in the Appendix to give some indication of the kinds of variation in movement involved).

According to Tubridy (1994), set dancing began to decline as a popular form of social dancing in rural areas in the 1920s and 1930s for a multiplicity of reasons; rural migration, clerical hostility, the creation of, and increasing popularity of an alternative 'authentic' canon of Irish dancing before and after national independence in 1922, the suppression of house dancing following the enforcement of the Public Dance Halls Act in 1935, and increased prosperity leading to changing patterns of consumption. It is interesting to note that set dancing, though a popular rural dance form, was to some extent ousted by what was regarded as a more 'authentic' canon of *céilí* dancing during the revival of cultural nationalism prior to political independence in 1922. Set dancing, in the context of an essentialist cultural nationalism, was seen as foreign because of its origins. Tubridy (1994) refers to the way in which even the names of the dances themselves such as 'The Lancers', 'The Victoria' and 'The Caledonian' would have militated against them during this period. According to Brennan (1994), both the Munster dance forms and styles were favoured over others by those members of the Gaelic League involved in the creation of the new canon. In the same context, she notes the response to the performance of four-hand and eight-hand reels at the annual conference of the League in 1901.

> Controversy ensued when some observers dismissed the dances as versions of the quadrilles which were classified as alien and thus unsuitable for nationalists. Also excluded as foreign were social dances such as the highland Schottische, the barn dance and the waltz, despite the fact that they were part and parcel of the repertoire of the ordinary people of rural Ireland among whom traditional dance was strongest. (Brennan, 1994, p. 23)

However, despite official efforts to exclude set dancing, there were pockets where it retained, and continues to maintain, its popularity, notably in Clare, West Cork, and Kerry (Tubridy, 1994).

Currently the four main types of venue for set dancing in Dublin city are (a) weekly set-dance classes, which usually run for about two hours, (b) *céilís*, i.e. dances where set dancing is the main form of dancing and which are also held at regular intervals, (c) weekend workshops held in a variety of venues often outside the city (sometimes as far away as Tory Island off the Donegal coast), where participants attend classes during the day followed by a night-time *céilí*, (d) a small number of city pubs which usually have dancing one night in the week. Some people attend classes only or *céilís* only, others combine all four. It is possible, therefore, to dance every night of the week if one so desires.

The socio-demographic profile of set dancers awaits further investigation since the sociological analysis of dance is still at an embryonic stage. From my own observations of the people who attend one particular class, there appears to be a range of groups which include people in their forties, fifties and even sixties who would have done set dancing as children in rural Ireland and are happy to have the opportunity for continuing their enjoyment: these might be married couples or married or single women.

There are also single and separated men who go for the social outing or with the hope of meeting a partner, and the dancing itself is of secondary importance. There are also a considerable number of women in their thirties and forties who come alone or with a female friend or friends. While this profile would need much more elaboration and systematic verification, what is clear is that there are variations in purpose among the participants and that the meanings and pleasures are likely to vary from group to group. For some the social outing and associated conviviality appears to be the most important element, for others the chance to meet a partner for a relationship is foremost, while for some the pleasures of dancing itself are primary.

In terms of age there is a range from twenties to sixties but it appears to be particularly popular among the over-thirties and amongst women. In accounting for the predominance of women doing set dancing two factors must be taken into account. One is the higher demographic ratio of women to men in Dublin city and the other is the historically greater interest in, and experience of, dancing by women. The gender ratios vary between class venues and between dance contexts generally, with a greater gender balance at *céilís* than at classes.

The following discussion is based on data from talking to ten women who attend or attended class in Dublin city centre on a regular basis. The data consists of transcripts from semi-structured individual interviews with five women and one group discussion with five women. It is also informed by participant observation, since I thoroughly enjoy set dancing and have been attending a class on a weekly basis for approximately four years. I also occasionally attend some *céilís* and weekend workshops. Some of the women to whom I spoke were learners and were attending classes only, while others also went to *céilís* and attended workshops, again, with varying frequency. These are women in their thirties and forties, professional women working in the service sector, some single, some with partners, some with children, others without. Generally speaking, the activity of dancing itself was very enjoyable for these women, as evidenced from the sheer enthusiasm and pleasure in talking about dancing. Set dancing was a new activity for all of them, though some would have had experience of learning step dancing as children. The discussion focuses on some of the main themes which emerged during the course of the interviews and group discussion.[2]

It is necessary at this stage to emphasise the exploratory nature of the findings presented here, since they are part of ongoing research where the main issues addressed will be developed in a more systematic way. However, despite the limitations of scale, it is hoped that the discussion will help to broaden the debates on women and dance, particularly since so much of the recent dance scholarship in the sociology/cultural studies area has been associated with 'youth culture'.

THE CONSTRUCTION OF 'COMMUNITAS'

Leisure activities such as set dancing are increasingly playing a role in the construction of community. In an era of late modernity or postmodernity, the 'traditional' communities based on the social interconnection of people living within a particular local boundary are on the decline. No longer, the arguments go, is our sense of affective identity based on the street or the parish, or indeed on other kinds of social formations such as social class, because of the changes which late capitalist development have wrought on our sense of time and space (see Giddens, 1991; Lash and Urry, 1994; Urry, 1995). In contrast to the ascriptive quality of 'traditional' community, we now exercise relative choice in selecting the kinds of communities with which we would like to be involved. This new way of inventing community is not a one-off activity but is rather one in which we are frequently involved (see Lash and Urry, 1994). Urry (1995) takes up this theme and explores some of the constituent elements in these new kinds of community or 'new sociations' which he claims:

> are not like those of traditional communities since they are joined out of choice and people are free to leave. People remain members in part because of the emotional satisfaction that they derive from common goals or experiences. Membership is from choice and many people will indeed enter and exit from such sociations with considerable rapidity. They provide important sites whereby new kinds of social identity can be experimented with. They can empower people, they provide safe social spaces for identity-testing, and they may provide a context for the learning of new skills. (Urry, 1995, pp. 220–1)

Examples of this kind of 'new sociation' would be environmental groups, women's groups, campaign groups, and leisure groups such as birdwatchers, choral groups and vintage-car enthusiasts. Urry draws on Gorz (1985) to make the point that the leisure activities are not merely passive and individualistic but depend upon 'communication, giving, creating and aesthetic enjoyment, the production and reproduction of life, tenderness, the realisation of physical, sensuous and intellectual capacities, the creation of non-commodity use-values' (quoted in Urry, 1995, p. 221).

The discussions on set dancing clearly indicated the quest for, and invention of, community. Indeed, one of most striking features of the discussions was the way in which both the ambience and the activity of dancing itself were seen to generate feelings of friendliness, inclusiveness and warmth which in turn provided a space in which women were empowered to communicate, learn new skills, experiment with social identity and express themselves in an aesthetically and sensually pleasing way.

One of the main ways in which this sense of community was achieved was through the breaking-down of hierarchical structures which form part of everyday life, the abolition of difference and the creation of a sense of 'communion'. Turner's (1974) concept of 'communitas' is useful in this context since it refers to ritual behaviour which generates a sense of togetherness, of unity and abolishes difference and distance. 'Communitas' involves rituals 'in which egalitarian and co-operative behaviour is characteristic, and in which secular distinctions of rank, office, and status are temporarily in abeyance or regarded as irrelevant' (Turner, 1974, p. 238).

Undoubtedly, most, if not all types of dancing, create some level of 'communitas'. For example, McRobbie notes the sense of universal communion which is a feature of 'raves', a type of social dancing which in some respects is very different from set dancing. She observes how in a 'rave', 'the atmosphere is one of unity, of dissolving difference in the peace and harmony haze of the drug Ecstasy' (McRobbie, 1993, p. 418). However, I would suggest that while there are similarities in the way in which 'communitas' is constructed (these might include the music which has a specific resonance with the dancers and is 'deeply felt', the pleasures of bodily movement in dance, and the sense of being in unison with a group of like-minded people), there are also differences. An obvious one is the absence of a drug culture in set dancing. Verbal and other forms of communication, particularly the sense of touch, are important aspects of set dancing (see discussion below), but are not present in rave.

The sense of 'communitas' in set dancing is expressed in a number of ways, the friendliness of the people, the ease of communication, etiquette and conventions surrounding the dance and the form and content of the dances themselves. For example, Mary,[3] in response to a question on the reasons why she likes set dancing, talks about the importance of *craic*, which can be loosely equated with fun, but it implies a conviviality and a sense of exuberance most often associated with music, lively conversation/banter and pub culture. She acknowledges that in order to have the *craic* one needs to be in the company of the right kind of people:

I think the music and the dancing, that's one thing but I don't think that's the prime reason .. motive .. I think the primary motive is just the 'craic' that goes on . . . ok . . the music and the dancing . . that's a likeable element . . but I think there has to be more than that . . I think it's just the whole scene around you and they are all people that are similar really to your own.[4]

The idea of 'communitas', that the community consists of people who may come from different social backgrounds but who are rendered equal by the nature of the set-dancing encounter, is taken up by Margaret:

meeting people from various backgrounds . . people in set dancing . . it's totally irrelevant what somebody's economic or social background is . . you're in there together . . very rarely do people actually end up discussing issues or debating things, your mind is not important . . it's very much yourself and you're taken as a person rather than as a just kind what your c.v. says . . you could be mixing with brain surgeons or you could be mixing with absolutely anybody . . from any kind of a background, and you'll never know and it's not important . . and people can form friendships and relationships based on their enjoyment of the music and dance which I think is fantastic . . it's a classless sort of activity really.

Margaret is well aware of the limitations of such contact but sees it as positive nonetheless: '[it's a] very superficial conversation . . but people grow bonds through that'.

The women were not unaware, though, of the negative aspects of this 'instant community' in the form of restraints on their behaviour such as the difficulty of refusing a dance because, as Kate indicated: 'you're likely to meet this person in a week's time or in a month's time at another *céilí* . . it just makes life awkward'. But, again, the positive aspect of community is reinforced by the fact that she feels free to ask someone to dance because you are bound to meet someone you know '*you will most definitely bump into somebody*'.

Another inflection of community was expressed in the sense of belonging and warmth felt in the presence of the other dancers. Helen speaks of the friendliness, the opportunity for talking and the ease of communication:

it doesn't matter who you are, everybody talks to each other, you know people by name, you don't have to know what they do, they're just nice to one another . . if you go to a disco, for a start, you can't talk to anyone at a disco.

Emma, like Helen, is attracted by the friendliness and the mix of people:

they're very friendly, old and young . . and there is a mix . . there's a good mix and everyone is so friendly . . might know their first name but

I wouldn't know their second name, what their surnames are . . or where they're from or anything else . . but everyone seems to get on well.

Nuala, contrasting her experiences of dancing in two different cities, claims that the fact of knowing more people enhances the possibility for fun:

maybe again, it was a long-term thing, when we started off in Galway we didn't know that many people either, then we got to know them all and it was really good fun . . 'cos they knew you and you knew them and whereas here I find I don't know as many . . and I go to a *céilí* maybe . . I know a few faces . . you wouldn't have the same feeling about it.

Noteworthy in the above extracts is the importance attached to friendliness, openness and inclusivity which generate a sense of belonging and security and the simultaneous acknowledgement that it doesn't have the constraints of a 'regular' community. It is sufficient to know people superficially, in fact, that is the attraction – the creation of an ephemeral and instant community which is based on voluntary association and personal choice.

The strong presence of 'communitas' is dependent not only on the friendliness and openness of the people who go, but also on the specific nature of the dances themselves. There was general acknowledgement that the form and content play an important role in the enjoyment of the dances. In response to a question on the appeal of dancing in a group formation Kate refers to a number of interlinked activities. She starts out by talking of the enjoyment of collaborative effort and production: 'I suppose it's probably that you're working as part of a team in producing this dance, in producing each figure of it.' She then continues on to talk about the opportunity for communication which is inbuilt into the dance:

you *are* communicating with people that you are dancing with, so, as I say, it may not be verbal all the time because it's not easy, but it might be a nod or a wink . . there are some dances where that particular movement is part of the figure . . for example in 'The Corofin Plain Set' . . turn to the opposite couple . . and coming back the second time you nod to the person opposite you . . so there is that kind of communication there.

She then mentions the opportunity for gradual and easy acquaintanceship, if so desired:

then again, you dance with each person you are meeting, seven new people *if you want it to be like that* [my emphasis] . . you may not ever talk to them but you'll recognise them and you'll meet them the next time and you'll dance with them and eventually they might make conversation or you might get to know them .. and I think that is very enjoyable .. the other thing is that when you go set dancing you might not dance with the same person all night, you probably wouldn't .. you might dance with lots of different people, you might be in lots of different circles, because it's open.

The feeling of achievement in co-operative effort mentioned by Kate is also addressed by Eileen:

I actually like the feeling of achievement that you get .. from being with somebody who can dance .. it's like an achievement, you've done something well .. there has been a contact with somebody you've done it as a unit .. it's not just yourself and not even in a couple .. there is also a solidarity in the set .. that you'll ... help each other out .. a feeling of accomplishment.

Anne likes the excitement generated by being part of the group:

the group idea, dance formation with others, for instance now, in the old days we used to be in pairs, 'cor-beirte', two people .. it was a beautiful, graceful dance .. not as exciting as dancing with others in a set .. with all of eight people moving in and out.

Helen associates one of the joys of dancing with her knowledge of the people in the set, equal levels of competence and a familiarity with their dancing styles: 'you might get into a set where you know everybody .. you know the way they dance .. you know the way they move and you get such a buzz .. eight people in the set at the same level .. to me it's fantastic'.

All of the above points to the importance of the 'group' nature of the dance in creating a particular kind of engagement with other dancers. It is very much a physical as well as emotional engagement being based on touch, eye-contact, talk, moving in time with other dancers, and so on.

A number of anthropologists and dance historians have pointed to the important role which group dancing plays in generating community solidarity (see, for example, Boas, 1972; Radcliffe-Brown, 1964; Rust, 1969; Lange, 1975). Dance as metaphor for the social body (see Douglas, 1976) was apparent when I enquired about favourite dances. The 'Clare Lancers' was mentioned a number of times and specifically that part of the fifth figure of the dance, the line up, side step, advance and retire (see Appendix), in which dancing within one's own set of eight people is transformed by

joining hands with members of the adjoining set – the choreography resulting in one continuous line of dancers along the length of the hall.
Kate says of the 'Lancers': 'to look at it from a balcony, for example in
Seapoint in Salthill, the international weekend, it's just amazing, you just
see a sea of people and they are moving together . . it's just unreal and it's
very nice'. Nuala also mentions the attractions of the line up: 'I love the
line up, the military line up and I love that . . . it's just so neat and it looks
lovely . . opportunity to look at it from a balcony . . it looks lovely . . . it's
so uniform.' Margaret refers specifically to the way in which it creates a
feeling of community:

> I love the Clare Lancers because . . . for me it is an extremely elegant
> sèt and I think some of the movements are almost like ballet actually,
> where the lines separate and dance across the room . . it's very stylish
> and elegant and at the end when people hold hands together the whole
> hall can hold hands at the same time . . so you get a great feeling of
> community from that one.

WOMEN, PUBLIC SPACE AND DANCE

The substantial literature on the gendering of public space highlights the
ways in which public space came to be appropriated by men and consequently considered out of bounds for women. From the mid-nineteenth
century on the department store became a safe haven for women in the
city – a place to be, feel comfortable and enjoy themselves. Not much
has changed since then. There are still relatively few public places where
women can go unaccompanied and feel a sense of ease and security. Dance
venues are potentially one of those spaces. As Thomas observes, '[D]ance
has provided women with at least the possibility of self-expression in public
spaces in a culture where women traditionally have been confined to the
private sphere' (Thomas, 1993, p. 81). However, not all dance venues are
perceived as being equally safe, as indicated by the discussion below. The
women to whom I spoke discriminated between the feelings of security
they experienced at set dancing and their relative vulnerability at other
venues, notably disco and line dancing. I think it is also interesting to note
that the topic of 'feeling safe' emerged spontaneously during the discussions. As indicated below, these feelings were generated by the general
ambience, the conventions and rules surrounding dancing, and the content
of the dances themselves.

Both Mary and Margaret touch on some of the sexual elements involved and the freedom to express themselves in a sexual way, however limited, with impunity. Mary talks of the freedom to flirt in a safe environment:

> half the fun in a set is the winking and the nodding and the messin' that goes on which is *total* flirtation . . that's half the fun of it . . but it's all very safe . . you know that there is not going to be someone at the door waiting for you . . . it's very false in a way but it's very safe and it's fun.

I find this statement particularly interesting because it seems to express the way in which flirting in 'normal' circumstances may be enjoyable but is circumscribed because it could be misinterpreted and have undesirable consequences. This is a classic example of the control over women's behaviour in public space. Margaret mentions the opportunity for physical closeness which is not risky because it is part of the content of the dance itself:

> you have the physical contact of being with somebody, holding another person . . a lot of people who don't have physical contact . . it's the only time that they get a chance to 'get a hoult' of somebody (*laughs*) . . it's funny because I've spoken to some people who've tried line dancing . . . but a lot of them would say 'No, I don't think it will take off because the physical contact is missing' . . it's a kind of safe way of still having some physical intimacy without . . the kind of, you know, attachment or whatever.

Here, again, we can note an explicit expression of the ways in which set dancing provides an opportunity for behaviour which might be risky in other circumstances but is made safe because of the context in which it takes place. It is also very tempting but highly speculative at this stage to suggest that this quest for intimacy without responsibility, or at least, over which one has some control, is part of the postmodern sensibility, and that set dancing within this framework is a form of sexual 'grazing' in which women can now participate.

In addition to the sexual elements discussed above, knowledge of, and adherence to, the conventions is seen to give women more control over interaction with any one person. Mary comments: 'it's totally a non-threatening type of interaction . . . I think the fact that you can walk away easily . . the time-limit is almost defined for every interaction . . and . . . everybody knows the rules.'

Margaret contrasts the formal conventions surrounding set dancing with the less clear and hence, more risky, behaviour at disco dancing:

> and another nice thing is that in a set dance it's organised in a sense that you know when you can leave the person . . if you are dancing with

somebody that you don't like, officially at the end of four figures or whatever, that's it .. you can go and say 'thank you very much', .. whereas in a disco situation if you're dancing with someone you don't want to be with, it can go on for ever . . . you're not sure when the point will come when you can leave him.

Anne, a married woman who goes to set-dance classes on her own, comments on the safety of going to the classes as opposed to a night-club: 'you couldn't really go to a night-club by yourself or with another woman friend . . and it's a place to go, and be, and dance . . it's kind of safe'. Kate points to the differences between the disco and the set-dance atmosphere:

I *hated* going to a disco, low lights, loud music, darkness or almost darkness, you couldn't see people, you couldn't have a decent conversation with them and I never really enjoyed that. I preferred set dancing from the point of view that you get a mixture of all ages there, it's much more sociable in that you can talk to somebody and you're not blasted out by the live music .. it's usually a nice, bright, airy and roomy atmosphere.

The women also spoke favourably of set dancing in contrast to disco or line dancing in terms of the 'presentation of self', particularly image and dress. These, being significant markers of sexual attractiveness and availability, are usually subject to strict control. Margaret claims that:

they [people at the disco] were also very conscious of how they look and their image .. set dancing you just don't have time and at the end of an afternoon or an evening set dancing most people look horrendous anyway (*laughs*) and it's a great leveller .. people sort of laugh at themselves and at other people .. 'look at the state of me here!' .. so it's a great way of .. how would I describe it? .. it tears away the superficiality of most dancing . . . when you stink to high heaven, well, there's no problem there .. you're accepted completely.

Orla refers to the fact that neither looks nor age, the two most salient features which men generally take into account when asking women to dance, are important in the set-dance scene:

you're rated on your dancing ability, not your age or your looks .. and I think if someone's an excellent dancer and she's sixty, she'll get asked .. certainly more down around the country .. if you're a good dancer, you're up for every set regardless of what you look like .. I mean it's not a glamour sport .. sweatin' .. a big red face.

Nuala thinks that set dancing is safer and more fun than disco because of the less disturbing nature of the male 'gaze', while simultaneously acknowledging that male surveillance does exist to some extent in set dancing:

> you can have great fun, you're under no pressure . . . whereas if you go to a disco you're certainly under pressure the moment you come in the door because of the context of where you're in . . you're on show, you're prey, literally, from the opposite sex . . you are being eyed up . . obviously it goes on in set dancing but not to the same extent . . at the end you can say, 'Thank you very much and goodbye' . . . you certainly feel safer.

One of Eileen's criticisms of line dancing is that one is the object of both the 'gaze' and of personal remarks:

> and also it seems to me that there are people on the fringes of line dancing they are just there to leer . . in 'Break for the Border' you're in this pit . . and then there's all these people up here and . . I spent a bit of time up there just listenin' to what people were sayin' . . an awful lot of 'pass remarking' going on about the people down there . . people's attributes . . whereas I find that . . set dancing people will get up and do it.

Personal identity construction is also referred to in terms of an opposition between a forced and contrived behaviour and behaving in a more 'normal' way. Nuala, in contrasting disco with set dancing, claims that there is:

> less posing in set dancing than in disco . . the crowd is much nicer . . people are friendlier . . there's less posing . . . and I find that I am that way myself then as a result of it . . I mean I'll go in there and I will behave as I normally behave . . whereas if I was at a night-club I would certainly behave more coy or . . than I would be in set dancing.

Margaret distinguishes between the kinds of people who do set dancing and those who do disco:

> I would have been a great disco-goer as well . . but what I do notice is a difference . . one very obvious difference I noticed was the time I did the weekend workshop in Galway I spent all day doing the set dancing, morning and afternoon, and in the evening I went to a disco and I could really see the contrast, because the morning session was full of people smiling, giggling, screaming, crying out with excitement and then in the evening I was kind of plunged into this room . . this dark room with people . . with serious expressions on their faces not wanting to be seen

to perspire or anything . . I thought it is extremely anti-social . . in fact people were more dancing with themselves than with anybody else.

Frank's (1991) distinction between the 'communicative body' and the 'mirroring body' might approximate Margaret's distinction between the two dance genres. In an attempt to arrive at an analytic model of the body Frank suggests four ideal types of body usage. The two which are pertinent to the discussion here are the 'communicative body' and the 'mirroring body'. Dancing he sees as one model of the 'communicative body'. The medium of activity for the 'mirroring body' is consumption. Frank arrives at his typology of body types by examining the various ways in which bodies deal with four tasks or dimensions of activity; control, desire, relation to others and self-relatedness. It is the 'relation to others' which is of most interest to me in the current context. The 'other-relatedness' for the 'communicative body' is a 'dyadic relation with others who join in the dance and it implies an associatedness which goes beyond one's own body and extends to the body of the other(s)' (Frank, 1991, p. 80). The 'other-relatedness' of the 'mirroring body', on the other hand, is 'open to the exterior world but monadic in its appropriation of that world' (Frank, 1991, p. 61). Frank is careful to stress the 'ideal' nature of his typology, and is aware that dance does not always attain this ideal. It seems to me that when Margaret talks of the disco dancers 'more dancing with themselves' she is describing the narcissism of the consuming 'mirroring body' in contrast to the 'associatedness' of the 'communicative body' in set dancing. The distinctions made by Frank between dyadic and monadic relatedness may also have more general use as a continuum along which to mark various genres and performance contexts in contemporary recreational dance.

It seems to me that there are two discourses emerging from the discussion so far. One is the clearly visible discourse of relative freedom from the constraints on women in public spaces. The other, perhaps less immediately obvious, is that of the 'natural' interlinked with a rural romanticism. I find Simmel's (1950) work on the metropolis helpful in attempting to understand the latter. In his insightful analysis of the qualitative difference between rural and urban sensibilities, Simmel claimed that urban life demanded an attitude of reserve and insensitivity to feeling because of the multiplicity and diversity of stimuli in the metropolis. He characterised the urban personality as being detached and blasé (Simmel, 1950) ('cool' would probably be the contemporary equivalent expression). If we can take it that rurality implies the opposite traits, such as passionate, involved and 'warm', then set dancing provides just that. In this sense, then, we can claim that it symbolises an ideal rural community; not the traditional community of gossip, mutual obligation and 'rural idiocy' but rather one in which all the negative aspects have been obliterated.

The distinction which Simmel (1950) makes between rural and urban could be neatly overlaid on the distinction which the women make between set dancing and other genres; the opposition between the superficiality and consciousness of image, and being accepted as you are, which was mentioned by Margaret, between the posing and coy behaviour, and 'normal' behaviour referred to by Nuala, between the darkness and the nice, bright, airy and roomy atmosphere mentioned by Kate (indeed, the darkness of the city has historically been a constant motif in the construction of rural romanticism, for instance see Williams, 1973), and between the dyadic and monadic relations suggested by Margaret.

COUNTRY DANCING IN THE CITY?

The emergence of a romantic rural discourse is further supported by explicit reference to the country. Indeed, one of the most remarkable features of the discussions, though not on my list of topics, was the way in which associations were made between set dancing and rural Ireland. However, only some of the women made these spontaneous references. Although further work would be necessary to ascertain the strength of such a discourse, I think it is of some consequence that those parts of Ireland, Clare, Kerry and West Cork, in which set dancing had been continuous, were being constructed as a romanticised 'other', the heartland of 'authentic' community and set dancing. The discussion is clearly reminiscent of Williams's (1973) observations on the representation of the country as the repository of 'organic community' and 'authentic' folk culture.

Margaret's reference to the country was in the context of her talking about her initial introduction to, and motivation to take up, set dancing:

> my first experience of set dancing was in Miltown Malbay years ago in 1983 . . I didn't know what set dancing was at the time, I'd never heard of it, seen it or anything . . I remember it was about three o'clock in the morning . . out all night . . we were just on our way back to the caravan and I saw this vision in the street of eight people of various ages and what struck me was there was an old man . . I don't know what age he was, late sixties maybe . . or early seventies, dancing furiously with a *young* one . . with a loose flowing skirt and hair . . a real Irish colleen . . and the two of them were tearing into this *wild furious* dance . . . and I just thought: 'God, it's incredible' . . for me it sort of . . it was some

kind of a symbol of the vitality of the Irish spirit, that's the only way I could describe it ... and I've always thought that that's also the Atlantic Ocean itself is the vitality and the passion of Irish people .. and that lashing of the waves against the rock is just what I see in set dancing.

Here we are in no doubt about the romance of the pursuit! I think a number of motifs are linked to produce a discourse of nature, the merging of the wildness of the dance with the wildness of nature to produce an association between the 'natural', the expressive, and the passionate.

The sense of connection with the rural was also expressed by Anne, who explained her preference for a particular kind of dance by her family's origins in that part of the country where it is popular: 'I just love polkas .. really I do .. I would be drawn to it anyway because I come from west Cork .. my father does .. that's how I feel I belong there.'

Eileen also refers to the authentic set dancing which she has observed down the country and which has acted as an inspiration to her: this was in the context of a discussion of preferences for reel or polka steps, and Eileen spoke of her reasons for preferring the latter:

I love Kerry you know, anything to do with Kerry, I just love .. I have this vision .. I mean the best dancers I ever saw in my life down in Connell's pub in Knocknagree .. and that's my image of them doing polkas down there .. and that's what I want .. they're not actually dancing on the ground, they're dancing on the air .. that's where I want to be.

Later on Eileen is talking about her desire to continue set dancing indefinitely:

I often think it's something I could do for my life .. the granny when I'm still in my zimmer-frame (*general laughter*) .. again to go back to that famous night in Knocknagree, in Danny Connell's .. in the corner of the room .. in the same room with all these people dancing up in the air was a group of what looked like to me .. ninety-year-olds dancing the same dance ... they were doing it at a slower pace and everything but I thought that was wonderful.

Here Eileen is expressing her admiration of those rural communities where a wide range of age groups can socialise together. In our ageist culture women often express regret that they don't have the opportunities to dance which they would have had in their youth and indeed, I think that set dancing provides just such an opportunity and is probably one of the main reasons why it is so popular among women over thirty.

Orla admires what she perceives as a sense of continuity in the country when she is talking about the harmony of dancers who have danced together for years, and feels that this harmony would be unlikely to be achieved in the city:

> it's lovely to see couples . . go down the country like you might see a couple . . they're married or whatever, they've danced together for years and they dance exactly the same . . couples in their sixties now who've gone out dancing together every Saturday night for the last twenty years . . . I mean you wouldn't have that up in Dublin . . the only time I can watch someone dance . . that is just fantastic to watch.

Since the women who spoke so favourably of the country were from the city it could be thought that it would have been easier for them to be involved in a kind of rural romanticism than for people who had their origins in the country and experience of country life. However, this is not necessarily the case, since it is probable that rural women, too, could romanticise rural areas other than the ones in which they were born and reared. I am suggesting this probability because those geographical areas which were singled out for mention – scenic areas of the western seaboard – have a long history of romanticisation both by British colonists in the nineteenth century and subsequently by the culturally dominant classes in the post-independent state (after 1922).

Remarks made by a few of the women who had spoken so highly of set dancing in the country made me realise, though, that there is a disjuncture, if not outright paradox, between the image of set dancing in the country and in the city. These remarks were made in response to a question about their opinion of the kinds of people who do set dancing. This was a much less flattering representation. Margaret, who had spoken earlier about her initial introduction to set dancing in Miltown, answered the question thus:

> my first impressions always at any of these workshops is 'Oh, my God, will you look at this lot!' (*laughs*) . . I remember my first workshop in Galway and I looked around the room and there was little old grannies in Aran cardigans . . and they were all practising the steps and I thought 'This is sad . . oh my God' . . all the square people of Ireland, you know . . were kind of gathered together and I just thought 'no, thank you' . . but the minute you get into doing the activity, that changes completely . . I mean it looks from the outside total boredom . . but once you actually get involved in the actual doing of it . . you know . . it changes.

This, in my view, is interesting because firstly, the image has changed, at least the female one, from the real Irish colleen to 'little old grannies in aran cardigans' from a representation which connotes beauty and freedom to one which has connotations of being 'square', drab and out of date. And secondly, there is a perceived tension between the image and the reality of the dancing itself, as if one loves the dancing but would be reluctant to be associated with the stereotype of the people who do it.

Margaret continues on in a similar vein to give even more damning detail of her image of the set-dance community, which includes:

> the female national teacher .. men who may be .. conservative .. no-where else to go .. didn't make it at the discos (*laughs*) ... people who are separated are coming back in to meet people again .. an air of need or loneliness sometimes.

Here again, there is a reluctance to be associated with such a conservative group and the tension emerges between her own self-image and her image of her dance associates:

> I look at my friends and we're doing it but we're really not that type .. and yet if they are doing it they are becoming set-dancing types .. but maybe they feel that they don't want to identify themselves with the old image that set dancing is about .. sometimes I go to *céilís* and I'm totally depressed .. I look at a roomful of post-menopausal women, single women .. the blouse is buttoned up around their head .. and the long skirt and the brown tights and I go 'Oh, God, is this going to be me?' and I start panicking.

However, she finally reassures herself by allowing for the fact that different kinds of groups are involved in set dancing:

> and then, on other occasions you go and there's a younger set of people or whatever .. or younger at heart .. you don't get that feeling .. but I suppose there's a mix of people doing set dancing .. people who have always done it and it's been a tradition.

Eileen makes a similar observation to Margaret regarding the tensions between her image of the stereotypical people who do set dancing and her own involvement in it:

> the first night I went into the Ierne it caused me all sorts of 'God, I'm not going to the Ierne [*tone of mock incredulity*]' (*general laughter*) and even into the Merchant [*pub popular with set dancers*] .. I would never have gone into the Merchant in a fit before last year .. even the bloody mural on the outside of the Merchant, people with skirts on down to here .. you look at the mural .. talk about an ancient stereotype of set

dancing . . . women in long skirts down to their toes . . and get inside and it's totally different.

Eileen goes on to relate how her teenage daughter thinks that set dancing is 'out of the Ark' and associates it with country people:

sometimes I'd be tryin' to practise my steps at home on the floor [*and her daughter would say*] 'Jesus, she's off again' . . she [*daughter*] was in Mayo last weekend . . thinks it's the ends of the earth . . ten-year-old hairstyles and ten-year-old clothes . . that's her perception of it, you know . . that would have been my perception.

Though it is a question worth raising, it is impossible to assess if the negative stereotypes above are related to the transference of the dance from a rural to an urban location: in other words, a breakdown of the romanticised 'other'. Certainly, some of the images conveyed – those of being dated, conservative, 'square', could be quite easily associated with rurality. However, the country could hardly be seen to have a monopoly of post-menopausal women and lonely men! The above extracts do clearly express, though, a definite reflexivity about personal-identity construction and the final triumph of the enjoyment of the activity of dancing over the negative images associated with it.

CONCLUSIONS

In contemporary society, sociologists claim, there is a tendency for the body to become increasingly central to the modern person's sense of self-identity (for example, see Falk, 1994; Featherstone *et al.*, 1991; Giddens, 1991; Shilling, 1993). There are also, in recent years, the increased efforts of women to liberate their bodies from the controls and constraints of patriarchal institutions and practices. Dancing can be seen as playing an important role in both agendas. For the women to whom I spoke the enjoyment of the activity itself is dependent on the provision of a safe environment, a space in which they can feel free to indulge in this form of bodily expression. Set dancing provides such a space. It does so in at least two ways. It enables them to exercise more control over social interaction with men than in other dance situations, and possibly in most other public circumstances. This relative freedom is achieved through the avoidance of potentially unpleasant encounters due to the rules and etiquette involved, the relative absence of male surveillance and relative choice in 'the presentation of self'. Since traditional dance is commonly believed to maintain traditional, i.e. patriarchal gender relations (see Hanna, 1988 and Frank, 1991) it is interesting to note the ways in which it can operate in a contrary direction. One could see this as an instance of the possible ways in which cultural forms can change and be adapted to different meanings and purposes over time and in keeping with the interests of the groups involved.

Set dancing also provides women with the opportunity for communication and physical contact with people in what they perceive to be an inclusive and friendly environment. In many ways this community could be likened to an idealised rural community which is contrasted favourably with other dance communities. The members of this community are perceived to be warm, natural and engaging as opposed to 'cool', coy and blasé. And germane to its attractiveness is its temporary and voluntary nature. It offers the best of both worlds in that this 'rural space' in the city provides women with an opportunity for dancing which would not otherwise be available to them and does not demand of them the continuous duties and obligations attached to being members of a rural community based on local residence. Perhaps there is a little irony in the fact that a dance form which is associated with tradition and rurality is a source of pleasure, freedom and individual expression for women in the city in conditions of high modernity.

APPENDIX

THE LANCERS

5th Figure   Reel – 192 bars

Opening Position: All four couples join hands in front and face anti-clockwise around the circle, gents on the inside.

A LEAD	All four couples dance anti-clockwise around until	
AROUND	back in original places.	
	During the last two bars each couple changes to the standard position by the gent turning the lady clockwise under both arms.	8 bars

B *SWING*	All four couples swing in place.	8 bars

C *FIGURE*   (a) *CHAIN & LINE UP:* Starting with a right hand to their own partners ladies and gents chain around clockwise and anti-clockwise respectively. Half-way around partners meet each other and swing once. The chain is then continued to bring all dancers back to their original places. They do not form couples again, but line up as follows:

LINE UP: On the first occasion the line forms up behind 1st tops lady, facing out of the set in the direction of 1st tops position. As each couple gets into place in the line each lady should be in front of her partner. (see page 84)

The line forms in the following order: The leading couple, the couple to the left of the leading couple, the couple to the right of the leading couple, and the couple opposite the leading couple, with each lady in front of her partner.   16 bars

(b) *SIDE STEP:* The line splits. Gents step sideways to the left and ladies sideways to the right, (4 bars). The lines then return in opposite directions, passing through each other to the opposite sides, and turn to face each other, (4 bars). (see page 84)   8 bars

(c) *ADVANCE & RETIRE:* Lines join hands and advance and retire twice.   8 bars

(d) *DANCE TO PLACE & SWING:* Each dancer dances back to their original place in four bars and then couples join up and swing in place for four bars. i.e. dancers at the end of the lines dance towards each other and meet in the centre. In the case of the other two couple the lady and gent that are in their correct places simply dance in place, and their partners dance across to them. (see page 84)   8 bars

D *FIGURE*	Repeat C, the line forming behind 2ND TOPS.	40 bars
E *FIGURE*	Repeat C, the line forming behind 1ST SIDES.	40 bars
F *FIGURE*	Repeat C, the line forming behind 2ND SIDES.	40 bars
G *HOUSE*	All four couples dance house around, doubling the last two bars.	8 bars

THE CALEDONIAN

5th Figure   Reel − 256 bars

Opening Position: All dancers face to centre, joining hands in a circle.

A *START*	(a) *CIRCLE:* Advance and retire twice.	8 bars
	(b) *HOME:* All four couples dance around at home.	8 bars
B *FIGURE*	(a) *HOUSE & HOME:* TOP COUPLES dance around the house inside (8 bars), and then dance around at home, (8 bars).	16 bars
	(b) *SLIDE & CHANGE PARTNERS:* TOP COUPLES advance and retire once (4 bars); then the couples seperate and the gents dances in an anti-clockwise direction around each other to pick up the side ladies to their left (4 bars). The side ladies dance on the spot for the last 4 bars.	8 bars
	(c) *HOUSE & HOME:* TOP GENTS and their new partners dance around the house inside (8 bars), starting and finishing at their new partners position, and then dance around at home, (8 bars).	16 bars
	(d) *SLIDE & CHANGE PARTNERS:* TOP GENTS and their new partners repeat (b). The gents move one place around again to pick up the opposite top ladies.	8 bars
	(e) *HOUSE & HOME:* TOP GENTS and their new partners repeat (c).	16 bars
	(f) *SLIDE & CHANGE PARTNERS:* TOP GENTS and their new partners repeat (b). The gents move one place around again to pick up the side ladies.	8 bars
	(g) *HOUSE & HOME:* TOP GENTS and their new partners repeat (c).	16 bars
	(h) *SLIDE & CHANGE PARTNERS:* TOP GENTS and their new partners repeat (b). The gents move one place around again to pick up their original partners.	8 bars
	(i) *HOUSE:* TOP COUPLES dance around the house inside.	8 bars
C *MIDDLE*	(a) *SLIDE:* ALL four couples advance to centre and retire once.	4 bars
	(b) *HOME:* SIDE COUPLES dance around at home.	4 bars
D *FIGURE*	SIDE COUPLES repeat B	104 bars

E *FINISH*   (a) *SLIDE:* All four couples advance to centre and re-   4 bars
tire once.

(b) *HOME:* All four couples dance around at home.   4 bars

(c) *HOUSE:* All four couples dance house around.   8 bars

Fifth figures of the Lancers and the Caledonian sets reproduced with kind permission from Terry Moylan, *Irish Dances*, 2nd edn (Dublin: Na Píobairí Uilleann, 1985).

NOTES

1. The lead dancers in the first run of *Riverdance: The Show*.
2. The list of topics on which the discussion here is based includes: patterns and frequency of dancing, the pleasures of dancing, favourite dances and music, conventions and behaviours relating to dancing.
3. In the interests of anonymity I have not used real names.
4. In the extracts two dots (. .) means a pause, three dots (. . .) means non-sequential commentary.

REFERENCES

F. Boas (ed.), *The Function of Dance in Human Society* (New York: Dance Horizons, 1972).

H. Brennan, 'Reinventing Tradition: the boundaries of Irish dance', *History Ireland* (Summer 1994), pp. 22–4.

M. Douglas, *Natural Symbols: Explorations in Cosmology* (London: Cresset Press, 1976).

P. Falk, *The Consuming Body* (London: Sage, 1994).

M. Featherstone, M. Hepworth and B. S. Turner (eds), *The Body: Social Process and Cultural Theory* (London: Sage, 1991).

A. W. Frank (1991), 'For a Sociology of the Body: An Analytic Review' in M. Featherstone *et al.*, *Social Process and Cultural Theory* (London: Sage, 1991), pp. 36–103.

A. Giddens, *Modernity and Self-Identity: Self and Society in the Late Modern Age* (Cambridge: Polity Press, 1991).

J. L. Hanna, *Dance, Sex and Gender* (Chicago: University of Chicago Press, 1988).

R. Lange, *The Nature of Dance* (London: MacDonald & Evans, 1975).

S. Lash and J. Urry, *Economies of Signs and Space* (London: Sage, 1994).

A. McRobbie, 'Shut up and Dance: Youth Culture and Changing Modes of Femininity', *Cultural Studies*, 7, 3 (1993), pp. 406–26.

T. Moylan (ed.), *Irish Dances*, 2nd edn (Dublin: Na Píobairí Uilleann, 1985).

A. R. Radcliffe-Brown, *The Andaman Islanders* (New York: Free Press, 1964).

F. Rust, *Dance in Society* (London: Routledge & Kegan Paul, 1969).

C. Shilling, *The Body and Social Theory* (London: Sage, 1993).

G. Simmel, 'The Metropolis and Mental Life' in K. H. Wolff (ed.), *The Sociology of Georg Simmel* (New York: Free Press, 1950).

H. Thomas, 'An-other Voice: Young Women Dancing and Talking' in H. Thomas (ed.), *Dance, Gender and Culture* (London: Macmillan, 1993), pp. 69–93.

H. Thomas, *Dance, Modernity and Culture: Explorations in the Sociology of Dance* (London: Routledge, 1995).

M. Tubridy, 'The Set Dancing Revival', *Ceol na hÉireann, Píobairí Uileann*, 2 (1994), pp. 23–34.

V. Turner, *Dramas, Fields, and Metaphors: Symbolic Action in Human Society* (Ithaca, NY: Cornell University Press, 1974).

J. Urry (1995), *Consuming Places* (London: Routledge, 1995).

R. Williams, *The Country and the City* (London: Chatto & Windus, 1973).

Part III
Border Country

10 Nazism and the Call of the Jitterbug

Les Back

The music of my race is something more than the 'American idiom'. It is the result of our transplantation to American soil, and was our reaction in the plantation days to the tyranny we endured. What we could not say openly we expressed in music, and what we know as 'jazz' is something more than just dance music. When we dance it is not a mere diversion or social accomplishment. It expresses our personality, and, right down in us, our souls react to the elemental but eternal rhythm, and the dance is timeless and unhampered by any lineal form.

Duke Ellington

Far from Harlem, from Chicago, from New Orleans, uninformed and naive, we served the sacrament that verily knows no frontiers . . . I can see them in their longish skirts, dancing and 'dipping' in the taverns of remote villages, with one fan always standing guard at the door, on the lookout for the German police. When a *Schupo* appeared over the horizon, a signal was given, and all the *krystýnky* and their boyfriends, the 'dippers', would scurry to sit down to glasses of green soda-pop, listening piously to the Viennese waltz that the band had smoothly swung into. When the danger had passed, everyone jumped up again, the Kansas riffs exploded, and it was swing time once again.

Josef Skvorecky

In 1931 Duke Ellington published an article – his first – in the pages of a British dance-band magazine called *Rhythm*. He emphasised that the culture of jazz is infused with experience of dislocation and oppression, but he also stressed the timeless non-lineal nature of jazz dance. He commended his British readers for their appreciation of his music but ended his first excursion in print with a caution: 'Remember that your most important asset is your rhythm' (Ellington, 1931, p. 22). By the 1930s and 1940s European dance-halls were no longer the exclusive province of the waltz and the foxtrot. A generation of young Europeans had assimilated the sounds, movements and sensibilities of swing. Jazz – a music born out of what Ellington called the 'white heat of our sorrows' (*ibid.*, p. 21)

– provided a resource for self-expression and dissent amongst young Europeans both inside Nazi Germany and elsewhere in Europe. It was the age of jazz, the jitterbug and generic fascism. Nazi propagandists found jazz simultaneously both threatening and useful. Jitterbugging youngsters drawn to the likes of Benny Goodman, Count Basie, Nat Gonella, Django Reinhardt and Duke Ellington became the focus of an anxiety about preserving the racial and national spirit. Swing could also be represented in propaganda as the exemplary symbol of decadent non-Aryan *Entartete Musik* – part-African, part-Jew, part-Gypsy – the mongrel creation of the American metropolis. Concerns about the politics of swing were not simply confined to the Reich. Jazz had established itself in Britain long before the outbreak of World War Two. In 1919 the Original Dixieland Jazz Band, a white ensemble from New Orleans led by Nick La Rocca, opened the Hammersmith Palais de Danse, attracting 5,800 dancers on its opening night (Goddard, 1979). Black dances like the Charleston and the Black Bottom had been introduced to Europe in large part through the fame of Josephine Baker, who performed at the *Folies Bergère* in Paris from the mid-1920s (Emery, 1988). From 1942 the presence of American GIs on British soil, some of whom were black, accelerated the introduction of black dance, posing a serious moral dilemma for the military and the political elite. There were sincere concerns about the import of the 'American race problem' and even antipathy towards the bigotry of white southerners. Yet the spectre of interracial jitterbugging – black soldiers dancing with white English women – revealed uncomfortable similarities between Jim Crow, John Bull and the racial phobias of Nazism. In what follows I want to look at the ways in which swing made these racial harmonies audible. At the same time I examine how the jazz subcultures that took hold in Europe registered dissonance within the demesne of race and culture.

In America swing had provided the context for the first racially-integrated dance-halls. For black people the opportunities for public dancing were few and confined to the after-hours 'jook houses', private parties and the dance-halls that served the black community. The Lindy Hop was innovated by the black dancer George 'Shorty' Snowden in 1928 during a dance marathon in New York. Snowden had developed a breakaway technique which involved separating, allowing for individual improvisation while holding on to one's partner with one hand. He named the step, which was danced to a 4/4 syncopated beat, after Charles Lindbergh's successful transatlantic flight. In the 1930s Lindbergh was an admirer of the Nazis. Ironically, the Reich would later brand the new step named after him degenerate and racially corrosive.

The Savoy Ballroom on Lennox Avenue in Harlem provided the context where these techniques were practised and developed (Sterns and Sterns, 1968). The dances innovated in 'cats' corner' at the Savoy Ballroom were not simply a response to the music of the time. The movement of the dancers affected and inspired the musicians on the bandstand. Complex forms of call and response developed, giving the interrelationship between music and dance an organic and antiphonic quality. The Savoy in Harlem provided one of the first contexts where dancers could enjoy an open dance-floor in front of large audiences. Swing brought black dance out in to the public domain in unprecedented ways (Hazard-Gordon, 1990).

The Savoy Ballroom was racially integrated and white dancers learned their steps – sometimes with black partners – on the dance-floor (Stowe, 1994; Malcolm X, 1968). As the dance spread to the white mainstream a new name was coined for it – the Jitterbug. The word originates in the 'jive talk' of swing musicians. It was coined by Harry 'Father' White who played in the White Brothers Orchestra and also in Duke Ellington's band. The story goes that before White took a solo he would step into the wings to take a snort of what he called 'jitter sauce'. He also had a jive name for all of his friends who he referred to as 'my bug'. The story goes that one day, while playing with the Ellington band, someone in the band hid his bottle. Dry-mouthed, 'Father' White returned to the spotlight and shouted 'Whoinhell took my jitterbug?' (Tucker, 1993, p. 467). Cab Calloway identi-fied himself with the emerging swing counterculture with his 'Song of the Jitterbug' (1935), which celebrated the dance and its connections.

The 'white jitterbugs' posed a significant moral panic. By the late 1930s some localities in the American Midwest banned the dance, prohibiting contact to be broken beyond arm's length on the dance-floor. But the hedon-ism of the Jitterbugs also offended some swing partisans, who saw the dance culture as shallow in terms of its musical appreciation. The impulse that drew young whites to the ghetto dance-halls were complex. Malcom X, in his autobiography, describes the impulse for these encounters as a combination of white voyeurism and sexual adventure (Malcolm X, 1968; Backstein, 1995; see also Hughes, 1958). David Stowe, in his excellent study of swing in 'New Deal' America, concludes:

> For the moralists, jitterbugs combined two unsavoury tendencies in American culture: the hedonism and uninhibited exhibitionism of African-American culture coupled with the mindless 'mass man' behaviour symp-tomatic of and conducive to totalitarian societies. 'Bugs' thereby conflated a racial and a political threat. (Stowe, 1994, p. 30)

Ironically, it was precisely the expressive nature of swing dancing that fed its allure and attractiveness to young people living under the totalitarian

universe of Nazism. The rhythms of Nazism insisted on a dif-
~at.

THE CHOREOGRAPHY OF NAZISM

Adolf Hitler did not and could not dance. He frowned on social dancing,
particularly when it involved the women that he took into his jealous and
suspicious guardianship. Hans Peter Bleuel, in his insightful study of sex
and society in Nazi Germany, described one such relationship. It involved
his niece, Geli Raubal. Geli enjoyed dances but Hitler only permitted her
to attend under the surveillance of his cronies and with a curfew. Her
uncle's strict rules and repressed desires created tension between them.
These longings were never realised as Hitler presented himself during the
pre-war years as being married to the German people and, by implication,
to all German women. Bleuel comments on the erotics of Hitler's appeal
to women and describes the response of German women to Hitler's call
for devotion and domination as almost orgasmic. This union, however,
proved fatal for Geli. After a quarrel with the Führer, the content of which
is not known, Geli shot and killed herself. Eva Braun, the woman who
Hitler eventually married on 29 April 1945 in his Berlin bunker, was also
a keen dancer. But like her predecessor, Eva lived in 'constant dread lest
he [Hitler] learn of the gay soirées in which she indulged during his
frequent absences, innocent but with an aching conscience' (Bleuel, 1973,
p. 50). Why was Hitler suspicious of Geil and Eva's penchant for a dance-
floor embrace?

It is my feeling that these private anxieties point to a larger unease
within the Nazi vision of the Aryan woman – the womb of the nation –
and her place within society. During the Third Reich dance took its place
within the pageant of Aryan purity. It became a public, mass activity in
which the German Girls' League would be put through their paces in front
of huge audiences. Dance was not a matter of individual pleasure, or
expression, but a collective entertainment and a demonstration of the national spirit and will. Events like the opening-night spectacle of the 1936
Berlin Olympic Games were staged by the high priestess of German dance
– Mary Wigman. The piece, entitled *Olympic Youth*, was conceived in
collaboration with Gret Palucca, Harald Kreutzberg and Carl Orff and
presented a national community unified through its allegiance to Hitler
(Manning, 1987). Some German dancers found this spectacle of mass ad-
oration a step too far. Martha Graham, for example, was asked to perform
but she refused. The Olympics, its festivals and symbolism provided a

international stage to advertise and entrench the regime (Mandell, 1987). Through such spectacles a model of Aryan masculinity and femininity could be exhibited. The mass dance of the Third Reich attempted to present an image of Aryan Germans into which the individual could project him or herself. These mass forms of dancing were not achieved through the invention of a new Nazi aesthetic of the body and movement; rather, the 'Nazification of art' (Taylor and van der Will, 1990) involved the recombination of German dance.

Unlike other arts forms the majority of leading dancers and choreographers – including those who were exponents of modernism – remained in Germany after Hitler took power in 1933. There were some notable exceptions. Martin Gleisner, who was Jewish, escaped to Holland and Kurt Jooss, who had left-wing affiliations, fled to Dartington Hall in England (Preston-Dunlop, 1989). While the *Reichskulturkammer* (*RKK*) attacked modernism in art and painting, the leading exponents German dance were accommodated within the new regime. Susan Manning has commented that twice as many leading dancers remained in Germany and collaborated with the National Socialists as did not (Manning, 1995, p. 175). This, she argues, disrupts the widely-held belief that Nazism cut short the development of modernism within Germany. The reasons why figures like Rudolph Laban and Mary Wigman remained and worked with the Third Reich are complex. While some key figures became exponents of Nazi dance, in the main modernist or expressionist dance under Hitler occupied an ambiguous position.

During the Weimar period expressionist dance, or *Austdruckstanz*, drew its followers from amateur students who were devoted to *Tanz-Gymnastik* (dance gymnastics). Dance gymnastics was extremely popular during this period and comparable in its mass appeal to aerobics in Europe and the United States during the 1980s (Manning, 1995). Within *Austdruckstanz* Laban blurred the distinction between professional and amateur dance and developed improvisational techniques which enabled new forms of mass participation. This combination provided the members and audiences for Laban's movement choirs (*Bewegungschor*), which were organised through a unique notation system entitled Labanotation or Kinetography. During the 1920s movement choirs were established in association with unions, political parties and religious organisations within a diversity of interests. Although the expressionist movement embraces mysticism and anti-rationalism, later to be exploited by the Nazis, from its inception the form was not explicitly connected with a particular ideological position. For example, expressionism was critical of the regulated nature of ballet and its internalised discipline. Equally, new German dance challenged the distinction between professional and amateur, performer and audience. Laban's dream was to emphasise community through dance and to establish movement activity at the centre of the life of every citizen, regardless of class, gender or age group.

Initially, the new regime seemed to express compatible aims. Laban was the Director of Dance and Movement for the Prussian State Theatres in Berlin and he immediately became an employee of the Nazis as Hitler took power. However, as Valerie Preston-Dunlop points out, his relationship with the fascists was ambiguous and complex. Laban found little in the ideologies of Nazism attractive, he had Jewish friends and was in a relationship with a Jewish girlfriend (Preston-Dunlop, 1989). He was a Rosicrucianist, a sect which emphasised a culturally eclectic spiritualism and promoted personal growth along with an ethos of not judging others. Within this world-view it is understandable that he naively thought it possible to serve his ideals within the regime (Preston-Dunlop, personal communication). However, tension became apparent between his vision of expressionist dance and the *Volkisch* Nazi dictates on movement culture. Dance became almost solely a female activity as the male membership of the movement choirs declined. Mass dance performance became the context in which the Aryan ideals of womanhood were represented and celebrated. Through the naked Venus in galas like the 'Night of the Nymphs', the athletic heroine in the Festival of the Amazons and the wholesome peasant-mother of community festivals: the gendered archetypes of Nazism were choreographed and set in motion.

Men's involvement in dance was relegated to folk dancing. Directives came from the *Fachschaft Taz* (Dance Department) of the *Reichstheaterkammer* (RTK), espousing and encouraging particular dances. They invented new Aryan steps and aimed to eliminate all non-Aryan and 'degenerate' influences (Preston-Dunlop, 1989, p. 5). Dance schools had to comply with these directives if they were to stay open. Gymnastic components of *Tanz-Gymnastik* were emphasised at the expense of Laban's commitment to self-expression. Under these circumstances it proved ultimately impossible for Laban to continue his work. He was investigated and offered an ultimatum to join the party or resign. He refused, and after two years in the wilderness he eventually fled from Germany to Paris and ultimately to England to join Kurt Jooss at Dartington Hall.

Mary Wigman, a Laban apprentice and the most prestigious German dancer of the period, also felt that Nazism offered a possibility to extend her artifice. Like Laban, she was ultimately to fall from favour. Wigman is an interesting and enigmatic figure precisely because Nazism initially appealed to her ideas about expressing German nature through movement.

Hedwig Müller (1987) argues that in order to understand Wigman's reaction to the Hitler it is necessary to locate her philosophy of dance within a wider intellectual context. Wigman adored Goethe, and she saw herself on a Faustian quest for truth and knowledge. She also was influenced by the ideas of Nietzsche, particularly the notion of becoming a spiritual and philosophical being. Through her dance she embraced spirituality and irrationalism as part of a collective tradition of national consciousness:

> This struggle turns on the essence of existence, of man and his fate, on the eternal and the transitory. This struggle opened up the path to the primeval source of existence . . . . Because this dance had the courage to confess to life, to life as the eternal mystique of weaving and working, because this dance searched for God and wrestled with the demon, because it gave form to the old Faustian desire for redemption as the ultimate unity of existence – because of all this, it is a German dance. (quoted in Müller, 1987, p. 66)

It is not surprising that Wigman was fascinated with Hitler's charismatic and demonic persona. In many ways she identified with the Faustian quest to realise his vision of a new German Reich.

She was disgusted by the anti-Semitism that raged in 1933. The bookburning and violence she saw as a result of baser instincts being unlocked in revolutionary times. Like Laban she had Jewish friends and students and fought to defend them. But the emphasis on individualism and selfexpression within new German dance came into direct conflict within the Nazi imperative of mass control. The Nazis wanted dance to be a diversion from – not a confrontation with – experience and emotions within everyday life. Ultimately, artists like Wigman were caught between the desire to further their art and the necessities of placating their political overseers. The result was that German dance was reduced to the choreography of obedience and submission: 'Choric dance no longer served to promote Gemeinschaft, community, but Volkgemeinschaft, the fascist community based on the spirit of the German Volk' (Manning, 1987, p. 94). Wigman became disillusion and marginalised and it was only her deep-felt love for Germany that prevented her from leaving.

While the dancers and choreographers who stayed were certainly complicit with the Nazification of German dance they were not always willing collaborators. Geobbels's insistence on submission, escape and entertainment came into direct conflict with the philosophy of self-actualisation through dance which was at the core of the modernist movement. The vision of inclusive community within *Ausdruckstanz* and movement choirs was lost in its vapid Nazi counterpart. The artifice of Nazism was its ability to ensure that politics was collapsed into popular aesthetics (Benjamin, 1968). Through its preoccupation with organising people within rows and circles these mass dances enforced a political as well as a physical line. Nazism produced an image of the German *Volk* into which individuality could be dissolved and where human conscience could be lost in the stencilled order of mass kinematics.

As the Nazification of German culture reached its height physical exercise took on a kind of messianic fervour. Nazi dance organised its participants within a geometric discipline: 'It place[d] a grid over the mass of bodies, which both arranged individuals and separate[d] them from one another. Clear lines confine[d] them to their places and prevented them from escaping' (Servos, 1990, p. 64). Within the starkly-gendered universe of Nazi aesthetics women were given ballet and folk dancing, while men were assigned to the marching ground. The spectacular rituals of mass dancing and the display of storm-troopers marching in perfect cohorts through the Brandenburg Gate anchored Nazism in the rhythm of the body. Through these choreographed rituals identities of race and gender were both embodied and publicly worshipped, producing a kind of racial narcissism. Bleuel concluded that in this climate personal awareness, so much at the centre of the expressionist dance of the likes of Laban and Wigman, was effaced by national anaesthesia (Bleuel, 1973, p. 92). These demonstrations were Hitler's rejoinder and stood as an answer to the very different rhythms that occupied the metropolitan night-clubs, where his *Volkish* reverie was less secure. The mute call of black culture – whether practised by white or black musicians and dancers – was answered in Germany with unexpected consequences.

'NEGRO TRIBES DO NOT MARCH': GERMAN YOUTH AND SWING SUBCULTURE

For the propagandists, jazz, or more correctly the big-band dance genre, swing, stood in contrast to the wholesome Aryan idyll. Swing and the Jitterbug were the 'mongrel creation' of the American city, the mark of a modern civilisation in the advanced stages of cultural decline. In contrast, the rural folk dancing and Nazi festivals were presented as the mark of national purpose, cultural health and racial authenticity. The Nazis filtered out the expressive elements of modernist German dance but swing offered a compensatory resource to young Germans. I want to suggest here that there is an arguable connection between Rudolph Laban and Duke Ellington. This is made less tenuous by the work of black dancers like Katherine

Dunham and Talley Beatty, who combined both modern dance influenced by Laban with the musical scores of jazz (Haskins, 1990). In both cases dance provides, in Mary Wigman's words, a means of 'perfecting the dance personality as an individual; and on the other hand, blending this individuality with an ensemble' (quoted in Manning, 1987, pp. 89–90). Here I am not suggesting any simple correspondence between these forms. Laban, in his piece *The Night*, performed in 1927, utilised a caricature of jazz to form the sonic backdrop to his representation of the depravities of city life (Laban, 1975). The sensibilities of the piece were not very far from the image of jazz in the big city so deftly utilised by the Nazi propagandists. Swing subculture, unlike the institutionalised forms of expressionist dance, was altogether more difficult to regulate and control. What was lost in the Nazification of *Ausdruckstanz* was nurtured and developed in the dance-halls, where the saxophone and syncopation reigned supreme.

Nazi musicologists attacked jazz and justified their opposition to it by arguing that its rhythm was unsuitable. They complained that, unlike Germans, 'Negro tribes do not march' (Kater, 1992, p. 31). This was also coupled with an attempt to show that jazz was the product of an abominable collaboration between 'Negroes' and 'Jews' with racially corrosive implications for Aryan Germans. The Nazi assault on jazz was not centralised and absolute. Geobbels himself was inconsistent on the matter. He condemned the degeneracy of jazz but he paid little attention to it. Jazz subcultures in Nazi Germany were consequently subject to cycles of persecution and harassment followed by periods where the regime was dismissive of their significance. While characterising jazz as another form of 'degenerate culture' the Nazi propagandists also attempted to develop their own saccharine form of swing.

By the middle of 1937 new forms of dancing inspired by the 'Lindy Hop' had been introduced into Germany and elsewhere in Europe through the popularity of Hollywood films such as *Broadway Melody* and *Born to Dance*. Through their newspaper the *Black Corp*, the Nazi military elite offered the party line on the dance. The article used a picture of a black Lindy-Hopper as evidence of the folly of America's flawed attempts at racial democracy: 'On the one hand the equality of all men; on the other, the Lindy Hop – a mixture of cannibalistic abdominal contortions and obscenity. Such a reckoning simply does not balance' (quoted in Crease, 1995, p. 211).

The RKT social-dance instructors set about providing an alternative to the 'foreign dances'. They planned to expunge the 'Nigger' [*sic*] and 'Jewish'-inspired foxtrot, Charleston and Lindy Hop, which were seen to be connected with lurid expressions of sexuality. The RKT revived long-outdated

German dance forms that 'stressed the desired communal animus at the expense of individuality and eroticism' (Kater, 1992, p. 102). Through organisations like the Hitler Youth state-sponsored dances became the party sanction version of youth culture. These wholesome Aryan capers included the *Deutschländer* – predictably performed in groups – and the *Marsch,* which was performed in pairs. Added to these were the staple polka, waltz and a more wooden version of the foxtrot entitled the *Marsch-foxtrot.* These steps were danced to the accompaniment of the mandolin, zither, harmonica and recorder. This vapid Nazi dance did little to turn young Germans away from swing. Local dance divisions of the RTK in Gau Essen and Düsseldorf circulated ordinances that banned the jitterbug. Other areas like Osnabrück and the Ruhr Valley later followed this example. Ultimately, state and party agencies including the Weirmacht, RAD, SS, Deutsche Arbeitsfront (DAF), the Nazi students' organisations and ultimately the Hitler Youth, joined the condemnation of swing dancing (Kater, 1992, p. 104). All of this condemnation fuelled the attraction of the jitterbug to nonconformist youth.

Swing was particularly popular in the city of Hamburg. This Hanseatic metropolis was a port town with a long history of cosmopolitanism. The participants in the jazz scene were often drawn from wealthy and middle-class homes, some of whom had travelled abroad with their parents. The swings were Anglophiles; they utilised English rather than German as their prestigious vernacular. They would greet each other on the street with the phrase 'Swing high!' or 'Hallo Old Swing Boy', and they took up nicknames drawn from American films. Swing style for men took the form of a caricature of the 'English spiv' and included sports jackets, crêpe-soled shoes, extravagant scarves, 'Anthony Eden' hats, an umbrella on the arm regardless of the weather, a dress-shirt button worn in the buttonhole, often with a jewelled stone. Women styled their hair long, shaved their eyebrows and pencilled them, dressed in flowing, luxurious gowns, wore lipstick and lacquered their nails.

The swings were scrutinised by the Hitler Youth who compiled 'ethnographic' reports on their un-Aryan behaviour and sexual degeneracy. One such account on a swing festival in Hamburg in February 1940 attended by 500–600 young people reveals the considerations of these youth spies:

> The dance music was all English and American. Only swing dancing and jitterbugging took place . . . . The dancers were an appalling sight. None of the couples danced normally; there was only swing of the worst sort. Sometimes two boys danced with one girl; sometimes several couples formed a circle, linking arms and jumping, slapping hands, even

rubbing the backs of their heads together; and then, bent double, with the top half of the body hanging down loosely, long hair flopping into the face ... when the band played the rumba, the dancers went into wild ecstasy. They all leaped around and joined in the chorus of broken English. The band played wilder and wilder items; none of the players were sitting down any longer, they all 'jitterbugged' on stage like wild creatures. (quoted in Peukert, 1989, p. 166)

The introduction of Hollywood styles of feminine beauty were viewed as particularly abhorrent by the Nazis and posed a serious challenge to the femininities associated with Nazi ideology and the state youth organisations. The body became the site for the expression of these gendered styles. Young women wore their hair long and flowing and openly rejected the homespun braids and German-style rolls. Equally, for young men their urban style challenged the dominant uniform of Nazi masculinity which combined the Aryan warrior hero with images of the responsible peasant patriarch.

In the midst of this hedonistic dance culture there was an important challenge to what Bleuel referred to as the 'edifice of tyranny by wholesome popular sentiment' (Bleuel, 1973, p. 245). This revolt was not just around style but through these 'forbidden steps' focused on issues of sex and sexuality. While the Nazis attacked bourgeois prudishness they were equally appalled by the sexual permissiveness of the swings. The police explained their conduct as the result of 'sexual license stimulated by dancing to highly syncopated music' (Bleuel, 1973, p. 243). By the early 1940s stories of dance-hall decadence and orgies of group sex were being circulated in reports composed by the authorities. The official statistics recorded a dramatic increase in juvenile delinquency, with more than twice as many cases in 1941 recorded than before the outbreak of war. Detlev Perkert concludes:

They carried over features of the music, and their response to it, into their everyday behaviour. Relaxed surrender to the rhythms; spontaneous bodily movements instead of coached dance-steps; unexpected discords instead of conventional harmonies – all these were expressive of a loose, easy-going attitude to life in general and a desire to escape from the rigid demands of social order, school discipline, the paramilitary drill of the Hitler Youth, the 'keenness' of Nazi officials and the ever-present call of duty. Their aim was to spurn the duties laid down by those in authority, to throw off inhibitions of behaviour, and to defy sexual taboos. (Peukert, 1989, pp. 202–3)

The swing subculture was not a self-consciously radical movement, despite the vicious suppression meted out to them by the Gestapo and the Hitler Youth. It was estimated that from 1942 to 1944, 75 Swing youths were sent to concentration camps by the SS, who classified them as political prisoners. For many it was only as the prison-cell door slammed shut that they realised that their music and dance – which they loved in equal measure – amounted to a ritualised form of opposition (Kater, 1992).

Within the context of the metropolitan night-clubs the jitterbug allowed for counter-hegemonic forms of bodily expression and individuality, so emphatically repressed within Nazi popular culture, music and dance. Josef Skvorecky, a Czech writer and jazz musician who lived under the shadow of both Nazism and Stalinism, has argued that it is for this reason that totalitarian regimes aim their ideological guns at those who danced to the song of the saxophone (Skvorecky, 1983). That is not to say that young Germans were attracted to jazz because of an overt political impulse or agenda. These style revolts were ultimately about nonconformism and individual expression, which had no necessary attendant political ideology. In Germany the jitterbug produced a culturequake of racial fears, but the same is true for its reception in Britain.

CHOCOLATE SOLDIER, VANILLA JITTERBUG: BLACK GIS, MILITARY SEGREGATION AND JAZZ PROPAGANDA

Swing went to war through Glenn Miller's band of the Allied Expeditionary Force (AEF) but it also exposed one the deepest flaws at the heart of the American dream. In Europe black GIs (Government Issue) served in segregated units, but outside their military bases the colour-bar was not observed. Indeed, in Britain the responses of military and political figures to young British women dancing with black American GIs reveals racial trepidation reminiscent of their professed enemy. Integrated dances where black and white mixed and swung together also invoked double standards within imperial Britain. The jitterbugging dance-halls became a context where these tensions were manifest, but they also enabled a momentary and alternative vision of kinship and intimacy to emerge beyond the colour-line within sound and motion.

The Allies and the Nazis put women to work during the war. With these new financial opportunities came partial escape from male authority. Women on both sides of the conflict became increasingly self-reliant, they had their own resources and many women exerted this new found independence in matters of sex as well. Bleuel illustrates this by quoting from an account of a young German soldier's Christmas leave, 1943–44:

New Year's Eve was frightful. The streets swarmed with females chasing field-grey uniforms. Many of them carried bottles containing their extra schnapps allocation and broke the ice by asking to borrow a corkscrew. If the soldier didn't have one, they produced one from their handbag. They weren't just young women either. There were forty- and fifty-year-olds among them. (Bleuel, 1973, p. 238)

The war had brought the sexualisation of community life in ways that threatened the *Volkish* ideal of German family life. The Nazi authorities mourned this situation but took little action except when this promiscuity involved German women crossing the barriers of race and nation. There were many thousands of foreign-indentured labourers working in Germany. Where there were instances of German women being caught having sex with French prisoners of war or Polish labourers they were viciously pilloried, often having their heads shaved publicly and being given severe prison sentences. For men caught having sex with foreign women workers their punishment was at most a verbal condemnation. The bodies of women and their sexuality became the site for concerns over miscegenation and racial hygiene. This was no less true in Britain.

British women were also conscripted into the war effort through the opening-up of industrial jobs that had been up until then the province of men. The presence of American GIs on British soil added another dimension to the processes of sexualisation that Bleuel identified in Germany. The dance-halls became the focus of concerns about the sexual probity of the GIs and also the effect that their presence was having on English women and the culture as a whole:

For older women during the war, dances, even before the Americans arrived, were oases of pleasure in a wilderness of work and worry; for younger women, after the G.I.s poured onto the dance floors, they became sheer fairyland. (Longmate, 1975, p. 262)

Britain was particularly well-equipped with dance-halls. The pre-war years had been the heyday of English dance-bands popularised by their regular broadcasts on radio (Rust, 1972). The most famous ballroom was the Hammersmith Palais in west London. The hallowed Covent Garden Opera House was also converted into an elegant dance-hall. Like their German counterparts, American soldiers found themselves surprised and a little thrown by the female assertiveness that the conflict had seemed to foster. Longmate quotes an account of a 'fantastic dance in Cricklewood' by a white airman from Plymouth, Massachusetts:

Even a poor dancer like I was could do well. When they had a 'Ladies Excuse-me' dance [in which women invited male partners to dance] it was chaos. You hardly had time to introduce yourself to the girl before you were tagged by someone as lovely or lovelier. (Longmate, 1975, p. 269)

The war had suspended some aspects of male power. In this context women were exploring quite new forms of autonomy in all matters, from spending-power to sex.

From 1942 until the end of the war some 130 000 black American troops were stationed in the British Isles. Graham Smith, in his ground-breaking history of the experience of black GIs in wartime Britain, has shown that the general public often reacted in a positive manner to, as one popular song of the time put it, the 'Chocolate Soldier from the USA' (Smith, 1987). Despite this the American command imposed a rigid system of racial segregation that transformed the English countryside. Military segregation was acute and actively enforced in East Anglia, where important combat units and air bases were located. Here black GIs were stationed and served as engineers, truck drivers and ordnance workers. The US army decided that the innocently named River Dove which flowed through East Anglia would provide the geographical expression of the colour-line. All areas east of the river were out of bounds to the black GIs who were stationed at Eye, Debach and in Haughly Park near Stowmarket (Smith, 1987, p. 108).

For black and white GIs alike the social centre was Ipswich, which boasted 150 public houses, of which fewer than ten were set aside for black soldiers. Black GIs formed swing-bands and hosted their own dances. Graham Smith (1987) has argued that the politeness of black GIs and events like these made the black soldiers extremely popular with the local people. While the US army attempted to impose racial segregation these integrated dances brought white English women on to the dance-floor, and within this informal social arena young white Englishmen were introduced to the culture of black America. Black GI swing-bands staged daytime performances and invited local children to a 'post party' to hear Count Basie and Duke Ellington tunes rendered in the heart of the English countryside. Each unit had its own band. For example, the black unit of 923rd Regiment of the Aviation Engineers formed a swing-band called the 923 Reveilleers. In addition to dances on their post they performed in local venues in and around Ipswich (Smith, personal communication). Informal forms of segregation also persisted in the dance-halls.

The Manager of the Dorothy Dance Hall in Cambridge effected the exclusion of black troops by maintaining that his floor was 'not suitable for jitterbugging' (Reynolds, 1995). Other dance-halls, including the converted

Royal Opera House at Covent Garden, put up 'No Jitterbugging' signs, but dancers mostly ignored them (Potts and Potts, 1985), and it did not discourage white GIs from attending. Black culture was embraced, albeit through white exponents. A good proportion of the popular orchestras of the period like Glenn Miller, Benny Goodman and Tommy and Jimmy Dorsey were white big-band exponents of jazz. *In the Mood*, arguably Miller's most famous tune, was composed by the black reed instrumentalist and arranger Joe Garland (Schuller, 1989).

Through the jitterbug black forms of dance had an unprecedented impact on English culture. As Brenda Deveraux remembers: 'American boys were the master of the Jitterbug craze. We English girls took to it like ducks to water. No more slow, slow, quick, quick, slow for us. This was living' (Gardiner, 1992, p. 114). The white GIs and their English dance partners elevated the jitterbug from a cult interest to a general fashion:

> In the process they changed the whole nature of the dance-hall phenomenon. Where formerly there had been graceful, circular movement of dancers around the floor, now there were wild gyrations of hip cats who pecked, trucked, leapt and dived. (Seidenberg, Sellar and Jones, 1987, p. 100)

Black music and dance could be tolerated and even loved within mainstream American and English culture, even with some reservations, but when it came to black people themselves this was quite another matter.

Walter White, the civil-rights activist, came to Britain during the war years and described what he saw in his book *A Rising Wind* (1945). White was light-skinned and could pass in white society. On entering a London cab, he asked to be taken to the Liberty Club which was near the British Ministry of Information. The driver, believing him to be white, responded 'You mean the Rainbow Club of the American Cross, don't you, sir?', the latter being a white club. After the confusion cleared the driver agreed to take him 'where the coloured boys go'. London's night-life was effectively divided up like a kind of racial checkerboard. The colour-coded hermetics of this geography was not, however, complete. On arriving at the Liberty Club, White struck up a conversation with a white GI from Georgia who had made friends with black peers whom he couldn't meet comfortably in other clubs. He wrote: 'I asked him about the continuation of these friendships when he returned to America. Ruefully he spread his hands, palm upward, and shrugged his shoulders. "I don't know," he said sadly' (White, 1945, p. 15).

There were other white GIs who also found the import of American racism all to close to the ideology of their fascist opponents (Reynolds,

1995). In the main white American troops found the presence of black soldiers threatening, and spontaneous violence – in the main instigated by whites – was commonplace (Smith, 1987).

The British, confronted with this spectre of racial violence and the institutionalised military segregation, more often than not took the side of the black soldiers. Walter White concluded that the brightest note of all in the stories told by his black countrymen was of the friendship with the British people:

> One had told of the distinguished British family inviting a group of American soldiers to their home for dinner and dancing. Everything moved smoothly during the meal, but when one of the Negro soldiers danced with one of the English women, he had been assaulted by a Southern white soldier. A free-for-all followed in which the British took the side of the Negroes.
>
> And there was the story of the pub keeper who had posted a sign over his entrance reading 'THE PLACE FOR THE EXCLUSIVE USE OF ENGLISHMEN AND AMERICAN NEGRO SOLDIERS'. (White, 1945, p. 11)

White figured that this could be explained by the sensitivity to material hardships that both British working people and black soldiers – three-quarters of whom came from the rural South – shared an understanding. This stood in stark contrast to the cocky garishness of the white GIs. He concluded that for many black GIs coming to England was their first experience in being treated with respect and friendship by white people. The stumbling-block, however, was the issue of the relationship between black soldiers and white Englishwomen, of which the Americans and the British expressed equal condemnation.

In 1943 several American newspapers, including *Life* magazine, published photographs of black GIs dancing with white Englishwomen. The response of the American military's Bureau of Public Relations was prompt. It ordered the censorship of any photographs which portrayed interracial dancing and social mixing. Black men could sacrifice their life in the fight against fascism but they could not be seen dancing with the natives! Towards the end of the war this policy was slightly modified after the protest of black troops both in western Europe and in Italy. This issue went up as far as to attract the attention of General Eisenhower, who countenanced the general principle behind the censoring of these photographs, and he proposed a compromise. Black GIs could post photographs home as long as they were stamped 'For personal use only – not for publication' (Roeder,

1993, p. 57). Black troops confronted with racial violence and military segregation were rendered publicly invisible through these forms of censorship. As I will show, the Nazi propagandists found the undoubted hypocrisy of the Allies over the question of race particularly useful. The meaning of jazz itself became an emblem of a wider struggle over the opposition between liberal democracy and fascism.

One of the paradoxes of the Nazi terror was that SS officers themselves demonstrated a fondness for swing. This went as far as to encourage the formation of jazz combos in the concentration camps of Terazin and Auschwitz, where prisoners performed swing tunes for the officers' pleasure (Vogel, 1961a, 1961b, 1962). Mike Zwerin, in his exploration of jazz under the Nazis, described a Luftwaffe pilot who switched on the BBC hoping to catch a few bars of Glenn Miller before bombing the antenna from which these forbidden sounds were being broadcast (Zwerin, 1985). Allied propagandists recognised the potential for exploiting the contradictory allure that jazz possessed within Nazi society.

The sound barrier of 1944 was marked on the one hand by the music of the Nazi marches and on the other by the big-band swing of Glenn Miller. The Allies attempted to exploit the popularity of swing inside Germany. On 30 October 1944 Miller's swing tunes were aimed at German soldiers through the American Broadcast Station in Europe (ABSIE) in an effort to persuade them to lay down their arms. These were transmitted under the title *Music for the Wehrmacht* (i.e. German armies). Major Miller addressed German soldiers in their own language, with the assistance of Ilse Weinberger, a German compère and translator. Ilse introduced Glen Miller as the 'magician of swing' and, through a strange act of cultural alchemy, tunes like *Long Ago and Far Away* and *My Heart Tells Me* were rendered in German by vocalist Johnny Desmond.

Miller's Wehrmacht sessions included a number of extraordinary exchanges between Ilse and the major. In one programme he denounced 'Nazi gangsterism' and claimed that 'there is no expression of freedom quite so sincere as music'. He presented the cultural diversity found amongst the musicians in his band as a microcosm of the American way of life:

Today they are true Americans sitting side by side with their buddies, no matter who they are or where they came from. This is a true picture of the great melting pot, America, and a symbol of unity in the fight for freedom.

Through a clumsy summary of these words Ilse unknowingly touched on a profound tension in the relationship between Glenn Miller, jazz and this image of America. Her German translation characterised the AEF band as: 'A true symbol of America, where everybody has the same rights – it is all equal regardless of race, colour and religion.'

True, Miller's band was made up from the sons of immigrants from Germany, Russia and Italy, and even included some Jews. But this micro-cosm of American freedom was not extended to include the very black musicians who had played a vital role in the development of swing.

Miller's musical gift transcended mere pastiche. Yet his music was invoked as an icon of American justice at the very time when racial se-gregation in the Allied armed forces was prevalent. The war had a dev-astating effect on African American jazz musicians, many of whom were drawn into the armed services not as prestigious musical tribunes but as common foot soldiers. Fearing military racism, some attempted to evade conscription. Buck Clayton, virtuoso trumpeter in Count Basie's Band, tried unsuccessfully to escape induction by eating soap and drinking Benzedrine and almost killed himself. Clayton later claimed that white officers treated German prisoners better than black Americans. This is borne out by the experience of band-leader Horace Henderson, and Lena Horne, who cut short a tour after finding that in Camp Robinson, Arkansas black soldiers were not permitted to see the show while Nazi prisoners of war were welcomed (Stowe, 1994).

Nazi propagandists hit back by proclaiming jazz as the product of an inferior black race. Prior to the D-Day landings posters were plastered over Dutch billboards representing the 'Allied Liberators' as the bearers of a dangerous cultural heritage. American troops were portrayed symbolic-ally as an 'uncivilised Frankenstein' that had a jitterbugging ape for its torso, a face hidden behind the mask of the Ku-Klux-Klan and black arms sporting a boxing glove on one hand and a jazz record in the other. They also tried to invoke racial fears amongst the peoples of occupied Europe through spreading a rumour that black American soldiers would play a prominent part in the invasion. Goebbels's Ministry for People's Enlight-enment and Propaganda produced a pamphlet entitled 'Greetings From England – The Coming Invasion'. Written in Dutch in the form of an Allied communiqué, it stated that the Germans had been duped into wrongly expecting a sea invasion and that a half a million 'Negro paratroopers' would spearhead the attack:

> It will be an enormous humiliation for Hitler, the prophet of racial theories, when his warriors will be driven from western Europe by the black race. Dutchmen, your co-operation will be counted . . . make your old jazz-records ready, because at the celebration of liberation your

daughters and wives will be *dancing in the arms of real Negroes* [my emphasis].

Jazz was equated with blackness and the presence of black soldiers on mainland Europe with miscegenation.

Aerial propaganda dropped by the Nazis in the first days of the invasion picked up these themes but the audience to which it was directed were white and black GIs respectively. A 'hold to light' card targeted at white American soldiers began with an image of a dead American soldier in the foreground. As the card was exposed to the light a bedroom scene was revealed showing a white woman on all-fours with a naked black man having sex with her from behind. The caption read: 'White Plays, Black Wins'. Equally, black soldiers were targeted. The dropped 'certificates' in both English and German guaranteed safe conduct to those presenting them to the Germans. Cards presented images of smiling, well-fed black GIs who had surrendered. Another showed two black babies with the commentary:

THEY WANT YOU BACK ALIVE

Well what chance have you to survive? Hardly any at all! Remember, back home the coloured man always had to do the dirty work. On the front it is the same Uncle Sam's coloured soldiers are just CANNON FODDER.

YOU HAVE ONLY ONE CHANCE

If you are fed up with the fighting, join the other coloured boys who are now waiting for the end of the war in modern sanitary prison-of-war camps. They are being treated decently like all the prisoners-of-war. They are getting good food and Red Cross parcels. They may write home and receive mail regularly. Above all they know

AFTER THE WAR THEY WILL BE SENT HOME TO THEIR FOLKS AS SOON AS POSSIBLE

The Nazi propagandists scorned American racism as a means to exploit the racial fear of whites and to get black GIs to turn away from the conflict.

For both sets of propagandists, swing provided the symbolic mechanism to ridicule the racial fears of the opponent. The Allies, through the big-band sound of Glenn Miller, attempted to capture the hearts and minds of the jitterbug-loving Germans. The Allies attempted to mock the Nazi prohibitions against jazz, but in doing so they sidelined the black musical innovators of swing and censored all trace of black GIs in Europe. The Nazis for their part used swing to expose American democracy as a sham.

They flaunted the blackness of the jitterbug as a means to invoke fears about miscegenation. White women would be 'dancing in the arms of real Negroes' or worse. Ironically, the Nazis used the racial apprehension of white men to expose American and European racisms.

CONCLUSION

> A rapid turning movement makes the surrounding objects vanish in the whirl, and the dancer with his inner wrestling seems alone in the world as if on an island, so dance-like thinking and feeling brings about a consciousness of one's innermost self. The fleeting pathway of the dancer is filled with ethical spirit. The trace, the pathway, the movement are the result of struggle, they represent the victory of an endeavour which, gentle and restrained or wild and abandoned, contains the gift of ethical understanding . . . . Dance is no static picture, no allegory, but vibrant life itself.
>
> Rudolph Laban

> The dance enhance.
>
> Dizzy Gillespie

The music of swing was answered emphatically on the dance-floors of Europe during the war years. As the jitterbugs hopped, dived and turned they found a rhythm that clashed with the time-signature of totalitarianism. Nazi dance filtered out the expressive dimensions of *Austdruckstanz*, leaving a regulating racial culture that designated men and women to specific gendered archetypes: submission was made obligatory and individuality impossible. Swing subculture offered young Germans an alternative to the state-sanctioned youth institutions and a means to ritually express contrasting gender identities and sexual mores. But why did this culture resonate so powerfully within the context of Nazism?

Paul Connerton has written that collective memories can be conserved in bodily automatisms and passed on in non-textual and non-cognitive ways (Connerton, 1989). Perhaps even in translation the jitterbug traced a living and embodied memory that went back to the slave master who exercised his chattels through making them dance under the whip (Emery, 1988). It is the transcendence of rupture, terror and suppression that is embodied within swing dance. This is why it was so attractive to the white jazz nonconformists who lived under Nazism. In those sounds and motions they discovered a living response to the terrorising racism that lurked in the shadow of modernity and which found its expression within the

Third Reich. As the dancers spun, broke away and turned they discovered an ethical understanding which valued the individual 'off-beat' – a syncopated sensibility.

I am not suggesting that there is a simple relationship between form and ideology. Jazz was conscripted to the Allied cause which showed little consideration towards translating their rhetoric of freedom and democracy into racial justice. Without any seeming contradiction capricious racists – on both sides of the conflict – could also be jazz fans. The jitterbug brought these tensions into focus where the dance-floor offered a place for interracial contact and sociability between black men and white women. These fragile associations were subject to scrutiny and censorship by politicians and the Allied military. Swing dancing was feared because it might lead to interracial sex and, ultimately, miscegenation. The humble jitterbug thus revealed the distinct but commensurable racisms that lay at the centre of both liberal democracy and Nazism.

Detlev Peukert has argued that National Socialism unwittingly paved the way for modern forms of youth leisure (Peukert, 1989). The history of swing subculture in Europe certainly disrupts the established wisdom that sees youth culture as a product of post-war consumerism (Abrams, 1959). In 1946 the cartoonist Stil published a series of cartoons which heralded a generation of young Englishwomen as sexually knowing and fully initiated in American popular culture and style. One entitled 'Tommy Comes Home' represented a dance-floor full of airborne, Lindy-Hopping women. Their newly demobbed English partners stood rigid, stuck to the floor and unable to follow their steps. The caption read 'What happened to you, Myrtle – you never danced like this before I went away!' Along with their increased spending-power the wartime dances had allowed English women to explore areas of self-expression and autonomy that had been previously unthinkable. This all changed as they were forced to give up their jobs and sacrifice their Saturday-night freedoms. While Britain knuckled down to post-war austerity the dance-halls would never be quite the same again. Future generations would answer the call of the jitterbug and its cognates in new and indeterminate ways.

ACKNOWLEDGEMENTS

I'd like to thank Graham Smith for his help and generosity with source materials for this article, and Valerie Preston-Dunlop who shared her insights into the life and career of Rudolph Laban. Also thanks to Irene Welch, Andrew Simons and Paul Gilroy, who in different ways helped me formulate these arguments. This chapter is drawn from research that is made possible by funding from the Harry Frank Guggenheim Foundation. I'd like to thank the Foundation for its support.

REFERENCES

M. Abrams, *The Teenage Consumer* (London: Routledge & Kegan Paul, 1959).
K. Backstein, 'Keeping the Spirit Alive: The Jazz Dance Testament of Mura Dehn' in K. Gabbard (ed.), *Representing Jazz* (Durham, NC: Duke University Press, 1995).
W. Benjamin, *Illuminations* (London: Harcourt, Brace & World, Inc., 1968).
H. P. Bleuel, *Sex and Society in Nazi Germany* (Philadelphia, PA: J. J. Lippincott, 1973).
P. Connerton, *How Societies Remember* (Cambridge: Cambridge University Press, 1989).
R. Crease, 'Divine Frivolity: Hollywood Representations of the Lindy Hop, 1937–1942' in K. Gabbard (ed.), *Representing Jazz* (Durham, NC: Duke University Press, 1995).
E. K. Ellington, 'The Duke Steps Out', *Rhythm* (March 1931), pp. 20–2.
L. F. Emery, *Black Dance from 1619 to Today,* 2nd edn (London: Dance Books, 1988).
J. Gardiner, *'Over Here': The GIs in Wartime Britain* (London: Collins & Brown, 1992).
C. Goddard, *Jazz Away from Home* (London: Paddington Press, 1979).
J. Haskins, *Black Dance in America: A History through its People* (New York: Thomas Y. Cromwell, 1990).
K. Hazard-Gordon, *Jookin': The Rise of Social Dance Formations in African-American Culture* (Philadelphia, PA: Temple University Press, 1990).
L. Hughes, *The Langston Hughes Reader* (New York: George Braziller, 1958).
M. H. Kater, *Different Drummers: Jazz in the Culture of Nazi Germany* (Oxford: Oxford University Press, 1992).
R. Laban, *A Life for Dance* (London: Macdonald & Evans, 1975).
N. Longmate, *The G.I.s: The Americans in Britain 1942–45* (London: Hutchinson, 1975).
Malcolm X, *The Autobiography of Malcolm X* (London: Penguin, 1968).
R. D. Mandell, *The Nazi Olympics* (Chicago: University of Illinois Press, 1987).
S. A. Manning, 'From Modernism to Fascism: The Evolution of Wigman's Choreography', *Ballet Review,* 14, 4 (1987), pp. 87–98.
S. A. Manning, Modern Dance in the Third Reich: Six Positions and a Coda' in S. Leigh Foster (ed.), *Choreographing History* (Bloomington and Indianapolis, IN: Indiana University Press, 1995).
H. Müller, 'Wigman and National Socialism', *Ballet Review,* 15, 1 (1987), pp. 65–73.
D. Peukert, *Inside Nazi Germany: Conformity, Opposition and Racism in Everyday Life* (London: Penguin, 1989).
E. D. Potts and A. Potts, *Yanks Down Under – 1941–1945* (Melbourne and Auckland: Oxford University Press, 1985).

V. Preston-Dunlop, 'Laban and the Nazis: Towards an Understanding of Rudolf Laban and the Third Reich', *Dance Theatre Journal*, 6, 2 (1989), pp. 4–7.

D. Reynolds, *Rich Relations: The American Occupation of Britain 1942–45* (London: Harper Collins, 1995).

G. H. Roeder, *The Censored War: An American Visual Experience During World War Two* (New Haven, CT: Yale University Press, 1993).

B. Rust, *The Dance Bands* (London: Ian Allan, 1972).

G. Schuller, *The Swing Era: The Development of Jazz 1930–1945* (Oxford: Oxford University Press, 1989).

S. Seidenberg, M. Sellar and L. Jones, *'You Must Remember This . . .': Songs at the Heart of the War* (London: Boxtree, 1987).

N. Servos, 'Pathos and Propaganda?: on the Mass Choreography of Fascism', *Ballet International Handbook* (1990), pp. 63–6.

J. Skvorecky, 'Red Music' in J. Skvorecky, *Talkin' Moscow Blues* (London: Faber & Faber, 1983).

G. Smith, *When Jim Crow Met John Bull: Black American Soldiers in World War II Britain* (London: I. B. Tauris, 1987).

M. Sterns and J. Sterns, *Jazz Dance: The Story of American Vernacular Dance* (New York: Macmillan, 1968).

D. W. Stowe, *Swing Changes: Big Band Jazz in New Deal America* (Cambridge, MA: Harvard University Press, 1994).

B. Taylor and W. van der Will (eds), *The Nazification of Art: Art, Design, Music, Architecture and Film in the Third Reich* (Winchester, MA: Winchester Press, 1990).

M. Tucker (ed.), *The Duke Ellington Reader* (New York: Oxford University Press, 1993).

E. Vogel, 'Jazz in a Nazi Concentration Camp', *Down Beat*, Part 1 (7 December 1961a); Part 2 (21 December 1961b); Part 3 (4 January 1962).

W. White, *A Rising Wind* (New York: Doubleday, Doran & Co., 1945).

M. Zwerin, *La Tristesse de Saint Louis: Jazz Under the Nazis* (New York: Beech Tree Books, 1985).

11 Aerobic Dance and the City: Individual and Social Space

Stacey Prickett

'Look Better Naked'

David Barton Gym logo, New York City

The desire to look better – clothed or unclothed – is a prime motivating factor behind the expanding aerobics phenomenon. After years of complaining about any dance class which began before 9.00 a.m., I took to my local fitness club at the unheard-of hour (for me) of 6.30 a.m. to obtain first-hand knowledge of my object of study. Fortunately, benefits have been increased lung capacity and looser-fitting clothes. A performance-dance background and education in American and English higher education institutions left me with a degree of elitism towards the fitness trend. However, the growing diversity and availability of aerobic exercise classes and increasingly, aerobic dance classes, challenged my initial reductionist metaphor of aerobics in the city essentialised by a step-aerobics class. Densely-packed classes, with platforms at various heights corresponding to an urban landscape of skyscrapers, sweating bodies responding to shouted commands in a seemingly automaton fashion – such images are bound in more complex relationships between aerobics, dance, urban (and suburban) life and the individual.

The local fitness club offers an antidote to the sedentary and car-bound lifestyle in which I find myself. Researching clubs to join, I was struck by the diversity of crowds and facilities, ultimately joining an institution which provides a full range of fitness and related amenities (including towels, hand-cream, cotton swabs, hairspray, etc.). Despite the enormity of the club (over 60 000 square feet) and large membership (over 3000), a camaraderie is evident among the regulars. High-tech equipment, raquetball courts, a basketball/volleyball court, an inside running-track and swimming-pool are available to members in addition to 76 classes per week, ranging from yoga to step aerobics. My shift from a dance-oriented training to a physical fitness/sports arena sparked an interest in the contrasts and similarities between the disciplines. Formal interviews were conducted with five aerobics instructors, four of whom have extensive dance backgrounds (one in England, a French-based Swiss modern dancer, a male dancer and an African-American woman who trained in American university dance programmes). Less formal discussions with numerous aerobic participants and instructors filled gaps in my knowledge of the aerobic, aerobic dance and fitness worlds.

Spatial considerations led to questions concerning issues of expressivity, postmodernist contradictions, consumerism and representations of the female body. Drawing on movement analyses, cultural studies texts and interviews, I examine aspects of aerobic dance in contemporary society. Beyond associations with city life, aerobic dance is also a suburban phenomenon, offering up different aspects of social space. Grounded in contemporary and classic sociological analyses of suburbia versus the metropolis, diverse aspects of space and community are examined below in reference to cultural pluralism and hegemonic influences. In addition to social space and constructs, essays on music videos and aerobic videotapes frame discussion of consumerism and representations of women.

Hargreaves's description of the fitness trend stresses visual and external appearances:

> Aerobics has been successfully packaged to persuade women, specifically, to participate in order to lose weight, and improve their sex-appeal, rather than for reasons of fitness and enjoyment or for competition . . . . The focus of publicity is on appearance (the athletic looking body), fashion (the rather trendy-looking image) and physique (the sexy-looking shape); rather than on movement (the active-looking woman). (Hargreaves, 1994, p. 160)

I argue below that a combination of dance and aerobic activity counteracts aspects of such analyses, wherein individualised expression and agency are perpetuated rather than diminished.

EXERCISE VERSUS DANCE: VIDEO AND LIVE INSTRUCTION

Combinations of popular or social dance evident in studios today are distinct from straightforward high-/low-impact aerobics, in part because of an interplay between broader society and the studio through dance. High- and low-impact aerobic classes offer stylised callisthenics, whilst a dance component fuses dance elements to cardiovascular intensity. Distinctions between a strict exercise approach, the aerobic videotape experience, live aerobic dance classes and performance/street dance are considered below. One dancer/instructor I interviewed defined five major differences between dance and her straightforward aerobic exercise classes: the class structure/ format, movement vocabulary/choreography, musical accompaniment, mental attitude-objectives for attending the class and the dynamic range within the class (Green, 1995).

A defining characteristic separating performance-dance styles from aerobic dance is the latter's emphasis on maintaining a heightened cardio-vascular rate. Aerobic exercise was initially defined in 1968 by Dr Kenneth Cooper, who is known for developing a 12-minute fitness test associated with military organisations. His book *Aerobics* has sold over 20 million copies in Braille and in 41 languages (Ikonian, 1993, p. 36). As one of 31 different aerobic exercises, aerobic dancing was created independently by Judi Sheppart Misset and Jacki Sorensen 'to promote health by increasing cardio-vascular stamina (aerobic), muscle strength, definition, and flexibility, and to provide a method for weight loss' (Kagan and Morse, 1988, p. 167).

'Queuing' upcoming exercises for students is a unique aspect of classes such as step aerobics and slide, since maintaining continuous movement is crucial to the aerobic element. (Step classes comprise exercises involving stepping on and off a plastic platform. Slide exercises imitate the side-to-side activity of skating, with a lateral sliding motion performed on a specialised board.) The seemingly instantaneous shouting of upcoming moves demands a refined sense of timing from the instructor. Advance knowledge of coming step changes reduces potential for injury by setting up proper weight placement. In step and slide classes, movement phrases are generally short, linked together at the moment. Aerobic dance classes, on the other hand, are structured more closely to a traditional dance class in which a brief exercise is taught and 'performed' from memory.

As noted above, a crucial difference between an ordinary aerobics class and a traditional dance class exists in its structure. The aerobics format is 'law' according to one instructor, 'it works, it is safe, and it has to be set' (Levenson, 1995). An elevated heart rate is sustained in part through 'marching out' between movement phrases. An aerobics class format includes a warm-up beginning with the head or feet, working up or down the body depending upon the starting-point. An aerobic phase of 20 minutes or more follows with a cool-down section to finish. For Fabienne, the Swiss dancer-turned-instructor I interviewed, the cool-down phase of an aerobics exercise class provides opportunities to integrate her dance background within a fitness-oriented structure where she focuses on expressive movement qualities. Dance training is also evident in her transitions with a continuity of movement in seamless shifts between exercises, literally choreographed to the music.

On a fundamental level, aerobic dance classes offer an alternative venue for learning street-dance styles in a sanitised environment, with dance steps broken down for the uninitiated. Ethnic-influenced and street-dance classes integrate hip-hop or techno-funk, Latin-American and swing styles into an exercise format. Techno-funk/hip-hop aerobics use music from popular charts by Paula Abdul, M. C. Hammer and Janet Jackson, among others, and integrate quick, intricate footwork and high virtuosity kicks and turns in place of callisthenic-type exercises. Salsa/Latin-American dance integrates lateral, swaying movements which help tone the legs and muscles of the lower back, abdominals and pelvis and 'encourages mobility of the pelvis — something we don't get by sitting in our cars and chairs', according to Elizabeth Larkam, director of dance medicine rehabilitation at St Francis Hospital in San Francisco (Brody, 1995b, p. 96). Aerobic exercises, in contrast to dance, are generally two-dimensional, with the limbs moving back and forth, up and down, in arcing or spoke-like patterns (Kagan and Morse, 1988). One instructor spoke of the increased workout her non-dance-based aerobics students experienced when she integrated exercises drawn from a Cunningham technique series. Curved torso actions on diagonal directions were alien to her students, thus intensifying a physical and mental challenge. Another dancer-turned-instructor spoke of being admonished by her supervisor, 'No dancing.' There is a strict distinction between dancing and aerobic exercise in the institution where she works, and her classes called for square movements.

Integration of specific dance vocabularies and rhythmic patterns into aerobic classes shape the movement into distinctive styles, with musical choices integral to the dance form. Instructors of various types of aerobic dance classes emphasised the significance of the music in shaping their class, in terms of a literal driving beat and, in less tangible terms, through creating an atmosphere. Additionally, within the aerobic exercise classes, speed is a significant factor in determining musical choices, as low-impact aerobic classes (keeping one foot on the floor all the time) are usually 130–140 beats per minute, while step classes are about 120–125. Copyright restrictions such as the Public Performance Licence in the UK also influence which music is used. As in the UK, fees are paid to musicians' organisations such as BMI and ASCAP for the rights to play recorded music within American fitness centres. While bootleg tapes abound, only professionally-recorded tapes are legally permitted, ensuring that royalties are paid to the recording artists.

ART DANCE V. AEROBIC DANCE

Increased availability of exercise and dance classes with an aerobic emphasis in private studios in the US and London mark a trend away from amateur dance-technique classes. Suspended activities of established dance companies such as the Joffrey Ballet also signal funding shifts and reduced attendance at performances, coinciding with a mainstream cultural shift of interest away from dance after the 1970s boom. The rise of aerobic dancing (in contrast to ordinary exercise/aerobics classes) offers a potential outlet for individual expression in the 1990s. This contemporary version of individuality stands in contrast to the 'inner landscape' variety of Martha Graham, however, with aerobic dance drawing on popular and social dance forms in contrast to concepts of high art integral to the early modern dance. Articles in women's magazines on dance-influenced aerobic exercises present movement descriptions separate from aesthetic principles. One article lists ballet's biggest benefits as improved posture and flexibility, along with toning and firming hips and thighs. In contrast, modern dance is offered up as free-form movement: 'Instead of telling your body what to do, why not let it move the way it wants? This is the philosophy of modern dance or natural movement to music and rhythm' (Guinot, 1994, pp. 29–30). Such misperceptions overlook the rigorous training demanded by many modern dance styles. Unlike ballet dancers, many modern dance performers began their training relatively late in life, thus perpetuating a vision of modern dance as a more accessible and less demanding dance form.

Current trends combine aerobics with dance forms for fulfilment of both aesthetic desires and physical fitness. Various classes echo the individualisation of dance techniques by being founded upon particular movement philosophies. The majority of instructors interviewed by the author or featured in fitness and women's magazines exemplify a trend away from rote repetition, evident in greater movement style diversity and multi-disciplinary combinations of forms such as yogarobics, NIA (non-impact aerobics), and bodysculpting. Blending opposite movement approaches, yogarobics is described as oxymoronic: 'Yoga is the yen: soft, maternal, female. Aerobics is the yang: hard, external and male' (Giddens, 1992, p. 54). The association of fit bodies with masculinity is a recurring concept in cultural studies and movement analysis, explored in more depth below. Individuals known (in the US) for their aerobic styles (Larry Lane for yogarobics and Karen Voight for bodysculpting) are familiar names not because of their celebrity status (e.g. Jane Fonda, Cher, Cindy Crawford, etc., who lend their bodies and names to videotapes) but rather for their stylistic appeal and pedagogic skills. Thus, live classes at local clubs and leisure centres do not generally promise aerobic activity as a path to an entire, glamorous lifestyle, as Kagan and Morse (1988), Winter (1995) and Buckland and Stewart (1993) discuss with reference to superstar videos. The local instructor is less likely to signify a lifestyle beyond the studio than is the celebrity on the videotape, yet wider publicity often perpetuates aerobics as sexualised and a pathway to romantic bliss.

An approach towards bodily and class discipline differs drastically between fitness clubs and dance institutions. Time out for water breaks, talking, and an essential concentration on bodily awareness are sharply contrasted between the two movement approaches. The student/teacher relationship in dance schools stems from a tradition of the dancing master who maintained absolute authority and power over the students. Dance teachers often prohibit late arrivals from participating in a technique class, and taking a water break during an exercise was unthinkable during my years as a dance student. In fitness clubs, on the other hand, people can enter or leave a class at will without reprimand, indicative of a freedom generally unavailable to the traditional dance student. An economic relationship exists between the aerobics instructor and student, one involving a wider degree of interchange than traditional dance student/teacher roles. Feedback is freely given by fitness students, with commentary on the difficulty of steps, musical choices and intensity of the workout. The switch can be disconcerting to instructors with a dance background as levels of critique from fitness students challenge norms in dance education institutions. The ultimate goal of each discipline contributes to their difference, with fun and tension release emerging as additional motivating factors for the aerobic student. Mastery of the dance technique for artistic purposes is the primary aim of the dance class, in training the body to be used as a tool for artistic expression.

Beyond fitness benefits, contemporary aerobic dance styles increasingly emphasise an ability to affect the human condition, whether through escapism, a connection with spirit or the soul, and/or through the intellectual exercise of focusing on the body and executing steps correctly. A didactic function for aerobic dance includes exposure to ethnic dance styles: Marla Bergh describes her African dance-influenced class as 'a painless way to introduce Minnesotans to African culture' (Graf, 1994, p. 28).

In addition to exposure to different cultural styles, a perception of fitness activities as a form of mental exercise is evident in recent publications. One editorial in a fitness trade magazine asks 'Can leg lifts make you dumb?' (Jordan, 1995, p. 7). Kagan and Morse's analysis of aerobic videotapes of the 1980s suggest that repetition de-emphasises individual expressivity.

As presented on the tapes, repetition deprives viewers of individual decisions as they follow the directives of the leader: 'the student overcomes resistance by borrowing the leader's will and the leader's voice to animate her body' (Kagan and Morse, 1988, p. 171). In addition to a 'follow-the-leader' surrender of will, a 'seen' body is emphasised over a 'felt' body, one which stresses visual imitation of patterns through mirror-like mimicry. The seen body 'sets in place a preoccupation with the values which determines the structuring metaphor of aerobics' (Kagan and Morse, 1988, p. 167). Rather than feeling bodily change and responses during the workout, an imitative visual experience is emphasised. I argue that live aerobic dance classes encountered in my research offer an experience distinct from videotapes. Intricate rhythmic patterns in hip-hop necessitate breaking down phrases beyond large muscle-mass movements of the leg or arm moving as an entire unit. In particular, a focus towards the front prevalent in videotapes is less evident in live classes which incorporate movements where the focus shifts to other parts of the room.

SPACE AND THE SUB-URBAN AEROBIC DANCE

A primary component of the aerobic phenomenon is the extent to which leisure centres and private health clubs function to create a sense of community for their clientele. As one journalist summarised, health clubs offer something 'more intangible than good health: a culture' (Steinhauer, 1995a, p. 41). 'Happy hours' and non-fitness events encourage socialising, and offers of food and beverages (including beer and/or wine) tempt patrons into spending more time (and therefore money) on the premises. On the other hand, leisure centres offer classes with broad accessibility without steep administrative and/or monthly fees. Amenities accompanying costly memberships are also absent, as the leisure and community centres present a less specific cultural ambience. The fitness club I currently frequent initially appeared beyond my budget, its lobby bearing closer resemblance to a posh hotel than the local leisure centres I attended as a student in London. An elegance not necessarily evident in other aspects of my life is available to me – at least during the club's opening hours. And as a newcomer to the area after living abroad, social aspects of the club were motivating factors in my choice, criteria equal to the club's proximity to work and home. My lifestyle change from struggling student to gainfully employed with an expendable income enabled me to opt for an institution with a moderately high fee. As a membership survey later revealed, I fit neatly into the demographic composition of the club's clientele in terms of average age range and salary.

Other significant aspects of the aerobics dance phenomenon include contextual analysis which locate the activity in debates about postmodern culture. Jameson's analysis of postmodern architecture and use of space in John Portman's design of the Los Angeles Bonadventure Hotel defines its aim of creating a total space, which 'corresponds to a new collective practice, a new mode in which individuals move and congregate, something like the practice of a new and historically original kind of hyper-crowd' (Jameson, 1988, p. 22). The mini-city of the contemporary hotel is replicated in the up-market fitness clubs, a self-sufficient environment in which guests have no need to step outside to eat, clothe themselves, conduct business or sleep. With food service, sportswear and equipment shops, showers, massage and personal trainers offered alongside the opportunity to become fit, a complete culture beckons.

Media representations of contemporary urban environments include images of youth, intensity and vitality, symbolised by the aerobics phenomenon. A fundamental distinction between the aerobic dance class and the aerobic exercise video is in a reliance on others for the class to occur. Aerobics classes grew out of market demands, requiring enough participants to make them economically viable and profitable. Some level of interaction is guaranteed in the class situation, whereas the videotape experience is formulated for solitary consumption, if desired. Videotapes additionally offer students chances to perfect moves, increase stamina and confidence in private prior to placing themselves on display in the public sphere in a live class.

Hanna's (1987) formulation of an urban ecosystem proposes that structural relationships exist between urban areas and the dance wherein 'sociocultural factors are the primary determinants of dance concept, process, product, and impact' (1987, p. 200). A greater level of creative freedom and diversity are available in an urban than a rural environment, resulting in urban patterns of social differentiation and interaction evident in the dance of particular cities (Hanna, 1987, p. 214). Differences premised upon locale were observed by instructors of aerobics and aerobic dance classes in the urban and suburban settings of San Francisco and its commuter belt, particularly in terms of prevalent attitudes towards exercise and fashion. Women in the city were perceived as more preoccupied with fashion than their suburban counterparts, wearing make-up, baseball caps, the latest trendy sportswear and shoe styles. Such observations reinforce distinctive ideologies associated with a suburban/city split, with an urban emphasis on appearance over functionality. Public/private differentiations between the urban/suburban environments are thus perpetuated in the aerobics phenomenon. The city as public space presents an arena for display, whereas the suburb is more associated with the private, as the place to where commuters return. Ironically, classes in the heart of San Francisco, away from the financial district with its large daytime commuter population, were slower-paced than those taught by the same instructor at the suburban clubs.

Simmel's classic 1903 essay on metropolitan life emphasises a fragmentation or 'compartmentalisation' of life in the city (Simmel, 1995). Aerobic classes offer an antidote to this through a chance to refocus on the body. At the same time, however, they typify aspects of urban life in offering a crowd-like interaction in terms of a physical closeness. A fleeting contact occurs in class, paralleled in Simmel's description of spatial bodily closeness with an intellectualised distance experienced in a dense, city crowd. A prevailing technique of reserve, a blasé attitude, is cultivated by urban dwellers in order to deal with the intense sensory stimuli of the environment.

Wirth (1995) argues that population density and crowds also provide a melting-pot of races, people and diverse cultures of urbanism, offered up as a celebration of difference. The city 'has brought together people from the ends of the earth because they are different and useful to one another, rather than because they are like-minded' (Wirth, 1995, p. 66). Compartmentalisation of life is intensified in the city, with face-to-face contact occurring on impersonal, superficial, anonymous and transitory levels. A sense of fragmentation is also evident in interest groups which function in relation to specific aspects of life. The fitness club fulfils recreational and or health needs, with a potential social aspect, whether or not it is acted upon.

Wirth's 1938 analysis of urbanism echoes Simmel in categorising the city as initiator and controller of economic, political and cultural life. The urban mode of life extends beyond its border, through the power of city institutions and personalities increasingly accessible through information technology and mass media. Aspects of a traditional urban/suburban split are disputed by theorists on the contemporary metropolis. Opposing perspectives centre on the degree and significance of heterogeneity in urban and suburban cultures. For example, Sharpe and Wallock (1994) criticise the concept that a traditional suburban economic dependence upon cities has vanished as suburbs are transformed into cities in their own right. Additionally, a city/suburb economic interrelationship still exists in an exchange of workers and a city's reliance on products and services which have moved outside urban centres. Strong distinctions between the city and suburbia are evident in degrees of 'diversity, cosmopolitanism, political culture and public life' absent from the suburbs while remaining defining characteristics of a city' (Sharpe and Wallock, 1994, p. 3). In contrast, suburbs reflect a rejection of diversity, in the US termed a 'white flight' away from negative aspects of urban life. Aerobic dance offers an element of otherness, however, the diversity of cultural expression in class is a mediated or watered-down version of that found in the streets.

A primary distinction between the city and the suburbs lies in the social construction of space. Within the US and Canada, Kasinitz (1995) argues that suburbs, as the dominant settlement pattern, are rich in private spaces and rare in public ones. A turn away from the street as a communal space is evident in the absence of front porches and prevalence of decks behind dwellings. To what extent does the fitness club function as a public space? The activities surrounding the class are private ones – such as showering and changing clothes. The leisure centre/fitness club provides a complex version of public space, combining diverse conceptualisations of the terms. But as Weintraub (1995) notes, acts can appear as visibly public and collective while performed for the individual. The class activity provides a group experience, yet there is a distinction in its level of collectivity – the benefit is for individual participants rather than the greater interests of a collective. To varying degrees, the concept of public space as one open to all enfranchised members of a community is applicable, yet an institution's admission charges place some limits on the notion of public. An additional spatial construct exists in the traditional association of private with feminine and the family, increasingly challenged with the arrival of more women into the sphere of the public workplace. The leisure centre/fitness club offers an intermediary location, one in which private activities occur outside the home.

The media and technology-shaped globalised village afforded through cable and satellite perpetuates a characterisation of aerobics as a worldwide phenomenon. International exposure to aerobic activities is enhanced through channels such as ESPN, which broadcasts aerobic competitions and fitness programmes (some with an eroticised emphasis). Although sportswear companies advocate a universalised concept of the world accessible through exercise, cultural difference is as evident in the studios as it is on the streets. For example, Japanese aerobics classes integrated elements of relaxation and meditation when they were introduced in the 1980s. On the other hand, Brazilian aerobics used a very fast tempo to help generate a party-like atmosphere, and Jamaicans drew on reggae influences (Ikonian, 1993, p. 36).

POSTMODERN DISCIPLINE AND DISPLAY

Elements of multiculturalism perpetuate a notion of aerobic dance as a postmodern icon. In defining prevalent concepts of postmodernism Kaplan (1988) exposes crucial contradictions in contemporary culture. While offering female spectators new arenas for desire and empowerment (exemplified by Madonna), Kaplan argues that postmodernism's benefits are counterpointed by a preponderance of masculine qualities in the broader culture, such as violence and destruction. In addition, contradictions of postmodern culture result in an assimilation of the masculine into women's experience. Binary oppositions such as male/female, public/private space are challenged. Thomas (1995) also identifies paradoxes which arise in cultural shifts away from modernity, highlighting postmodernism's links to consumer capitalism with an emphasis on style, representations and the commodification of culture in contrast to modernism's disdain of mass culture. Pluralism within postmodernism, it is argued, can lead to an absence of rigour, while providing for 'the possibility of other (marginal) voices to be heard and accepted as legitimate (dance, women, bodies)' (Thomas, 1995, p. 19).

This contradiction within postmodernism is made vividly apparent in some recent analyses of aerobics and the body, with specific focus on the feminine body. Hargreaves (1994), for example, examines the gender disintegration of binary concepts in the play on words, 'musculinity'. Female athletes' challenge to stereotyped images of the feminine involves the social construction of gender, strongly defined in sports and athletic activities from childhood. In addition to strong gender delineations, the athletic female body also reveals the postmodern contradiction by symbolising both women's empowerment and submission to dominant bodily ideals. Part of the contradiction lies in an increased physical strength and changing ideals of the female body. The slender, muscular female body symbolises empowerment, control, and a break from traditional concepts of femininity and domesticity. On the other hand, representations of the sporting body in consumer culture are sexualised and objectified in the media (Hargreaves, 1994, p. 161). An emphasis on the sexualised body can function to disempower women by focusing on appearances rather than processes of exercise for health benefits. As the female sporting body is stronger and 'musculinised', the ideal shifts to accommodate the new look. Such reductionism and objectification become a means of control integral to the representation of gender. As Foucault (1980, p. 57) summarises, the new 'mode of investment' of the body is one of control by stimulation rather than through repression: '"Get undressed – but be slim, good-looking, tanned!" For each move by one adversary, there is an answering one by the other.' The empowerment to reveal the body entails a turning-back on the body, to refine or redefine the physical.

Kagan and Morse (1988) reveal a similar contradiction in the ideals of a mobile, active femininity acquired through aerobic dance activity which combines static and passive concepts of femininity. Jane Fonda's body posture and exercises call for an immobile torso and tucked pelvis, and the videotape covers picture Fonda as a muscular, slender woman in static, precariously balanced poses. While the analysis of her pose and the exercise defines a stiffness, Fonda evokes a dancerly image through her leg-warmers, leotard and tights. In contrast, readings of the advertisements and the video-tapes present images of submissiveness alongside those of power (Kagan and Morse, 1988, pp. 167–8). According to Bordo (1990) a tension exists between a minimalist look and the fit athletic body, wherein the two ideals are 'united in battle against a common platoon of enemies: the soft, the loose; unsolid, excess flesh' (Bordo, 1990, p. 90).

With aerobic activity described as militaristic (Kagan and Morse (1988), Buckland and Stewart (1993), Winter (1995), characteristics of the discipline demanded to achieve a fit body correspond to Foucault's analysis of a docile body – one which can be 'used, subjected, transformed and improved' (Foucault, 1979, p. 137). Foucault focused upon military, pedagogic, monastic and penal systems, yet his definition of bodily discipline has parallels to aerobic exercise: 'exercise is that technique by which one imposes on the body tasks that are both repetitive and different, but always graduated' (Foucault, 1979, p. 161). The imposition of bodily discipline within institutions is generally imposed from the outside, by others upon the individual. A fitness enthusiast attends classes by choice, for a myriad of reasons, but has the ability to leave or not attend at all, choices unavailable within the disciplinary systems Foucault analysed.

Despite the element of personal choice in the physical fitness activity, there are influential societal pressures which a number of authors argue undermine a sense of agency. For example, Wolf's (1991) discussion of a 'professional beauty quotient' exemplifies the extent to which societal expectations surround external appearances. A chronicle of legal and legislative battles in the UK and the US detail employment discrimination actions arising out of perceptions of beauty and superficial looks over and above ability to perform tasks or physical fitness. Bordo (1990) argues that class connections to bodily ideals have changed over time, where a muscularity signifying manual labour is replaced by the 'yuppie' pursuit of 'working out'. In addition, 'the size and shape of the body has come to operate as a personal, internal order . . . as a symbol for the state of the soul' (Bordo, 1990, p. 94). Bordo integrates Foucault's concepts into cultural analysis of the slender body wherein various representations of the body in society comprise the intelligible body, through which social constructions are shaped and communicated. The useful body, adapted and formed through social institutions and processes, emerges as a normative social body.

The fit body signifies an individual discipline beyond the visible. Although not demanded as a requirement in most jobs, an emphasis on physical fitness among American workers is evident in an increasing number of employer-paid or subsidised fitness-club memberships. Health plans in the US entice enrollees with offers of discounted membership to clubs such as the YMCA. Physical demands in the information-technology age result in a range of work-related injuries, the late twentieth-century version of industrial accidents on assembly lines. The threat of repetitive motion injuries such as carpal tunnel syndrome and other stresses on the wrists, arms and neck acquired by hours at a keyboard, are strong motivators for today's intellectual labourer to be physically active.

Furthermore, shifts in disciplinary processes from one aspect of life to others is evident in Foucault's analysis that 'the disciplined body is the prerequisite of an efficient gesture' (Foucault, 1979, p. 152). Temporal regulation, degrees of precision in the breakdown of gestures and subjugation of the body to discipline are evident in the institutionalisation of training techniques and disciplinary processes. Disciplinary control 'imposes the best relation between a gesture and the overall position of the body, which is its condition of efficiency and speed' (Foucault, 1979, p. 152). Good handwriting is cited as an example which demands attention to the entire body in order to best fulfil the gestural detail of the activity. Foucault's analysis poses parallels to processes of dance training, in which turn-out, the use of centre, and other essential foundations of a technique are laid down as a framework upon which to build a vocabulary of steps. Such rigour is absent in the aerobics dance class, as the rhythm shapes the movement rather than being broken down into clearly-defined components. Completing the movement within the set counts is stressed over the shape of the gesture as it is being performed. Thus, the relationship between the gesture and the body is less rigidly defined in terms of the angle of a limb, or the stretched line of a leg. On an amateur level, attention to some aesthetic and technical concerns inhibit the exercise form. One instructor noted that dancers who cross over into the realm of step classes often tried to involve the whole body, mind and emotions in the movements, resulting in embellishments which were potentially dangerous within a strictly indicated step vocabulary (Green, 1995).

Within the education system, aerobics classes are categorised as 'female appropriate', perpetuating a function of fitness for the sake of improving one's image. Sports such as gymnastics, ice-skating and synchronised swimming emphasise 'balance, co-ordination, grace and flexibility', affirming popular images of femininity in contrast to masculinised sports (Hargreaves, 1994, p. 159). Kagan and Morse also argue that 'aerobics are at once the preparation and the end activity, perhaps because the ultimate goal is maintenance of (or return to) a youthful appearance in the body itself' (1988, p. 169). Running, weightlifting and swimming are offered up by Kagan and Morse as examples of activities in which the goal is mastery over some aspect of the environment, whereas in aerobics the mastery is aimed over an individual's inertia. In contrast to a callisthenics-style exercise class, however, aerobic dance forms integrate elements of mastery of the steps.

An increasing emphasis on physical appearance for women as the aim of aerobic activity is supported by a self-esteem/body-image study on 11- to 17-year-olds. Shifts in physical activity are apparent between young girls and adolescents, as the former reject team sports such as soccer and basketball in the US, choosing aerobics and lifting weights during later teenage years (Brody, 1995a, p. 137). New food labelling requirements in the US provide detailed breakdown of a product's nutritional composition for increasing scrutiny by the consumer. As Brody explains, 'the modern teenage girl learns to measure her worth on the scale – the lower the number, the higher the score' (1995a, p. 98). Along with eating disorders such as anorexia and bulimia, scarring oneself with a knife or razor is an increasingly widespread and disturbing trend among young females. Anorexia nervosa and bulimia are manifestations of efforts to control the body to the utmost extreme, through restricting caloric intake and ridding the body of food already eaten, respectively. Self-cutting is another expression of self-loathing, directing anger at the physical self as another aspect of bodily control. Bulimia and self-cutting have been brought into heightened public awareness in part through Princess Diana's revelations of her struggles with such destructive disorders.

Sportswear styles contribute to the concept of fitness activities as display linked to external images. As Hargreaves (1994) notes, the tight-fitting yet stretchy fitness clothes both cover and reveal the human form. Wolf (1991) and Wilson (1985) link a fashion emphasis on a revealed body to the decline of *haute couture* in the 1960s. The cultural revolution which freed the body and sexuality in new ways resulted in a shift in fashion emphasis. A postmodern contradiction is evident today, in the increased desire for a muscular, slender body, accompanied by new lines of undergarments which lift and shape. As the aerobic activity results in reduced body fat and decreased breast size, implants and bras are available to reverse what some may consider a negative outcome of improved fitness. New-age underwear externally reshapes hips, thighs and the pelvic girdle, held in by high-tech fabrics rather than the stiffness of older corsetry. The body-hugging properties of Lycra, for years associated with the dancer's uniform of leotard and tights, is transferred to Wonderbras and body-shapers where they control and lift without being obvious.

It is also through fashion that individuality can be expressed in the aerobic studio. Instructors have commented on the shift in clothing away from baggy sweats and oversize T-shirts to body-hugging tights and thong leotards to coincide with a reshaped body. Regular aerobics classes such as step and slide are strongly associated with Reebok due to specialised equipment requirements. Aside from clothing and footwear, aerobic dance classes do not require weights, slides or steps. As with dance-technique training, however, the body is the only equipment in aerobic dance, therefore it offers opportunities for perpetuation of a fashion-consciousness as a companion economy.

INDIVIDUALITY AMONG THE CROWDS

Stylistic diversity is apparent in the live classes of the 1990s, marking a difference to the aerobic exercise video trend of the 1980s. Today's off-screen instructors look less to an idealised and global model for inspiration, emphasising unique elements such as teaching style and musical choices. While Jane Fonda tapes helped spark a trend, they also established a wide-spread ideal: 'In the 80's, teachers seemed to base their routines on a Jane Fonda model, which meant the repetition of a few basic steps "danced" to Madonna . . . [1990s] class styles are so varied that a typical aerobics schedule reads more like a syllabus for a pop culture class' (Steinhauer, 1995b, p. C1). Competition is stiff among teachers for more students, the best time and prime location, therefore establishing a devoted clientele is critical. Instructors interviewed did not view themselves as 'aerobic gurus'; however, each had well-formulated teaching philosophies. They perceived themselves as facilitators for the fitness student to develop bodily aware-ness, and concurrently, to evolve into a happier person as a result of the new-found knowledge.

Diversity helps overcome the boredom of repetition for long-time aerobics participants, although the cultural pluralism is presented in modified form, paralleling the breakdance trend of the 1980s. Banes's (1994) analysis of the transformation of breakdancing as a street form into a theatrical dance form highlights the intense physicality of the style. Significantly, a social function existed for the dance form, in 'using your body to publicly inscribe your identity on the surfaces of the city' (Banes, 1994, p. 145). As breakdancing is one aspect of a wider hip-hop culture of music, poetry and movement intertwined, Banes argues that it is also grounded in a moral and aesthetic code. Removed from its social context with an individualising function, the hip-hop dance steps performed by predominantly white, middle-class patrons of a private health club conveyed a sense of awkwardness. An alienation from the form was evident among newcomers to the class instead of emanating a sense of identity and commonality of experience apparent among members of a hip-hop subculture. The removal of one aspect of a broader cultural style – namely the dance steps – from their social context was glaringly apparent in classes I attended. We were consistently encouraged to adopt an attitude, use some of that 'hip-hop brain power' absent in the day-to-day activities of most class participants. Normative behaviours in contemporary offices tend to constrain exuberant expression through movement, and sedentary practices (at work and home) minimise bodily awareness.

Subcultural appropriation and assimilation into mainstream culture result in certain degrees of homogenisation, yet integration of dance styles also enables alternative economies to flourish in conjunction with the big business of sports. McRobbie's (1994) discussion of rave and cultural production identifies dominant trends in cultural studies on issues of authenticity and cultural production, in which commodification of the subculture for a mass market results in its depoliticisation. Conventional cultural studies models establish a separation between the 'pure subculture' and the 'contaminated outside world', which collapse upon closer examination of those involved in the cultural production (McRobbie, 1994, p. 161). While employment opportunities arise for the street dancer-turned-instructor, the reverse exchange between the street and the studio is evident. The university-trained contemporary dancer is advised in her rap music choices by others for whom a hip-hop culture is a way of life.

Despite links to the sports equipment and corporate clothing world, aerobic dance classes offer alternative employment for a traditionally economically-challenged subcultural member – the dancer. Rather than sports/physical fitness backgrounds, the dance component of aerobic dance necessitates dance training, whether it be institutionalised through the higher education system or whether it comes directly from the street. Long after the rigours of rehearsal and performance have taken their toll on the dancer's body, s/he can continue teaching in a venue which demands a different type of rigour than that of the Western performance dance world. Jim Karanas, group exercise director of the San Francisco-based Club One fitness corporation, explains that the influx of dancers into the industry raised the standards of teaching overall, due to their high degree of bodily awareness and musicality often absent among teachers during the early years of the aerobics phenomenon (Karanas, 1996).

Increasingly, the institutionalisation of aerobic dance results in conformity to licensing standards and certification requirements concerning aerobic rather than dance training. The extent to which education and conformity result in a watering-down of diversity and individuality associated with street dance ultimately depends upon the management of each institution. A street element already emerges as doubly mediated – initially through the entertainment industry via music videos and a second time modified for performance by fitness enthusiasts. Stylistic appeal is linked to familiarity and exposure to music and movement styles via the entertainment industry.

The relationship between the mass media and the aerobics dance trend is examined by Buckland and Stewart (1993) in representations of the female body in music videos. A connection exists between dance and the rise in popularity of the music video, in which 'dancing gains wider currency, fuelled by the media, as a desirable means of achieving both healthy fitness and the "body beautiful"' (Buckland and Stewart, 1993, p. 55). Although the live classes are not bound to the media in terms of their transmission, strong links exist between music videos, the popular music and dance moves used in classes.

Idealised bodies are the dominant representations of fitness enthusiasts in the media, yet advertised as accessible and attainable. The viewer is enticed to become a member of the initiated, as Reebok invites readers to reveal the 'athlete in all of us'. Other advertising campaigns use professional dancers to promote a product's difference and refinement. Ballerinas on pointe (Seiko watches) or dancers captured mid-air in the inventive photographs of Lois Greenfield (Raymond Weil watches) celebrate physical strength and beauty. Beyond the amateur, international competitions offer elite versions of aerobics as performance in which aerobic routines are judged for technical merit (60 per cent) and artistic impression (40 per cent). The three-minute routine is scored on the basis of 'alignment, execution, intensity, difficulty, skill, music, choreography and originality' (Nix, 1995, p. 53). Combining subjective and objective components poses problematic issues similar to those involved in judging sports with artistic components such as ice-dancing, ice-skating and gymnastics while competitive aspects draw corporate sponsorship from Nike, Reebok and Danskin, thus perpetuating a fashion/sports link.

EXERCISE FOR THE MASSES

Accessibility is a significant aspect of the aerobics trend, with easy reference to statistical and scientific information about fitness activities. Details of the caloric expenditure of different activities are published in daily newspapers, while magazines include articles on fitness and aerobics or are devoted solely to the subjects. A *Washington Post* article explains that only five calories are burned per minute if the arms are held at the sides during an aerobics class, while twelve are burned per minute if the arms are raised overhead (Squires, 1993, p. WH20). In another article, caloric expenditure and injury rates are compared between jogging, step and aerobics classes (Squires, 1994, p. WH16). Technological and scientific studies continue to support the need for aerobic exercise to maintain good health. A mind–body connection and cultural links to exercise are established in other articles, advocating a didactic purpose – a functionality extending beyond physical benefits of counteracting an otherwise sedentary lifestyle.

With such emphasis on the physical, the scientific, and keeping the body moving, is there a connection to expressive movement, or is aerobic dance merely another cog in the big wheel of sports? My opinion has shifted since beginning research for this article. Merce Cunningham's maxim that all movement is expressive would support a contention that aerobic dance functions as individualised expression in today's world. And while some crossover is apparent between concepts and manifestations of the avant-garde or high art and the popular, the thought of a thong leotard in a Cunningham or Graham technique class strikes a note of incongruity.

Comparison of high-impact aerobic classes to those with a popular/ social dance element led to an unscientifically grounded conclusion that the latter style evoked more that mere sweat and strain. While attention to developing an aesthetic dimension, a transformation associated with performance dance, was not apparent in the aerobic form, a reintegration of dance into life takes place in the class. So whether the dance element exists in a leisure centre, a private fitness club, on stage, or the dance-floor of a local night spot, its continued practice in the city and suburbs and widespread availability emerge as significant, above and beyond aesthetic and expressive issues.

REFERENCES

K. Anderson, 'Express Yourself', *Shape*, 11, 5 (January 1992), p. 72.

S. Banes, 'The African-American Connection' in *Writing Dancing in the Age of Postmodernism* (Hanover, PA and London: Wesleyan University Press, 1994), pp. 121–61.

S. Bordo, 'Reading the Slender Body' in M. Jacobus, E. F. Keller and S. Shuttleworth (eds), *Body/Politics: Women and the Discourses of Science* (New York and London: Routledge, 1990), pp. 83–112.

L. Brody, 'Are We Losing Our Girls?', *Shape*, 15, 3 (November 1995a), p. 94.

L. Brody, 'Mild, Medium or Hot?', *Shape*, 15, 2 (October 1995b), p. 96.

T. J. Buckland with E. Stewart, 'Dance & Music Video' in S. Jordan and D. Allen (eds), *Parallel Lines: Media Representations of Dance* (London: John Libbey, 1993), pp. 51–79.

K. Dohney, 'The Fitness Doctor is In', *Los Angeles Times*, 113 (7 June 1994), p. E3.

M. Foucault, *Discipline and Punish: The Birth of the Prison*, trans. Alan Sheridan (London: Vintage Books, 1979).

– 'Body/Power', reprinted in C. Gordon (ed. and trans.), *Power/Knowledge: Selected Interviews & Other Writings, 1972–1977* (New York: Pantheon Books, 1980), pp. 53–62.

S. Giddens, 'Yogarobics', *Women's Sports & Fitness* (January/February 1992), p. 54.

P. D. Graf, 'Cultural Workout', *Minneapolis/St. Paul*, 22, 5 (May 1994), p. 28.

C. Guinot, 'Dance!', *Weight Watchers Magazine*, 27, 5 (May 1994), p. 28.

J. L. Hanna, *To Dance is Human: A Theory of Nonverbal Communication* (Chicago and London: 1979, University of Chicago Press edn, 1987), pp. 199–229.

J. Hargreaves, *Sporting Females: Critical Issues in the History and Sociology of Women's Sports* (London: Routledge, 1994).

T. Ikonian, 'Stepping Across Borders', *Women's Sports and Fitness*, 15, 1 (January/February 1993), p. 34.

F. Jameson, 'Postmodernism and Consumer Culture', reprinted in E. A. Kaplan (ed.), *Postmodernism and its Discontents* (London: Verso, 1988), pp. 13–29.

P. Jordan, 'Editorial: Can Leg Lifts Make You Dumb?', *American Fitness*, 13, 4 (July/August 1995), p. 7.

E. Kagan and M. Morse, 'The Body Electronic, Aerobic Exercise on Video: Women's Search for Empowerment and Self-Transformation', *TDR*, 32, 4 (1988), pp. 164–80.

E. Ann Kaplan (ed.), *Postmodernism and its Discontents* (London: Verso, 1988).

P. Kasinitz (ed.), *Metropolis: Centre and Symbol of Our Times* (New York: New York University Press, 1995).

C. Krucoff, 'From Bubba Funk to Cardio Combat: Trend Setting Classes Feature Street Dance, Sculpting and Step', *Washington Post* (3 August 1993), p. WH16.

A. McRobbie, *Postmodernism and Popular Culture* (London: Routledge, 1994).

W. Melillo, 'The Battle of the Fitness Videos', *Washington Post*, 115 (10 November 1993), p. WH12.

A. Nix, 'World Class Aerobic Athletes Face Off in Japan', *American Fitness*, 13, 4 (July/August 1995), p. 53.

L. Paul, 'Funky Fitness: Victoria Johnson's Technifunk Aerobics', *Women's Sports and Fitness*, 14, 1 (January/February 1992), p. 50.

J. Servin, 'Members' Muscle Only', *The New York Times*, 142 (4 January 1993), p. V8.

W. Sharpe and L. Wallock, 'Bold New City or Built-Up 'Burb? Redefining Contemporary Suburbia', *American Quarterly*, 46, 1 (March 1994), pp. 1–30.

G. Simmel, 'The Metropolis and Mental Life' in P. Kasinitz (ed.), *Metropolis: Centre and Symbol of Our Times* (New York: New York University Press, 1995), pp. 30–46.

S. Squires, 'Fitness Benefits Make Step Aerobics Popular', *Washington Post*, 116 (9 November 1993), p. WH20.

S. Squires, 'Aerobics is Aerobics in Test of Intensity', *Washington Post*, 117 (1 November 1994), p. WH16.

J. Steinhauer, '90's Anthem: So Many Gyms, So Little Time', *New York Times* (1 January 1995a), Section 1, p. 41.

– 'For Aerobic Die-Hards, No Substitute Teachers', *New York Times* (February 1995b), p. C1.

H. Sweet, 'Muscle Ballet', *Harper's Bazaar* (March 1992), p. 16.

H. Thomas, *Dance, Modernity and Culture: Explorations in the Sociology of Dance* (London: Routledge, 1995), pp. 1–30.

D. Umansky, 'Step Power: A Guide to Step Aerobics', *Weight Watchers Magazine*, 27, 6 (August 1994), p. 26.

Weintraub, Jeff, 'Varieties and Vicissitudes of Public Space' in P. Kasinitz (ed.), *Metropolis: Centre and Symbol of Our Times* (New York: New York University Press, 1995), pp. 280–319.

E. Wilson, *Adorned in Dreams* (London: Virago, 1985).

T. Winter, 'An Exercise in Contradiction: Reading the Aerobics Video', compiled by J. Adshead-Lansdale, *Border Tensions: Dance and Discourse*, Proceedings of the Fifth Study of Dance Conference (Guildford: Department of Dance Studies, University of Surrey, 1995), pp. 345–54.

Wirth, Louis, 'Urbanism as a Way of Life' in P. Kasinitz (ed.), *Metropolis: Center and Symbol of Our Times* (New York: New York University Press, 1995), pp. 58–82.

N. Wolf, *The Beauty Myth: How Images of Beauty Are Used Against Women* (New York: Doubleday, 1991).

OTHER SOURCES

Erica Green, personal communications with the author, June and September 1995.

Jim Karanas, interview with the author, January 1996.

Connie Lambrecht, interview with the author, September 1995.

Fabienne Levenson, interview with the author, August 1995.

Teela Shine-Ross, interview with the author, September 1995.

12 Dance and Erotica: The Construction of the Female Stripper
Sherril Dodds

INTRODUCTION

Over the past ten years I have become increasingly fascinated by the role of women in the sex industry, and this appears to have come about for two main reasons. The first is fuelled by an interest in feminism, and one of its central paradoxes of whether women are either fundamentally exploited or else empowered through the sale of their bodies for sexual gratification. The second, I am afraid, is far less noble. It is based on simple curiosity, and the somewhat illicit and taboo status of the British sex industry has clearly appealed to my inquisitive nature. As a nineteen-year-old, I would spend an hour or so nervously wandering around the red-light district of Soho as I peeked into sex shops, stared at the women who sat in the doorways of strip clubs, and collected the odd calling-card for 'Lady Whip' or the 'Lovely Denise' as a souvenir. It therefore came as a perfect opportunity to undertake some serious study into female striptease, when I was required to observe and analyse a 'dance event' as part of my research in dance anthropology.

The research, which forms the subject of this chapter, takes the shape of an ethnography, and is based on my fieldwork experiences in which I attended a number of striptease performances. The fieldwork was conducted in 1993, and took place at two venues in London, in which women would remove their clothes to a state of nudity whilst dancing before a public audience. The first is a theatre bar which is situated in a known red-light district in central London. Its shows take place during the evening and cost approximately £15 per seat. The second is a pub venue located in southeast London that charges no entrance fee. The pub is licensed for all-day opening and there is a continuous rotation of strippers throughout the day.

I have divided the chapter into two parts. The first constitutes an analysis of how the stripper is socially constructed, through which description and analysis are used to create an ethnographic 'picture' of the dance event. The second section deals with issues of power, and how such power is distributed in the striptease context. Because of the taboo nature of sex within our society, and the plethora of codes and values surrounding sexual practices, there are many controversies and contradictions within such a study. Therefore at times it is necessary to offer more than one interpretation of a particular phenomenon. It is also crucial at this point to state my belief that we exist and operate within a patriarchal social structure, and as the collection and analysis of data can never be value-free, the study adopts a theoretical bias towards a feminist perspective.

THE SOCIAL CONSTRUCTION OF THE STRIPPER

The construct of the stripper would appear to involve the interaction of three parties: the stripper herself, the audience members, whom I refer to as the 'clients', and the agents who work for the establishments, whom I refer to as the 'hosts'. The following section, therefore, considers each of these three parties in turn. As the study focuses on two separate venues, I have used a comparative analysis rather than a general summation of events.

The Stripper

At the theatre bar, when the clients have been seated, the show is introduced by a dynamic male voice set against a pulsating disco theme. Such a build-up gives an immediate sense of spectacle and theatricality. The theatre-bar show lasts for one and a half hours and comprises several acts, with an interval half-way through. Each act is based on a theme and the different costumes are designed in relation to this. The costumes are highly elaborate and theatrical, which convey notions of glamour and artistry. Much of the theatrical attire that is traditionally associated with the female mystique is employed: fur coats, feather boas, and plumed head-dresses. The stereotype of feathers and fur has symbolically linked women to slang names such as 'bird', 'chick', 'pussy' and 'bitch'. It is therefore significant that within our society animals are subject to man's 'right' to make them captive and domesticated at his will. If certain animals are effectively controlled and manipulated by 'man', then to call women by 'pet' names perhaps implies that they too belong to a similarly subordinate position. At the pub venue the strippers are given no formal introduction. They often wander around the pub beforehand, and appear to begin their act in their own time. As a result there is little sense of theatrical tension. There are about three or four sessions of striptease a day and each session is divided between two strippers who alternate slots at about five- or ten-minute intervals. The women at the pub venue must provide their own costumes and as a result this attire is quite varied. In general, the costumes exuded less glamour than the theatre bar by tending towards the everyday. They ranged from denim shorts and vest tops, through to the striptease cliché of suspender belts and stockings. There was clearly less sense of luxury and the exotic, as they appeared to be the type of garments that could be bought across the counter at cheap fashion outlets.

Although there was a qualitative shift between the theatre bar and the pub venue, both adhered to a dominant feminine representation which has been historically applied to women: the duality of woman as virgin or whore. The former image was constructed through garments such as a pink baby-doll gown and white lace underwear, whilst the latter was conveyed through scarlet hot pants and black fluffy G-strings. The virgin construct, which draws on images of youth and purity, places women in a position of vulnerability, whilst that of the whore colludes her with sexual assertiveness and immorality; the virgin represents a challenge to deflower, and the whore becomes a challenge to tame. On another level it has been suggested that in striptease the female body becomes masculinised and in turn, the male client identifies this as his self-image: the phallic stiletto heels and the various images of captivity manifest in bondage wear (Kroker and Kroker, 1987).

At the theatre bar there is a uniform application of make-up: heavy foundation, dark shades of eye colour and red, sticky lips which are a symbolic display of sexual arousal. The women also wear gold body glitter which gives the skin a sense of luxury and price that warrants it desirable. The heavy application of make-up creates a mask-like face, and the near-identicalness of the strippers diminishes their sense of individuality. Although on one level this is a common theatrical practice, it may also be read as a conscious means to protect the stripper from any kind of recognition and resulting harassment outside the workplace. This sense of discretion perhaps highlights the potential risks of the profession. Another perspective would suggest that the conveyor-belt of identical women effactually objectifies them through the representation of woman as mass-produced ornament and decoration.

At the pub venue the make-up was applied according to personal taste, and tended towards an everyday look, which made the women more recognizable as individuals. There was clearly a range in skill and style which varied from a heavier, punk look, through to a stripper who wore no make-up and had a large cold-sore on her chin. The everyday style and the qualitative fluctuations once again served to diminish notions of artistry and mystique. Although the pub venue was at the cheaper range of the market, in general the women still pertained to a female stereotype. One woman had bleached her hair to such a degree that it had become yellow and wiry with split ends, but, as the saying goes, 'blondes have more fun'. At both venues the women were between sizes 8 and 12, were approximately between 5'6"and 5'8", and were generally of youthful appearance. The theatre-bar strippers all appeared to have well-toned bodies, and whilst some at the pub venue had visible cellulite, or slightly sagging breasts, their overall sizes reflected the late twentieth-century consumer ideal of the nubile female: young, feminine and petite. At the theatre bar there is a clear divide between the clients and the strippers. The clients face a raised stage on which a curtain rises to reveal the strippers. After the routine, the curtain lowers again to seal the strippers off. This boundary, which neither party ever attempted to cross, gives the strippers a sense of the exotic, the unavailable, and what may be termed 'the other'. At the pub venue the strippers also performed on a stage, but to get to it they had to walk through the bar area, which is the client's domain. On the one hand this close-range availability diminished any sense of mystique, especially as the strippers often walked back to their changing room naked; yet this may account for the sociable atmosphere that permeated the pub. In terms of proxemics, the pub-venue strippers were placed in a more approachable position, which allowed for an informal degree of social interaction. Once again this highlights one of the fundamental differences between the two venues. The way in which the strippers at the theatre bar are distanced from the clients adds to the element of theatricality, while the close proximity of the pub-venue strippers emphasizes the everyday.

It is interesting to note that both venues had a stage, and this may be analysed from two perspectives. On the one hand the strippers are placed in a higher physical position and are therefore elevated in status. The notion of them being central to the attention, and a focus for action is potentially a powerful position; yet there is also a sense of them being placed on a pedestal, separated as ornaments and thus objectified into a passive position.

The routines at the theatre bar were highly choreographed and professionally executed. The choreography drew upon simple disco steps, mimetic sexual gesturing and cabaret motifs. The women undressed fairly soon into the act and the whole effect was of an extremely fast and slick operation, which negates any sense of tease and eroticism. There was an obvious use of sexual symbolism in a number of phallic props which lacked the degree of subtlety required for a climactic build-up of erotic tension. When the strippers caressed either the props or each other, the gesture was highly superficial. It came across as routine and surface symbolism, without any act of intention behind the movement. Likewise, there was little sense of interaction with the audience; the strippers simply stared out at the audience with plastic smiles, and during the group routines, they even further excluded the clients by having a wry smile among themselves.

The acts at the pub venue were all improvised solos and the strippers brought along their own choice of records. A vast range of movement was displayed depending upon the individual: some merely wiggled along to the music whilst others executed more gymnastic routines; some were sexually explicit and played with their breasts and genitals, whilst others would exploit the element of tease. The routines were slower in general and there was more sense of self-arousal whilst doing the movement. The women's facial expressions suggested that they too were sexually stimulated by their performance. I would imagine, however, that this is based on good acting ability rather than any degree of genuine arousal.

Regardless of the disparity between the two venues, both made clear display of women as sexual objects. The focus was constantly directed towards the breasts and, more predominantly, the genitals, through positioning the women's bodies in such a way that these body parts would be the centre of attention. The strippers arched their backs, spread their legs and protruded their buttocks so that there was no sense of an erotic whole, or a celebration of the total female body; rather, they were persistently reduced to an exposed and available display of their sex: their genitals.

As the strippers at the pub venue often wandered around the bar area, I spoke to several of the women over a period of time. They were very accepting of my interest in the field and, almost in every case, were extremely willing to divulge information. The women spoke quickly and although we were usually limited by time constraints, the conversation poured out. This desire to speak perhaps highlights the sense of social stigma that is still attached to the sex industry and as a result, women are silenced by it, or feel the need to defend their position.

Most of the women used false names for work, and one of the strippers, 'Cindy' always wore a black Cleopatra-style wig. She said that it was not to disguise herself, but to separate her work identity from her private life. It is debatable, however, as to whether she would construct a false persona if the profession was of a higher status in society. Although many of the women took pride in their work, there is still a social stigma attached which could potentially affect their position in society. 'Suzie', a blonde stripper who was studying for a university degree, said that only close friends knew about her work. This is because she had once been sacked from a bar job when it became known that she also worked as a part-time stripper. Suzie also mentioned that she had once auditioned to work at the theatre bar, but dismissed it by saying, 'it's like a proper job there, and you have to rehearse through the day and learn new routines'. It is interesting that she did not want her stripping to constitute a 'proper job', and therefore undermined the status of the profession.

It appears that a striptease position at the theatre bar does carry a degree of prestige. One hopeful interviewee said to the manager, 'I've always wanted to see the show', which perhaps highlights its reputation. The women at the pub venue clearly had no delusions of glamour, and in general were quite scathing of the place. Cindy simply stated, 'it's tacky here', and seemed to have little respect for the type of dancing that was performed. She said that it was not 'proper dancing' because she just 'posed around', which required little stamina.

The various women appeared to be working in the industry for a number of reasons but, at some point in the conversation, they all mentioned the financial benefits. Suzie stated that she could earn more in a night from stripping than she could in a week if she was waitressing, and as a result had become used to the money. Some of the strippers said that they enjoyed the work, and clearly had a degree of pride in their profession. Cindy explained that they are only paid for the striptease, but she adds that mixing with the clients is part of the skill of the job, as it creates a good atmosphere. Yet it is notable that the strippers were aware of the various stereotypes to which they conformed. Cindy said that she would not normally wear such feminine attire, and Suzie was very conscious of the dichotomy of being a respected and intelligent woman in the context of her university, and then having to behave as a 'bimbo' at the pub venue.

The strippers also highlighted various drawbacks to the work. Cindy was extremely concerned that I should not stay too late as she cited several incidents in which strippers had been followed on their way home from the pub. On the subject of sexual harassment she said that it may occur anywhere, regardless of the class of the establishment. The apparent availability of the stripper is demonstrated as the men clearly feel at liberty to touch the women up. It appears that this is not an acceptable practice and many of the women respond by swearing, or hitting out at the men. Cindy felt that this was both risky and not particularly diplomatic (although she had once assaulted a client herself) as the men were often drunk and aggressive, and outnumbered the stripper with their companions.

In general the women appeared to 'look out' for each other, yet this necessary precaution still highlights the vulnerable position of the female stripper. Whereas Cindy appeared to take it all in her stride, and believed it was just part of the job, her colleague 'Jeanette' said that she could not bear to be touched by the men, and that she found this difficult to deal

with. Cindy summed up her work as a stripper like this: 'You need two
things for this job: a good sense of humour and a broad back.'

The Client

The theatre bar has an almost exclusively male clientele and, across several visits, it became apparent that the audience is about 60 per cent white
European and about 40 per cent Japanese. The majority were middle-aged,
but there were also a few younger men. Although several clients wore
business suits, the majority wore casual trousers, shirts and jumpers. In
general their appearance was clean, smart and well-groomed, and they probably represented a fairly middle-class range.

The clients at the pub venue were exclusively male and were divided
into approximately half white European and half Afro-Caribbean. Many
were regulars and in general, the age range was younger than that of the
theatre-bar clients. They were mainly in their twenties and thirties and
tended to be less well-groomed. They wore cheap-looking trousers with
old sweatshirts and jumpers, and appeared to represent a mainly working-
class audience. In many ways, the dress code of each establishment was
determined by the venue. For instance it was clearly acceptable at the pub
venue to wear shabby, old clothes whereas anyone in this type of dress at
the theatre bar would most probably be refused admission. There were,
however, some exceptions. Occasionally there would be a small group
of men at the pub venue constituting a 'lads' night out'. They would be
dressed in smarter clothes which suggested that they would be going on
somewhere that required a more formal dress code, and that the pub venue
was just a taster for the night ahead. On one occasion a group of business-
men appeared who clearly represented a more middle-class background;
they were well-spoken, smoked cigars and drank spirits in preference to
beer. This ties in with the notion of them coming for a 'bit of rough'.

At the theatre bar the men responded politely to the show. There
was orderly clapping at the end of each act, but never any wild bouts of
enthusiasm. Although the manager insisted that the show sometimes sold
out, there were usually only about 30 or 40 clients in the auditorium which
had a capacity of 200. At times their response was verging on the lack-
lustre, which perhaps had something to do with the small audience numbers, and in some instances the men would look quite bored. In between
acts, when the house lights came up, they would glance around awkwardly.
This may result from either the formal set-up of the show, or the sense of
social stigma that is still attached to the sex industry.

The pub venue had a far more relaxed atmosphere and there was a clear difference in the behaviour of the men who were there as regulars, and those who were specifically there to see the show. The regulars played pool, chatted to the bar staff, drank with their companions, and only sometimes glanced over at the stripper. The latter group, however, watched far more intently and, if they were accompanied, would joke and encourage each other, and call out to the stripper. Both groups of men appeared to be on familiar terms with the strippers, and would chat with the women and buy them drinks. It is interesting that the men at the pub venue clearly felt at liberty to express a sexual desire for the women and would openly flirt or request a kiss or a cuddle.

Although the men at the theatre bar showed little visible appreciation, the three clients whom I interviewed were initially very enthusiastic towards the show. They unanimously agreed that it was high-calibre entertainment for its genre and commented upon the professional dancing and impressive costumes. Although the three clients praised the artistry of the show, they also referred to the heavy make-up, the plastic smiles and how the impact of seeing the women's breasts and genitals diminishes through the constant display of them. It is perhaps the fast turnover of material, the repetitive structure and the relentless sexual display which dulls the audience into a state of passivity. Yet although they recognize the very mechanics which de-eroticize the performance, there is still a sense of witnessing the unavailable, and a desire for titillation; one of the men winked and said, 'We had the chance to come here and thought it was a good opportunity.'

Between the two venues there were a variety of responses towards the striptease act, but one position remains common to all of the clients: they all have the right to look at their will. They are permitted to 'look out for' or 'have an eye for' the women at their discretion which places them in an active role. The act of looking suggests selection, possession and evaluation (Kroker and Kroker, 1987). The film scholar, Laura Mulvey (1989) has analysed the construct of visual pleasure in relation to narrative cinema, but the theoretical model may be applied equally to striptease. She begins with the notion of scopophilia, which is the pleasure of looking. Freud saw this as a fascination with the human form in which a person becomes objectified when placed under a gaze. Mulvey then suggests that our society manifests a sexual imbalance in the very act of looking: men look, and women are looked at. She posits that the female role is to exhibit visual and erotic impact which is described as 'to-be-looked-at-ness' and, therefore, women are placed in a passive role, whilst the 'male gaze' remains active. As men are not objectified within the symbolic order of society, the active gaze is therefore always male. To some extent in female striptease, this division of roles is very much apparent. The strippers are constructed as an erotic spectacle which is intended to appeal to the gaze of a male audience. Yet it is perhaps too simplistic to see the strippers as completely passive. After all, the very act of dancing to incite sexual pleasure in the spectator suggests an element of 'activity'.

The Host

The function of the theatre bar as a striptease venue is clearly advertised, with its publicity posters and neon signs outside. The venue is made to seem attractive with its plush red carpets, computerized box office, and two doormen dressed in black tie. This sense of respectability pervades the establishment. The staff are polite and their service is discreet and efficient.

At the pub venue there is no indication that it is a strip venue. From the outside it would appear to be a normal pub, except for the windows, which are boarded over. This is obviously a legal requirement but it gives the place a sense of the illicit and taboo. The bar staff were similar to any other staff of a working-men's pub. They were casual and, in general, quite friendly. In a couple of instances, however, it lacked the discreet professionalism of the theatre bar. In one situation the bar staff were obviously concerned about my presence and made an awkward attempt to refuse service on the grounds that I was under-age.

As a public-service operation, the theatre bar was extremely efficient by many standards; yet whilst interviewing the manager, he reiterated several times, 'We like to think we're professional.' He almost overemphasized the point so as to suggest that although the sex industry has seedy and immoral connotations, the theatre bar has tried to place it within the realms of respectability. It was very apparent that he considered the whole operation to lie in the hands of the men. When asked if the women were professionally-trained dancers, he replied, '[The choreographer] could teach a cabbage to dance.' He also impressed upon me the fact that the choreographer was a trained ballet dancer, therefore placing him within the realms of high art rather than commercialism. The emphasis on classical training implies skill and learning which again adds to the manager's claims of professionalism.

In interviews both the manager and choreographer conveyed a degree of competition between the women. This was not as obvious rivals, but in the sense that they were constantly required to compete for, and maintain, male approval. For example, when the choreographer auditions the strippers, there are always more women present than he is able to employ. He lines the women up and immediately dismisses them if they are too short or too fat, and sometimes suggests that they re-audition when they have lost weight. So although they may not even gain employment, he exercises control over the women beyond the parameters of the venue. In many ways this is not unlike the audition and employment procedures of traditional dance companies.

The notion of skill is placed low on the list of priorities, as it is only when the women have passed the tests of physical appearance that they are required to dance. Even then it does not appear to be an essential requirement as the choreographer stated that if a novice is unable to pick up any of the steps, then he is quite happy to alter them for her ability. Once the stripper has become a full-time member of the show, her position is only secured for a one-year contract. If she does not live up to the expectations of the men in control, then she is asked to leave. The manager commented on the regrettable nature of this: 'It is one of the hardest things in the world when we have to let a girl go.' It was not only noticeable that his over-sympathetic tone verged on the insincere, but it also reasserted that the men are in the position of control and, with it, have the right to hire or fire the women.

In discussing the creative process the choreographer emphasized the artistic concept rather than the need to create an erotic product. It is interesting that on the one hand he was indifferent to the fact that he himself had quite an accomplished technical background, but was dealing with dancers of little or no technical experience. He dismissed the matter by saying that he is not trying to say anything with his choreography as that is not the intention of the show. Yet there is a dichotomy as he constantly reinforced the sense of artistry in the work.

The choreographer mentioned that he has been offered a lot of work in pornography, but said he was uninterested in that area of business, although the money is very good. It is interesting that he drew a line between the notion of the erotic, in which he considers the theatre bar to be situated, and the pornographic. He suggested that two movements may be identical, but if performed 'artistically', with beautiful costumes and subtle lighting, then it is erotic. Whereas the same movement, set under stark lighting and executed without any sense of performance, places it within the realms of pornography. The feminist writer Andrea Dworkin finds faults with such definitions: 'In the male sexual lexicon, which is the vocabulary of power, erotica is simply high-class pornography: better produced, better conceived, better executed, better packaged, designed for a better class of consumer' (1981, Preface).

The above quotation would appear to encapsulate the fundamental difference between the theatre bar and the pub venue; both provide the opportunity for men to gaze at women's nude bodies, except that one venue offers a more 'tasteful' version.

POSITIONS OF POWER WITHIN THE STRIPTEASE CONTEXT

The previous section provides a detailed analysis of two female striptease venues in London. This section aims to use this material in order to analyse positions of power within the striptease setting. Firstly, it must be noted that no person in the striptease context is completely without power. All of the individuals involved may influence or alter the state of things in some way, but the distribution of power inevitably shifts according to whether the analytical focus is taken from the stripper, the host or the client. This section therefore does not intend, or even attempt, to discuss every area of power within the striptease phenomenon, but to highlight some of the more central issues in relation to the fieldwork data.

One of the most basic arguments used to defend the sex industry in general is that it operates on a mutual relationship of supply and demand. That is, men are in demand of sexual fulfilment, and women are in a position to supply it in return for monetary payment. Many arguments are used along these lines, but it is necessary to question whether a reciprocal financial transaction is too simplistic a justification, and to consider what other implications are involved.

Women are undoubtedly able to earn more money through stripping than they would in relation to other unskilled labour. At the theatre bar the strippers earn approximately £300 per week, and at the pub venue, they receive £12 per hour, plus tips. Other unskilled service jobs usually offer between £3 and £5 per hour. Were it not for the high pay, it is debatable whether women would necessarily choose striptease as a profession. It may simply be a case of economic submission as women are generally undervalued in the workplace: whereas women only constitute 32 per cent of managerial and administrative positions in Great Britain, they make up 76 per cent of clerical and secretarial positions (Equal Opportunities Commission, 1995).

The placing of a woman's body within a financial transaction reduces her to a commodity and it is questionable whether this inevitably places the clients within a more powerful social position. Several theories have emerged which both recognize and celebrate the sexual objectification of women and see this as a position of power in its own right. Debi Sundahl, an American stripper, argues that being a sex object is acceptable within the striptease context, as it is part of a profession and should be respected as such (Delacoste and Alexander, 1987). Her job is to express her sexuality in a skilled and meaningful way, and if she fails to arouse, then she has failed at her job.

In the order of the everyday world, men usually only see women with whom they are familiar take their clothes off. This act of undressing is generally part of a utilitarian function: so there is rarely a sense of performance. In the striptease context, however, the women consciously make a display of the very act of undressing. In fact this image is one that is widely used throughout soft pornography in which women are 'caught in the act' of undressing. Permitting men to witness this spectacle could be seen as putting them in a position of power. There is also a notion of pride and freedom in revealing the female form.

These various arguments are all based on notions of women being at liberty to express their sexuality on their own terms. It is therefore important to locate the ways in which a woman's sexuality is constituted. The post-structuralist thinker Michel Foucault defines the body as an 'inscribed surface of events' (Kroker and Kroker, 1987, p. 169). He posits that the body is a site of discourses which are socially, historically and culturally constituted. Therefore, the female body is not inherently erotic, but has been posed, dressed up and written by the society in which it exists. As our society operates as a patriarchal system, the female body both literally and metaphorically constitutes a man-made construct. This theory dissipates the very idea of stripping being a personal expression of an innate female sexuality. Women do not possess a 'natural' self, but instead are constructed through predetermined gender identities.

Within our culture there is a duality between mind and body, and the two are seen to be distinct. The mind is cerebral and associated with rationality and order and historically men have represented the thinking sex. Women on the other hand are more closely associated with the body and nature. This is perhaps linked with their bodily cycles and their natural capacity to reproduce. Traditionally the body is considered a sensuous and passionate instrument which aligns it with evil, the uncivilized and a number of other negative attributes. This is echoed in the symbolic links between the womb and hysteria which has deemed women erratic, emotive and irrational. So whereas the rational male has been placed in the public domain of worldly affairs, the emotive female is confined to the private domain of the home, as the provider of both domestic and sexual labour (Adair, 1992). It has therefore become the social norm for women to be defined in terms of service and sexuality, which are in effect the roles of the striptease artist.

The feminine beauty ideal within our society serves to maintain male dominance as it is weak and passive in comparison to the male ideal. The current ideal of feminine beauty and attractiveness demands that the female body be small, slim and attractively decorated, and the image of the stripper, both at the theatre bar and the pub venue, perpetuates this ideal. Men are believed to be physically stronger than women and traditionally choose partners who are smaller than themselves. Although women obviously have a degree of physical strength, a powerful and muscular frame is considered unfeminine and unattractive. It is perhaps also seen as a threat to masculinity.

As women are constantly presented with this feminine ideal, they are required to undergo a number of time-consuming activities in order to achieve and maintain it. Diet-management and cosmetic ornamentation have encouraged the growth of a massive beauty industry. A whole consumer culture has developed which may be economically exploited by the male, capitalist system in which our society operates. This constant manipulation of women may be said to result in the production of 'docile and disciplined' bodies (Featherstone, 1991, p. 170). By creating a society in which women are actively encouraged to develop a time-laboured obsession with preserving and decorating their bodies, it conveniently prevents them from presenting any other type of political challenge. In response to this, however, it could be argued that women take a certain pleasure in 'dressing up' which effectively negates this idea of women as 'docile ornaments'. To take pleasure in something implies an element of personal agency and therefore a resistance to being constituted as completely passive.

Foucault posits that when people are placed in a position of surveillance, eventually the surveillant is no longer required to be physically present as the individual has learnt to watch herself; so the gaze becomes internalized (Gore, 1993). This notion of the 'internalized gaze' may be applied to the social construction of women. The slim, adorned body of the ideal construct created by men, and proliferated throughout the media, is the equivalent of the gaze; in effect women internalize this male projection of slenderness, youth and beauty, and as a result women merit their success and failure in life depending on how they match the ideal. This ideological process based upon the 'body beautiful' may be said to be a means of suppressing the position of women in society.

The final area of social construction that is important to consider is in relation to language. It could be argued that striptease easily lies within the parameters of the pornographic, as pornography has been defined as 'explicit representation of sexual activity visually or descriptively to stimulate erotic rather than aesthetic feelings' (Allen, 1984, p. 572). It is therefore interesting that striptease is frequently referred to as erotic entertainment or exotic dancing, rather than pornography. It would seem that the word pornography carries with it associations of immorality and degradation; so the former phrases conveniently place it within the realms of the artistic and the respectable. This appears to highlight our phallogocentric society in which language is biased towards men. The 'erotic art versus pornography' debate has been well documented within feminism (see Segal and McIntosh, 1992).

The various ways in which women have been socially, culturally and historically constituted all appear to maintain the patriarchal equilibrium and as a result, women are placed in a position of little power. The gender construct of the feminine ideal, to which the stripper conforms, would seem to be a reflection and acceptance of women's subordinate position within the symbolic order of our society. It therefore could be argued that all the strippers at the theatre bar and the pub venue are able to express and be proud of is a gender construct determined by a patriarchal system.

Yet it could be argued that the striptease phenomenon is in fact an inversion of the everyday world, in which women are placed within a position of power to which men are subordinate. Firstly the female stripper is placed in a position of power as she takes on attributes that are traditionally associated with men. The stripper becomes sexually assertive and takes control of the sexual offer, whilst the man is reduced to a passive state of voyeurism. The stripper then instigates a loss of control in the man. Whether it is a public display of desire, or a private erection or act of masturbation, this places her in a position of power. There is even a notion of collusion, in which the sisterhood of female strippers are effectually duping the clients through their distinctly unerotic acts.

This notion of female strippers as being a challenge to the dominant male order is reiterated elsewhere (Delacoste and Alexander, 1987, Kroker and Kroker, 1987). It has been suggested that the way in which the stripper's body has been written signifies a sexual insatiability. The constant references to sexual desire, and its relentless offers become a threatening proposition to the client: 'These statements challenge the privileged masculine position within sexual discourse by imposing sexual demands, unsettling certainly to even the most confident of readers' (Kroker and Kroker, 1987, p. 180).

These various theories which assert that female strippers are powerful in their position to control and manipulate men's desire are nevertheless negated when applied to the theatre bar. The whole concept of the show is designed by men, for men, in which the women are manipulated as the puppets of a male fantasy. There is more potential at the pub venue for the women to assert control over the men as they have a greater degree of liberty to design their own acts. Some of the women teased and mocked the men. Yet these various arguments, which suggest that the female strippers are in a position of power because they are challenging and causing men to lose bodily control, is perhaps an over-simplistic justification for striptease. The alibi of losing bodily control becomes a convenient disclaimer for men to justify any consequences of his sexual arousal, and the implications of it within the real world are potentially detrimental (Dworkin, 1981).

Nevertheless, there are still other ways in which striptease has been said to challenge the symbolic order of men and women. Kroker and Kroker (1987) suggest that the analysis of 'the look' in relation to the traditional duality of male/female, seeing/being seen, does not apply to the pornographic genre. Instead it is suggested that the stripper must solicit a look from the client which becomes a mutual exchange of eye contact rather than the active/passive relationship of the 'male gaze'. This two-way process of gazing is defined as 'ocular penetration'. The implications of this theory place the stripper in a position of power as she is able to close, or avert her eyes, which serves to exclude or deny penetration to the spectator. Yet this could be simply read as an aspect of the tease, as ultimately the client remains clothed, and therefore armed, whilst the stripper becomes naked and completely exposed to his gaze. Her eyes may remain shut, but there are many other orifices on her body where he may apply his penetrating stare.

It is perhaps this notion which highlights the fundamental imbalance of power in striptease. Regardless of whether men are ridiculous for allowing themselves to be financially exploited in their desire for titillation, or demonstrated to be weak and passive as they succumb to the sexual control of the stripper, it is ultimately the woman who must offer her body for the purpose of male pleasure. The men are at liberty to cast their eyes across her naked body, which has been reduced to an exposed and vulnerable display of her genitals.

REFERENCES

C. Adair, *Women and Dance: Sylphs and Sirens* (London: Macmillan, 1992).
R. Allen, *Pocket Oxford Dictionary*, 7th edn (Oxford: Oxford University Press, 1984).

R. Barthes, *Mythologies* (London: Paladin, 1973).

S. Browne, 'I'm Working my Way through College', *Sunday Times* (11.4.93).

F. Delacoste and P. Alexander, *Sex Work* (London: Virago, 1987).

A. Dworkin, *Pornography: Men Possessing Women* (London: Women's Press, 1981).

J. Elsom, *Erotic Theatre* (London: Secker & Warburg, 1973).

Equal Opportunities Commission, *Some Facts about Women* (Manchester, 1995).

M. Featherstone, 'The Body in Consumer Culture' in M. Hepworth and B. Turner (eds), *The Body: Social and Cultural Theory* (London: Sage, 1991).

G. Gore, *Postmodernism: Dance and Popular Culture* (unpublished University of Surrey Lecture, Research Week, 22–26 March 1993).

A. Kroker and M. Kroker (eds), *Body Invaders: Panic Sex in America* (Canada: Oxford University Press, 1987).

M. Meyer, 'I Dream of Jeanie: Transsexual Striptease as Scientific Display', *The Drama Review*, 35, 1 (Spring 1991), pp. 25–42.

L. Mulvey, *Visual and Other Pleasures* (London: Macmillan, 1989).

L. Segal and M. McIntosh (eds), *Sex Exposed: Sexuality and the Pornography Debate* (London: Virago, 1992).

13 Let's Face the Music – and Dance?: Torvill and Dean – 'Champagne on Ice'

Stephanie Jordan and Helen Thomas

Frank Keating, sports writer of the *Guardian,* wrote in February 1984 of the daftness of winning an Olympic medal for enacting the scenario of 'Two young people unable to marry, who climb a volcanic mountain to hurl themselves into the blazing inferno' (Parry, 1984, p. 17). He was referring of course to the Torvill and Dean *Bolero* and pointing to the craziness of winning at sport on pure style. Certainly, the dance critics have been more than happy to claim Torvill and Dean for themselves as exponents of high art. There are of course other big things to celebrate. For instance, writes Alastair Macaulay (1984, p. 20), 'Romance has made them national heroes.' It should be noted that we are avoiding here the old arguments about 'is it sport or art?' This is because the immediate arguments about how Torvill and Dean situate themselves between these boundaries now seem tired, and there is also a useful body of literature about technical differences between dance on land and on ice (see Best, 1974; Reid, 1970). Instead, we would like to point out new facets of these borderlines, between skating, dance and sport, to discuss some remaining untapped boundary issues. Our ultimate aim is to reach a more subtle answer to the question of what is Torvill and Dean. Complementary forces are acting here between the ice dance itself, the culture of sport, and the highly important media trappings of sport. We write from the perspective of dancers rather than of skating experts.

Potentially, many inherent features of ice dance rub shoulders rather easily with sport, more subtle ones than the up-front feature of competition structures. Torvill and Dean are no exception in embracing these features. If they sometimes experimented with the habits of their game, like using single pieces of music rather than bits and pieces of scores cobbled together, daring at the edge of the rules on tempi, or creating small variations rather than straight repetitions in Original Set Pattern (OSP) dances, a certain kind of spirit, akin to that in sport, which they hardly ever combated, at least in the competition context. Some kinds of 'dance' dance project this kind of spirit. The important point here is that Torvill and Dean kept it within the core of their work and made a creative issue out of it, found in it artistic liveliness.

We are speaking here, and, incidentally, too, only with regard to the competition dances – about the frequent metaphor of striving in their work, the 'joy of effort', the determination to be free of physical limitations, daring, cleverness, the issue of difficulty being on display (virtuosity is often a part of the subject-matter), the celebration of teamwork, and an overriding sense of idealism, the person competing with the self for something bigger and better – perfection in the harsh terms of ice dancing, a row of 6.0s – and working in harmony with someone else in order to do so. In skating, by its very nature, the directional forces that make for this kind of impact are especially strong. Skaters are nearly always travelling, and usually fast, they are emphatically going somewhere or leaving somewhere, heads flung back and chests lifted, they communicate up and out to a huge crowd all around them, or, in pairs, they swing out from each other with an enormous centrifugal force. Put bluntly, you can go places faster and turn faster on skates than without them. In any particular dance, Torvill and Dean might be pressing back the air in excitement and fun (*Mack and Mabel* and *Barnum*), or sadly reaching into the goodbye direction (*Summertime*), or journeying with weighted, effortful tread as if yearning for the unobtainable in a situation of tragedy and violence. In 1984, with the OSP *Paso Doble* and the *Bolero* as free dances (ending with that fall into the volcano), they shifted powerfully into this last expressive direction. With Torvill and Dean, nearly all is out; even in the collapse to the ice, the energy of motion reaches desperately way beyond the body. *Bolero*, it will be recalled, is structured to develop its sense of desperation and tragedy as it progresses. Alastair Macaulay, who has written eloquently about this dance (1984), compares it to the love duet and *Liebestod* in Wagner's *Tristan and Isolde*, with its theme of always the 'beyond'; and he adds, 'it's just right for the ice too, where every stroke is a step into the beyond' (Macaulay, 1984, p. 41).

Sarah Montague (1985, p. 72) has observed that in *Bolero*, line is 'turned into motion with a rapidity possible only in skating'. This means that sculptural moments can streamline directional forces still further. Although this is clearly visible in *Bolero*, perhaps the most extraordinary example of all can be seen in the *Paso Doble*, with Dean dragging Torvill (the matador's cape) behind him; she pulls back and down and he presses forwards and onwards: there is a Concorde-like spatial thrust through the couple.

Other formal means contribute to the expressive statements of Torvill and Dean: the complex scribble of steps and intertwined bodies, the determination to keep up with a tight rhythmic pattern in the music, these too are features that speak of passionate ambition, striving, daring – and, of course, we applaud them. Rarely, if ever, have ice dancers presented that imagery of idealism, power and virtuosity (so close to the images of sport, which ironically often fails to live up to such metaphors) as part of a cogent, expressive, poeticized statement. But there is also the more subtle ambition of musicality, or rather dynamics, rhythmic play, and phrasing and in this respect there was a major development in their work between the 1980s and 1990s. The 1994 *Rumba* shows the most remarkable gradation of pressure from creamy shifts between skates that almost eradicate the impulse of weight shift, to huge, flamboyant accents (a sudden dead stop, or him falling into the centre of a turning circle to clutch her waist – shades of imminent tragedy again) to scribbles of steps in irregular rhythmic patterns sometimes weighting the weak beat, sometimes the strong, in the music, a lot or just as a slight hint, always with unpredictable results. And there's a striking passage of steps working hard to keep up with every note in the melody.

This last aspect, rhythmic/dynamic subtlety, was the prime feature of the first version of *Let's Face the Music* in 1994, and maybe here, the couple were really getting away from the overt metaphors of striving and daring that we have been discussing in relation to their earlier competition work. Experience in the European Championships suggested that the judges just didn't find this sort of thing interesting, or that they didn't see it, or that the judging goalposts had shifted. By the time of the Olympics, a radically revised dance incorporated plenty of moments that brought Torvill and Dean back into the former aesthetic arena.

While the television camera, which has brought the pair their biggest audience, captures detail and the rush of movement close by, the live experience in the vast arena, set upon the gleaming frozen surface, magnifies the imagery that has been referred to. There is nothing in the theatre either, to compete with the impression of exhilarating speed and the illusion of power to achieve that speed over the mass of ice, the danger of moving full-pelt up to the barrier, not to forget the quieter thrill of purring skates, and the rapturous applause and delight of a huge live audience in Wembley Arena.

It is at this point useful to compare John Curry, who, after his Olympic victory, and starting from a figure-skating base further away from what traditional aestheticians would call art, chose to get as far away as possible from this border with sport, even to evade any expression of difficulty. You could see his motivations even at the Olympics, light, restrained, limbs calmly placed within rather than reaching beyond his kinesphere. Later, he said that, while enjoying the illusion of defying gravity, he cherished simple movement, quality not tricks, silent skating rather than effort fully on display (Curry, 1978). His is quite a different order of expression. And it is significant that the focus of his career was towards theatre, towards high art. He invited important choreographers like Tharp and MacMillan to make dances for him, used high-art music – some of it not so well-known, Albinoni, Berlioz, Liszt, Stravinsky – and devised his written programme material as you would expect in informative dance programmes. On the other hand, Torvill and Dean kept in professional competitions, as well as big arena shows, before their very public Olympic return in 1994. They toured their show *Let's Face the Music* with deliberate references to their competition winnings – a row of 6.0s and rave headlines on a cloth pillar dropped to the ice – and offered a programme book about their history, including greetings from sports and showbiz celebrities, and not a word about the dances that they performed or the music that they used. No dance choreographers of note were invited to work with them on their shows. Dean, however, has choreographed for other ice-dance professionals and has recently choreographed a dance work for English National Ballet. In general they remained firmly in the world of ice dance, sport and its showbiz conventions of popular and pop-classical music.

In recent years, however, Torvill and Dean have expressed a desire to push the boundaries of their ice dance further towards the edges of innovative contemporary choreography of dance itself in their own shows. In their autobiography (Torvill and Dean, 1995, p. 139), the skaters indicate that they first became aware of the possibility of making their ice dancing 'less of a sport and more of an art' after witnessing a performance of the Sydney Dance Company in Australia in 1984, a short time after their Olympic victory. But they have also been astute enough to recognize that to certain extent they are constrained by the conventions of the ice-show context and the audiences' expectations. The audiences want their greatest hits, as they do with other popular entertainers like Sinatra and Streisand, and *Bolero* is a must for every show. Although Torvill and Dean may be tired of it after all these years, nevertheless, they are shrewd enough to keep it in the show. As Dean noted in the 1991 *Omnibus* programme on their work,

> if we want to go and perform to a large audience, there is a certain format . . . it's mass appeal and in some ways safe . . . but where we are heading now in an experimental way, will maybe alienate that audience and people will come and say 'Oh no! I don't like this . . .'.

In the next breath however, he said, 'but sometimes, if it's there you have to do it, regardless'. So there is a sense of working within the conventional expectations, but at the same time pushing towards the dangerous lines of the boundaries and the margins which provide a challenge to themselves and to the audience. This is very clear in works like *Missing* and in their stunning *Tango* at the 1991 Professional World Championships.

Tango begins without music and with an inward focus. Torvill and Dean are standing back-to-back and some distance away. Then they turn on the spot to face each other. Striking a pose which suggests they are holding an invisible partner, they skate towards each other, pass face-to-face, and although they move in unison, they seem oblivious to one another. They make a quarter-turn and travel back-to-back in a straight line, in opposite directions, and circle in on themselves. They continue to cross and encircle each other's space, crushing the blades into the ice as they stop. The rhythm is created by the swish of the blades as Torvill and Dean travel in short bursts across the ice and by the blades grinding into the ice as the skaters come to a sharp halt, stamp on the ice or pierce it with the tip of their blades. This section lasts over a minute and sets up an extraordinary tension. Some members of the audience are uncomfortable, there is shuffling in the seats and a number applaud before the end of the section, thinking that it has finished. You can almost hear a collective sigh of relief when finally, the music starts up and the skaters glide towards each other to prepare for the first lift. The audience applauds politely as it is lulled back into the safety of the conventions of ice dance. Although even here, the conventions, at least those of gender, are slightly disrupted when, soon after the dance begins, Torvill supports Dean's weight and leg as he moves through an arabesque sequence.

Although the media-hype that accompanied Torvill and Dean's re-entry into the world of the Olympics, a decade after their initial 'gold' triumph, was very clearly orchestrated, the chords that were struck were not always harmonious, at home or abroad, and they were exceedingly noisy. The media show began to gain momentum in January 1994 as the National Championships were coming up and continued unabated until the end of March, a month after the Olympic finals. If we examine the home press coverage in particular, we can see certain patterns in the reports and comments that may be categorized in terms of a set of tensions between amateurism and professionalism; sport and entertainment, 'lay' and 'professional' knowledge and judgement (audience and IOC judges) and national pride and Euro-scepticism. And it is to these issues that we now turn.

In terms of their profile as 'professional' ice dancers, the rumours circulated that their return to the competitive 'amateur' arena, made possible by a change in the rules the year before, was nothing short of a massive publicity stunt, a 'trailer', to fuel audience interest for their planned 1994–95 world tour which would make them a great deal of money. Broadsheets such as *The Times* and the *Independent* began to publish letters from their defenders and detractors alike. Torvill and Dean, it was revealed, invested around £100 000 to support their six-month preparation period. Although this demonstrated their commitment to the project, how many 'amateur' skaters could afford to have *Let's Face the Music* professionally rearranged to their particular specifications? The 'real' amateurs, we were reliably informed by a mother of a young skater, take their music tape along to someone who will doctor it accordingly for a fee of around £25. It is almost certainly the case that the entry into the competition arena of these former shining (but, to some, tarnished) stars, effectively displaced, or deposed, the 'real' amateur British skaters, Humphrey and Lanning, who would (some said should) have gone on to represent Britain. Alternatively, as was pointed out in the Letters pages of the *Independent,* Torvill and Dean's presence could benefit the sport in several ways (Oundjian, 1994, p. 46). If they succeeded in Europe and in the Olympics (and no other British couple could), they would then be eligible to take part in the 1994 World Championships in Tokyo, and if they were placed in the top five, then three British couples (instead of one) would be eligible to take part in the 1995 World Championships, which just happened to be scheduled to take place in Birmingham. Moreover, because of public interest in Torvill and Dean, a flagging sport which had received little media attention in recent years now had a two-year coverage deal with the BBC and the number of sponsors had increased (Irvine, 1993, p. 44).

Torvill and Dean's border crossing into the amateur skating world also drew out old controversies as to whether skating was indeed a sport or simply 'another branch of show business' (Wilson, 1994, p. 9). Indeed, the debates often raged within the pages of a single paper. Just as dance critics like Anna Kisselgoff (*Omnibus,* 1991) have noted the similarities between Torvill and Dean and other innovative contemporary dance choreographers, so a number of sports journalists pointed out the absurdity of a sport that gives 50 per cent of its marks for artistic merit, one in which the 'look' of the sports man/woman seems to take precedence. Other more sympathetic sports writers, however, suggested that if other sports like football awarded marks for artistic impression, then certain former more stylish players would not have been tossed aside too readily and would have lived on longer in the sporting hall of fame (Cleary, 1994, p. 2).

The is-it-sport-or-show-business debate was given further impetus after the judges' decision to award Torvill and Dean a bronze medal at the Olympics in Lillehammer. The theatrical 'aesthetic' style of competitive ice dancing that Torvill and Dean had become identified with since *Bolero* that, as we have indicated, they had continued to heighten, refine and change over the years, had unfortunately been copied to death by the next generation of skaters in the amateur competitive arena. So much so that the rules were changed in 1992 in order to ensure a return to 'strictly ballroom' and the demise of 'aesthetic' ice dance.

Concerned not to be seen as 'show-business swanks', Torvill and Dean went 'back to basics' with their first version of *Let's Face the Music and Dance* which gained them a row of sixes in the British championships. However, when they reached the European Championships they found that the goalposts appeared to have shifted, because it was precisely the showy dynamic style of the Russian couple, Gritschuk and Platov, not 'strictly ballroom', that the judges favoured, if not the audience (Rowbottom, 1994, p. 40). As a result of this, and the fact that they only won by the narrowest of margins, Torvill and Dean made 80 per cent changes to the free dance for the Olympics. They aimed to provide the judges with the 'gimmicks' they seemed to want (Springs, 1994, 3) and thereby enhance their chances of winning a gold medal. Dean admitted:

> The old trick thing seems to get applause. As much as we don't like to do it, that's what they're [the judges] telling us, that we must be more flamboyant. We concentrated on technicalities and intricate footwork but it seems they want more flourishes and show business. (Springs, 1994, p. 3)

But the changes they made still did not inspire the judges at the Olympics, except perhaps for the British judge, who awarded them 5.9 for technical merit, while the others marked them between 5.6 and 5.8. They were placed third, not first. The inconsistencies in the marking astounded both the audience in the stadium, who whistled and, booed the judges, a large proportion of the British press and, presumably, the 23 million people who watched it on British television, a record audience for a single sporting event. The television switchboards were jammed with complaints; a teletext poll recorded that 98 per cent of the 13 000 callers believed that they should have won, despite the fact that most people cannot tell the difference between a triple axel and a toe-salchow.

We are not concerned here with whether Torvill and Dean should have won, rather what interests us is that *they* invoked such passions. And these passions were shrouded in a cloak of nationalism and ethnocentrism. Their award of the bronze medal led the newspapers at home (see the *Independent on Sunday*, 27.2.94, p. 10, for a compilation) to pronounce that it was 'Gold Robbery' (*Daily Express*) and calls went out to 'Hang Those Judges' (*Sun*). A number of newspapers attempted to lay the blame squarely on the shoulders of the judges, and cited as evidence the fact that six ISU judges had been suspended in 1993 and that a 1993 statistical survey showed un-equivocally that ice judges were biased towards their own country (Coleman, 1994, p. 2). Such was the concern that the ISU was forced to call a press conference to 'untangle some of the confusion which surrounded the ice dance judging' (Corrigan, 1994, p. 11). Other less enthusiastic comment-ators used the very public judging controversies as further ammunition for questioning the validity of ice dancing as a sport. Nevertheless, the over-riding message in the print media was that they were robbed, and as they represented or stood for *us* in our imagination, we too (the British), so the story went, were robbed – it was yet another example of a European conspiracy, like the Common Agricultural Policy.

But the vociferous partisan views from within were not always echoed from without. Just as the British press thought Torvill and Dean wonder-ful, so a number of the foreign press considered them well past their sell-by date, with comments like 'too old, too fat, too slow' and 'too tedious and too sluggish (Mullin, 1994, p. 20). The French, England's historical adversary, seemed particularly delighted that the British pair had not capped their European gold. As an article in *The Times* (Bremner, 1994, p. 15) noted, 'while overt nationalism is deemed distasteful among the European allies, no holds are barred in sport'. Moreover, the French were rather tired of the Francophobia expressed through the British press and this was their opportunity to engage in some 'Anglo-bashing'.

The general consensus in the French media was that 'justice has been done' (Bremner, 1994, p. 15) at the Olympics because Torvill and Dean would not have won the European title in the first instance, if the judging had not been biased in their favour. Thus, once again the judges are called into question, although from a different side. Although ageist comments were directed at both skaters, Torvill bore the brunt of the attacks and, as usual, these were directed at her shape, make-up, dress and weight, rather than her skating skills: 'Chubby-cheeked and bloated, wearing far too much make-up and in an ill-fitting costume, she [Torvill] looks like a London housewife attending the wedding of one of her children' (quote from *Le Figaro* cited in Mullin, 1994, p. 20). It is not simply that sport is considered to be the province of the young, rather, as studies of women performers have demonstrated (Thomas, 1992; Thomas and Klett-Davies, 1995), the message seems to be that if women wish to succeed in the media after they have reached the age of thirty, they should stay slim and keep looking younger than their actual age.

The overt nationalism that was unleashed by their return to the competit-ive arena at home was underpinned by a fierce loyalty for their former achievements, admiration for the boldness of their risk, the working-class suburban dream come true, a conspiracy about a romance off-stage that didn't exist, intensified by the policeman background and girl-next-door image, and a no-nonsense 'Britishness' behind superstardom that flattered us all at home. All that and more fed back into the dancing, how we read what they did for *us* out there on the ice. And it was a very broad 'us' that read the dancing, by virtue of the sports context and its ravenous media, a wide community cutting across class/age and gender differences. If we left our examination here, however, we would be in danger of relegating their work and our reading of it to the realm of the dominant ideology and ignoring the power of the aesthetic component with which we began (for a fuller discussion of this issue see Jordan and Thomas, 1994).

Our chapter suggests the playing of a number of forces with and against each other, and all contribute in some way to the experience of Torvill and Dean. Within *Let's Face the Music*, it was as if our stars knew just what kind of multi-faceted image they presented and worked right with it, acknowledging that their image is part history – in postmodern *bricolage* fashion, references, for instance, to the old *Barnum* and *Mack and Mabel* numbers. History as originality – the judges missed that one. 'Instant global gossip has it that they were penalised by the judges for recycling old choreography', wrote Anna Kisselgoff of *The New York Times* (cited in the *Independent on Sunday*, 27.2.94, p. 21). Yet, for all that, Torvill and Dean are of the present, radiating aura, magic, the mystique of the inseparable. The transformation from ordinary to extraordinary remains – a final border crossing.

REFERENCES

D. Best, 'Aesthetic of Sport', *British Journal of Aesthetics*, 14 (1974), pp. 197–213.

C. Bremner, 'Frosty French Roast Torvill and Dean: A Gallic View of the Ice Event', *The Times* (23.2.94), p. 15.

M. Cleary, 'Perfect Match of the Day', *Observer: Sport* (9.1.94), p. 2.

M. Coleman, 'Judging Row cools Lure of Ice Dancing', *Sunday Times* (27.2.94), p. 2.

Comment, 'As Others See Us', *Independent on Sunday* (27.2.94), p. 21.

P. Corrigan, 'Outrage goes against One's Better Judgement', *Independent on Sunday: Sport* (27.2.94), p. 11.

C. Irvine, 'Flags Raised for the Return of Torvill and Dean', *The Times* (10.9.93), p. 44.

S. Jordan and H. Thomas, 'Dance and Gender: Formalism and Semiotics Reconsidered', *Dance Research*, 12, 2 (Autumn 1994), pp. 3–14.

A. Macaulay, 'Love Scenes', *Dance Theatre Journal*, 2, 2 (Spring 1984), pp. 36–41.

S. Montague, 'Art of Ice', *Ballet Review*, 13, 1 (Spring 1985), pp. 64–73.

J. Mullin, 'Past it or Not, a "Step too Far" Cost Torvill & Dean Olympic Gold', *Guardian* (23.2.94), p. 20.

H. Oundjian, 'Welcome Return', sports letter in the *Independent* (27.1.94), p. 46.

J. Parry, 'Athletes or Artists?', *Dance and Dancers* (May 1984), pp. 17–19.

L. A. Reid, 'Sport, the Aesthetic and Art', *British Journal of Education Studies*, 18 (1970), pp. 245–58.

M. Rowbottom, 'Ice Skating: Britons Face the Music', *Independent* (18.2.94), p. 40.

S. Springs, 'That's Show Business', *Observer: Sport* (23.1.94), p. 3.

H. Thomas, *Equal Opportunities in the Mechanical Media: A Research Report* (London: British Actors' Equity Association, 1992).

H. Thomas and M. Klett-Davies, *Unequal Pay for Equal Parts: A Survey of Performers in the Theatre and the Electronic Media* (London: Goldsmiths' College, 1995).

J. Torvill and C. Dean [with J. Man], *Facing the Music* (London: Simon & Schuster, 1995).

P. Wilson, 'Way off the Mark', sports letter in *Observer Sport* (27.2.94), p. 9.

OTHER SOURCES

'Bladerunners: Jayne Torvill and Christopher Dean', *Omnibus* (BBC Production in Association with Thirteen/WNET, 1991).

J. Curry [interview with Walter Terry, New York City] (30.11.78), tape held in New York Public Library Dance Collection.

Face the Music: The Tour (videotape), directed by David Mallet (Inside Edge Productions Ltd, 1995).

The Very Best of Torvill and Dean (Video Collection International Ltd, 1994).

Index